21 DEC

LE BOURGET
22 FEV 1960
FRANCE

25 OCT 1963

JUIN 1961
FRANCE

AOUT 1961

IMMIGRATION OFFICER
22 FEB 1963

19 OCT

FRANCE

OUT 1963

25 FEB 1963
LONDON AIRPORT

19 OCT 1963

24 OCT 1963

FOREIGN
MISSIONS
of an
AMERICAN
PROSECUTOR

From Moscow to Morocco
and Paris to the Persian Gulf

JOHN HAILMAN

University Press of Mississippi / *Jackson*

The University Press of Mississippi is the scholarly publishing agency of
the Mississippi Institutions of Higher Learning: Alcorn State University,
Delta State University, Jackson State University, Mississippi State University,
Mississippi University for Women, Mississippi Valley State University,
University of Mississippi, and University of Southern Mississippi.

www.upress.state.ms.us

The University Press of Mississippi is a member
of the Association of University Presses.

First printing 2019

∞

Illustrations are from the author's collection.

Library of Congress Cataloging-in-Publication Data

Names: Hailman, John R., 1942– author.
Title: Foreign missions of an American prosecutor : from Moscow to
Morocco and Paris to the Persian Gulf / John Hailman.
Description: Jackson : University Press of Mississippi, [2019] | "First
printing 2019." | Includes bibliographical references and index. |
Identifiers: LCCN 2019000822 (print) | LCCN 2019018334 (ebook) | ISBN
9781496823977 (epub single) | ISBN 9781496823953 (epub institutional) |
ISBN 9781496823984 (pdf single) | ISBN 9781496823991 (pdf institutional)
| ISBN 9781496823960 (hardcover : alk. paper)
Subjects: LCSH: Hailman, John R., 1942– | Public prosecutors—United
States—Biography. | Hailman, John R., 1942-—Travel.
Classification: LCC KF373.H228 (ebook) | LCC KF373.H228 A3 2019 (print) |
DDC 340.092 [B] —dc23
LC record available at https://lccn.loc.gov/2019000822

British Library Cataloging-in-Publication Data available

This Book Is Dedicated to My Parents,
Who Sacrificed So Much
So That Their Son Might See the World

And
To Their Beloved Granddaughters,
Family Physician Dr. Allison Hailman Doyle and
French Professor Lydia Hailman King

And
To My Loving Wife and Companion of Fifty Years,
Waverly Regan McGrew Hailman,
Who Kept the Home Fires Burning While I Traveled;
A French Professor, Gourmet Cook, and Caterer;
Innkeeper of a Thriving B & B;
Thoroughbred Horse Breeder and Longreen Foxhunter;
Sole Designer of Our Beautiful Homes
Outside Oxford and in the South of France

And
To Our Own Grandchildren:
Blond-Haired, Blue-Eyed Cousins, Artist/Chef Abbey McGrew Doyle and
Brilliant, Athletic Leland Alexander King;
And Raven-Haired, Violet-Eyed Magdalena Louise King,
Our Next Generation of Travelers.

ON TRAVEL

Travel . . . is one of the liberal arts . . . a spiritual necessity.
—Robert Byron (a cousin of Lord Byron)

For my part, I travel not to go anywhere, but to go.
I travel for travel's sake. The great affair is to move.
—Robert Louis Stevenson, *Travels with a Donkey*

The Sentimental Traveller (meaning myself), of whose travels
I am now sitting down to give an account, travels as much
out of necessity, and the need to travel, as anyone in the class.
—Lawrence Sterne, *A Sentimental Journey*

Farewell, Monsieur Traveller. Look you: lisp, and wear
strange suits, and disable all the benefits of your own country.
—Shakespeare, *As You Like It*

Who travels widely needs his wits about him.
The stupid should stay home.
—Attributed to the Norse god Odin in the Icelandic saga *Edda*

There is no magic like traveling alone, without friends
or colleagues to condition one's opinions. It is the
very aloneness that makes travel worthwhile.
—Robert Kaplan, *Eastward to Tartary*

If you want to go fast, go alone.
If you want to go far, go with companions.
—African proverb

Travel makes one modest. You see what a
tiny place you occupy in the world.
—Gustave Flaubert

CONTENTS

Contents

PREFACE: TRIPS TAKEN AND NOT TAKEN

After my earlier books on wine and on my experiences as federal prosecutor, this one, my fifth, is the only one entirely devoted to my other favorite subject: international travel. Like the other books, this one begins with a brief prologue, setting the scene for my travels. The focus quickly shifts from youthful train travel in the US to the cultures and court systems of eight faraway, exotic countries. Courtesy of the Justice Department, we travel together from modern Switzerland and bustling Paris to Interpol Headquarters in Lyon, France, where I received my international law certificate from the National School for Magistrates. We next explore three very different Islamic cultures in the colorful societies and legal systems of Tunisia, Algeria, and Morocco in the northwest corner of North Africa known to Arabic speakers as the Maghreb, "land of the sunset."

From North Africa we move to the chaotic world of the former Soviet Union, a new world of old countries trying to rediscover their independent pasts while adjusting to a complex and confusing future. We begin with Moldova, the most unknown country of all modern Europe. A desperately poor but beautiful farming country which looks to me a lot like France might look if its traditional wine-rich economy had been hamstrung for seventy years by Soviet bureaucrats. Moldova, called Moldavia and Bessarabia by the Russians, lies in the heart of the historically volatile region known as the Balkans, the Turkish word for "mountains," the crucible for centuries of bitter wars between Christians and Muslims. It helps if you picture Moldova as bordered on the east by modern Ukraine, the hotly contested "borderland" country of the warrior Cossacks, as much a battleground today as ever.

Not far from Moldova is the most spectacularly beautiful country in the book: the Republic of Georgia, strategically situated on the south side of the magnificent, snow-clad Caucasus Mountains. An ancient and complex country, Georgia was the first country in Europe, in the third century, to adopt Christianity. Georgia has always had one foot in Asia. Its capital Tbilisi [tuh-BLEE-see], called Tiflis by the Russians, was for centuries the final stop on the ancient Silk Road linking China with the West. My photos of Georgia are among my favorites of the more than a thousand original photos I took of all these little-known countries. The deep-green alpine meadows of Georgia climb the sides of the mighty Caucasus beneath snow-white peaks, which dwarf even the Alps, more resembling the towering Himalayas. To complete the stunning picture of the visual differences, Georgia has real "Caucasians," fair-skinned people in contrast with their often darker neighbors to the south. Funny how long I'd been called a Caucasian without ever meeting a real one. Georgia also has its own uniquely beautiful alphabet, descended from neither Latin nor Greek, but from Aramaic, the language of Jesus.

It is in western Georgia, at Colchis, its second city, where Jason and the other Greek Argonauts found the famed "golden fleece," said to be derived from Georgians sieving the river with sheep's wool to harvest the thousands of flakes of gold which washed down from the Caucasus. Of all the countries and peoples I've visited, including Greece and the Greek islands, Georgia and Georgians most remind me in spirit of the ancient Greeks. The Georgians are a handsome people with dark-haired, assertive, almond-eyed women. The men tend to be warlike mountain men who write poems to their daggers more often than love songs to their women. Georgia is also the ancestral home of the *vitis vinifera*, the great wine-vine responsible for all the world's great wines, from Europe and the US to Australia and South Africa.

As if Georgia and Moldova were not unique enough, in 1997 two colleagues and I were privileged to be invited as the first Westerners ever to attend the Russian National Prosecutors' Conference in Moscow. While there, during that happy period when Russia under Boris Yeltsin sincerely tried to become more open and democratic, I attended several of its new, experimental jury trials, never before attempted under either the tsars or the Communists. The trials were fascinating, but with what now begins to look like a new Cold War upon us, they may have just been one brief moment of brightness in the dark, troubled—but also inspiring and courageous—history of the Russian people. All of that remains to be seen, but we did see for one happy moment the "New Russia" described here, just before that hopeful window to the West began to close.

If I were forced to choose just one favorite country of all the exotic ones I visited, it would have to be the Sultanate of Oman. Located at the entrance to the Persian Gulf between violent Yemen and the oil-rich United Arab Emirates, Oman faces Iran across the narrow gulf. Despite its location, Oman is one of the most peaceful places on earth. It practices a unique, quietist version of Islam called Ibadi [ee-BAH-dee], which features low-key prayers in a melodious major key rather than the anguished minor-key wailings of most Muslim calls to prayer. On the south, Oman has miles of unspoiled, nearly deserted white-sand beaches facing the mild Indian Ocean, where I often swam. On its northern side Oman borders the spectacular desert mountains and dramatic deep sand deserts of Saudi Arabia, which are so trackless that for hundreds of miles no border is even marked. I wandered with great pleasure in those mountains and deserts for days with a trusted Omani sheikh as my guide. My favorite traveling chef/explorer of cultures, the late Anthony Bourdain, called Oman perhaps his favorite undiscovered country in the world. I could not agree more.

Next the book moves to the faraway islands of Indonesia, which is both the world's largest democracy and its most populous Islamic country, where I report in depth both from Jakarta, the bustling capital on the island of Java, and from the most spiritual place on earth: the Hindu island of Bali, the most enchanting place I've visited and possibly the closest place on earth to paradise. Of course even paradises have problems if humans live there, and I try to describe fully and fairly the troubles in paradise.

Asked how I could remember so much about so many places and so many people, I wondered about it myself, but upon reflection, I think I know. In my desk drawer are *twelve* well-worn US passports dating back to 1960, all filled with visas and stamps, in various languages and alphabets, showing dates of entries and exits to all countries I visited, several of which we used as "end papers" for this book. For the last few trips I still have my official mission reports, which I excerpted extensively, along with my little pocket-size repertoires, or personal address books.

Richest sources of all are my letters to my parents, which my mother faithfully kept in a heavy fireproof box, organized chronologically and by dates received, which she left to me in her will in 1992. Sharing the family hoarder award turned out to be a benefit after all, as did the habit of trying to be a dutiful son. One ironic result of reading those old letters was to see how often I deceived my parents by concealing how dangerous some of my travels really were and how I shamelessly asked for more money. Also funny was how few were my references to the beautiful women I encountered in my youthful travels. But I did, just in case, keep many of their letters back to me also, which are quite a consolation to an old traveler looking back on his life.

If I have regrets, and I do, it is that circumstances prevented me from visiting the legal cultures of several of the countries I most wanted to visit. My long-held hopes of visiting India came close, but two times my carefully laid plans to slide into the country from next door fell apart, first due to a civil war in Nepal, and then to severe flooding in Bangladesh. Earlier, in 1965, I had applied for both a Woodrow Wilson Fellowship at Tulane in New Orleans and a Fulbright Scholarship to study in India. The Wilson came through, but Fulbright put me on a lengthy waiting list. Months later, long after I had moved to New Orleans, they actually offered me the Fulbright, but it was far too late to accept.

In another instance, our US envoy to Haiti, a former Argentine ambassador, called me on a Friday night to tell me my trip scheduled for the next morning to Haiti had to be canceled because we'd just landed several hundred Marines there to stop the violence. Not a dream trip, but Haiti is still unique for its colorful art and I hated to miss it.

Twice I had tickets to Israel to interview witnesses in terrorism cases when the Intifada and other events caused our government to cancel them as too risky. Perhaps, as the Arabs say, it was just "written" (i.e., *mektoub* [MEK-TOOB], or fate). Considering the always-uncertain state of our modern world, I know I was extremely lucky to see as much of it as I did, and under the favorable conditions described here. I didn't make it everywhere, but I really saw a lot *very* far from Guntown.

My biggest regret of all was not seeing China. After years of reading the wonderful novels of Robert van Gulik based on Judge Dee, a true historical Sherlock Holmes–like Chinese magistrate from traditional, Ming Dynasty, pre-Communist China, I thought in early June 1989 I finally had it made. I even had my plane ticket. Then came the Tiananmen Square protests and massacres, which caused the Justice Department to cancel my visit. But there is no way I can omit from this book at least a taste of classical Chinese learning and legal and political wisdom, so I'm including a quick summary of Confucian thinking on law and justice as an epigraph to the Prologue.

USEFUL ABBREVIATIONS
AND FOREIGN TERMS

ADR—Alternative Dispute Resolution, a method of settling lawsuits informally without courtroom trials, now very popular for reducing the high cost of trials but much less fun for cynical trial lawyers.

Aîd (Eîd)—Important Muslim holiday

Berbers—Mixed-race natives of North Africa, occasionally blond and blue eyed, but most often darker with curly hair. Their many related dialects were recently traced to ancient Egyptian. Politically powerful, especially in the southern, mountainous regions, but in large cities as well. Many speak Arabic in public, but Berber at home.

Chargé d'Affaires—Acting Ambassador.

DCI—Director of Central Intelligence, recent office created by President George W. Bush after 9/11 to oversee and coordinate all other intelligence agencies, including the CIA, NSA, DIA, etc.

DCM—Deputy Chief of Mission, i.e., Deputy Ambassador.

DOJ—Department of Justice, a.k.a. "Main Justice."

Diwan—Seat of Islamic government.

FISA—Foreign Intelligence Surveillance Act, a federal law allowing international wiretaps and other highly effective law enforcement measures to combat terrorism and other international threats. Administered from a SCIF (see below) deep inside the Main Justice Building by a special FISA court of hand-picked federal judges.

Henna—Washable, dark-red dye used by Muslim women to decorate their hands for special occasions, like washable tattoos, often quite elaborate. Also much used as hair dye.

Ibadi—An independent Islamic sect more related to Shia than Sunni, prevalent mainly in Oman.

ILA—Intermittent (temporary) legal advisor who travels to a country or regional periodically.

Imam—Islamic prayer leader.

KGB—Former Soviet spy agency now called officially in English translations the FSS or FSB (Foreign Security Service or Bureau).

Legat—FBI legal representative to a country or region.

Maghreb—Northwestern states of Africa, especially Morocco, Tunisia, Algeria, Mauretania, and Libya. Means west or "sunset" in Arabic.

Majlis—Consultative assembly, somewhat akin to an early parliament.

Mektoub—Fate, as in "It is written."

Mufti—Top influential religious/political figure now often appointed by a nation's ruler. Some are called "Grand Mufti."

NGO—Nongovernmental organization, usually charitable, at least on the surface.

NSA—National Security Agency collects intel mainly electronically rather than "humint," or human intelligence using people as agents. Previously referred to, because of its secretive ways and refusal to admit its existence, as "No Such Agency."

OSS—Office of Strategic Services, predecessor of the CIA until 1947.

Plenipotentiary—Having full powers (in theory) to act for a government.

Qadi—An Islamic judge, somewhat comparable to traditional Chancellors in Equity under old English law, who still exist in a few states such as Mississippi.

Rial—Currency common to Saudi Arabia and several Gulf States.

RLA—Department of Justice Resident Legal Advisor to an ambassador, usually assigned for one or more years full time.

RSO—Regional Security Officer of the US State Department, responsible sometimes for one country, often for an entire region.

Saracens—Arabs from the eastern end of the Mediterranean, or "Sunrise" region in Arabic.

SCIF—Secure Compartmentalized Intelligence Facility, a special insulated office built to prevent interception of discussions of top-secret matters. Known on the old television spook show *Get Smart* as the "Cone of Silence" room.

Sharia—Islamic religious law.

Shi'a [SHEE-ah]—The minority sect of Islam, centered in Persia (now Iran), who profess that Ali, son-in-law of Mohamed, was his only true successor. The name applied to them by their rivals, the Sunnis, means "heretic" in Arabic.

Sufi—A mystical sect of Sunni Islam known for their *darwish*, or "whirling dervish" dances, during which they enter religious trances. It is now based especially in Turkey.

Sunni—The orthodox, majority sect of Islam named for the Arabic word for "path," or "way," stressing that the *Sunna*, or acts and sayings of Mohammed, are as binding as the Holy Koran itself. Blood enemies of the Shi'ites, with whom they have been in internecine wars for centuries, somewhat resembling the ancient Catholic-Protestant blood lettings of old.

USIA (USIS)—US Information Agency (or US Information Service outside the US). Formerly the most effective arm of the US State Department, but now abolished with its highly effective officers folded into the regular foreign service officer corps by a misguided Congress, seriously damaging our ability to establish closer relations with friendly countries.

Wazir, Vizier—A government minister under the Ottomans.

FOREIGN
MISSIONS
of an
AMERICAN
PROSECUTOR

PROLOGUE

Lessons for Travelers on Foreign Missions
from the *Analects* of Confucius

Confucius (551–481 B.C.E) served as minister of justice for one year in the State of Lu (500 B.C.) but was dismissed by the emperor for questioning the emperor's judgment, much like Socrates. His life was spared, however, and he became the world's most famous traveling teacher of anyone who would listen to his wisdom, which was both theoretical and practical. The *Analects* are his collected sayings, which he described as "small seeds that can grow in every man's garden."

Some of my personal favorite *Analects* are these highly useful thoughts on what to consider as you travel:

"Having a book is like having a garden in your pocket."
"By teaching and continuing to seek truth, I never notice that I am getting old."
Best method of teaching? "Thorough discussion."
We learn best by "reasoning, not memorizing."
We get information best "by gentle willingness to listen."
"The art of government consists in making people happy."
What should the ruler do for the people? "First, make them rich; *then* teach them."
"It is easier to be kind when you are rich."
"When the people are needy, how can the ruler bear to have enough?"
"If you want peace, prepare for war."
"Do not do unto others that which you do not wish done unto you."
On growing: "At thirty we should *know* something;
    At forty we should *be* something;
        At fifty we should *have* something."
"Practice modest luxury."
"He had no rules about wine, but no one ever saw him drunk."
"Music is like the inner motion of the soul—it must be harmonious."
"The thinking man seeks enjoyment; the wise man simply enjoys."

3

Prologue

A Traveler from a Family of Travelers

I am a traveler from a family of travelers. Even during the Great Depression, my mother's father used to get a cheap ticket on a Greyhound bus and be gone for weeks, traveling all around the United States. My father, an engineer from a strict Amish family who never left their simple farms or their buggies, became the first of his clan ever to travel *anywhere*. From age sixteen he traveled each day by interurban train to Purdue University, where he met students from India, China, and South America, not to mention Europe, and promised himself he'd visit one day all the countries of his classmates. As far back as I can remember, he kept a huge collection of intricate maps of both the US and the world at large.

Moving decades forward, our two daughters now have the travel bug. My older daughter, Dr. Allison Hailman Doyle, toured *every* country in Europe, including several I never visited. I recall vividly her phone calls from places I'd scarcely heard of, asking me to send money via Western Union, since that way she could pick it up anywhere she happened to be. Later she served three years as Chief Naval Medical Officer in Sasebo, Japan. Our granddaughter Abbey will probably be a traveler too, since she spoke baby Japanese long before she spoke English.

Our younger daughter, Lydia, both a Phi Beta Kappa and a state champion cross-country runner with a Parade of Beauties Award at Ole Miss, spent her junior year abroad in Montpellier on France's Côte d'Azur, then taught English for a year in a lycée in Le Mans, home of the famous road races, then was awarded a Rotary Ambassadorial Scholarship to Lausanne, Switzerland. An Honors College Scholarship later sent her to Japan, Hong Kong, and Taiwan. We often wonder where our daughters' three children will travel, and how soon.

Returning to my father, his first interest was the USA because his job paid him to travel across the country teaching engineering as a consultant and testifying as an expert witness. By the time I graduated from high school, we had visited all forty-eight contiguous states, missing only Alaska and Hawaii, which I somehow have still never seen. But my father's real dream, which he could never afford, was to visit the most faraway continents, the mysterious ancient domains of central Asia, especially what are now the new republics of Uzbekistan, Tajikistan, and Turkmenistan, which he knew mainly by the names, from old books, of the ancient cities along the Silk Road: Tashkent, Bokhara, and especially Samarkand. Very early on my father introduced me to books like *The Golden Journey to Samarkand* by James Elroy Flecker and *The Royal Road to Romance* by Richard Halliburton, whom I learned much later was from Memphis, just up the road from our current home in Oxford.

My father loved a board game called Risk, where you tried to conquer the world with money and soldiers. It was played with dice and little wooden men representing soldiers of various countries on a big, spread-out map of the world. On the map of each country were vivid names like Vladivostok and Irkutsk, although the names Russia and the Soviet Union were not even mentioned on the map. No need provoking them by getting too specific, we supposed. My father and I played two-man Risk constantly for two or three years, then for some reason it kind of disappeared. I wish I was better at twenty-first-century searches like Google so I could locate newer versions and other games to enhance my recollections even further. In any case, it certainly gave me some very intense ideas about how the world worked and a powerful desire to visit the exotic places we rolled dice for—not to conquer them—just to experience them.

We definitely were not born anywhere exotic. Maybe that's why we wanted to travel so much. My birthplace was Huntington on the flat plains of northern Indiana, now known mainly as the birthplace of one of our less-traveled vice presidents, Dan Quayle. When I was two, we moved to the three-story home of my great-grandmother in Indianapolis. She was married to a Virginia descendant of former President Woodrow Wilson, most internationalist of our presidents. I remember vividly the big, double-sliding doors between her two large sitting rooms, copied from Thomas Jefferson's at Monticello. They were very heavy and hard to open. Once I thought it would be challenging to close them all. When my frail mother got through reopening them and heard me snickering behind a couch, she gave me a good thrashing to teach me never to do that again. When my father got home, his reaction was the opposite: "Look at how strong that boy is. He pulled all those heavy doors closed, the ones that you were hardly strong enough to reopen. But you did right; he needs to learn not to make trouble for his mother." As she left the room, he winked at me behind her back.

When I was six, we moved to a little prairie town of five hundred people, which proudly announced that precise number on the sign at the city limits. We lived there till I graduated from high school at age eighteen. My earliest and only memory of our local legal system in Indiana comes from a Saturday morning in the local pool room, the social hub of Linden. One morning while shooting a relaxing game of snooker, several of us watched the town marshal escorting to the back room an irate motorist dressed in a suit and tie. His new Cadillac was sitting outside. The man was complaining loudly that Linden was nothing but a "speed trap" for unwary city dwellers from Chicago and Indianapolis. People from nearby cities like Lafayette, home of Purdue University, knew better than to zip through Linden, with its one block of stores and absence of stop lights. But this guy didn't. Hearing his complaining, we wondered what he would think of our backroom "courtroom." It was a big, ratty oblong room whose only furniture was a large square table covered with green felt and a few broken-down metal chairs. At one end was a low wooden wall against which players threw dice.

Presiding over the table was the owner of the pool room, who was also the local justice of the peace. He was said to be half Shawnee Indian and rumored to carry a bowie knife in his boot, but that may have just been a boast. He was a big boaster. How a straight-headed little town like Linden had chosen such a man I never learned. Probably no one else wanted the job. The well-known local custom was for the town marshal to bring the speeders to the backroom for their "trial." From my later experience I would have called it more of a plea-bargaining session between the accused speeder and the justice of the peace. My buddies and I stuck our heads through the dirty curtain that separated the pool room from the gambling house/courtroom. The justice was in his usual attire: dirty t-shirt and leather vest topped by the green eyeshade he always sported when presiding over a game. The other players didn't move, just sat there with their cards lying on the table in front of them, waiting for "justice" to take its course.

The judge asked the marshal for the "evidence." It was brief: "This old boy was doing sixty-five in *our* thirty zone," he said.

"The usual fine for that is $200," said the judge. "How did he treat you?"

"He was disrespectful, sir," said the marshal, a burly man who always had a big holstered pistol on one hip and a long, black nightstick on the other. His name, appropriately, was Harshman.

"That will be another fifty dollars for resisting arrest."

The speeder was speechless. The fight had gone out of him entirely.

"Fortunately for you, the local bank is open Saturday mornings. It's right across the street. We don't take checks from out-of-town folks. They tend to bounce." The card players laughed quietly at the judge's little joke.

Without saying a word, the out-of-town driver turned for the door to head for the bank. My buddies and I nearly fell over each other ducking out of the way. The judge saw us. "You fellows get on out of here." Stern local morality at work. My friends and I headed straight home without waiting to witness the inevitable outcome. I had known such things went on but never actually seen them till that day. I reacted strongly with a feeling in my stomach that was immediate and lasting: Something dirty had been going on, right under my nose, and I had never noticed it. I don't believe my friends and I had ever talked about it even once. When I told my father about it later that day when he got home, he said, "That sorry devil. We'll get someone else appointed next year. I'm sorry we tolerated him, son, but it won't be for much longer." Sure enough, the next year the JP and his son moved away, and the local barber, whose shop faced the highway and hid the pool room, took over the poolroom too. But the poker and dice games continued—just not presided over by a judge.

My mother's father, Raymond Trulock, traced his traveling ancestors back to the late 1600s, when they were indentured servants from England on a tobacco plantation on the eastern shore of Maryland. One of them supposedly fought with General Washington. The rugged English Trulocks were long lived. My uncle Harold lived to be ninety-five, as did his mother, my grandmother.

My father's first ancestor in the US, John Adam Heilemann, also fought in the Revolutionary War. Exactly how or why the Heilemanns of Hesse became the "Hailmans" from Alsace, or why or how some of them joined an Amish community slightly respelled as "Heilman Dale" in Lebanon County, Pennsylvania, is disputed, but they apparently never traveled very much again until my father came along. Sturdy farmers, they were long lived. My grandfather William Hailman died at ninety-five. I recall only his burning blue eyes and how I fell through the back of a folding chair at his funeral when I was two.

The Trulocks, on the other hand, produced many travelers—and many lawyers. My uncle Harold, a prominent newspaper editor who often appeared as a commentator on the PBS NewsHour, first went all across the US by motorcycle, then rafted down the Mississippi River from Minnesota to New Orleans just to write a series of columns about it. His father, my grandfather, loved to drive his big, dark-blue Packard with its huge metal spare tire on the side above its "running boards," little footsteps that ran along below all four doors with us grandchildren hanging on. In the Depression, when he could not afford to travel by car and took the Greyhound bus across the US, Grandpa Trulock sent us postcards from all over, including Mississippi, where I happily ended up many years later after going to school at Millsaps College in Jackson.

My own earliest memories of travel are more local. From ages three to six, when we lived in Indianapolis with my great-grandmother, her big, three-story house was filled with deep-colored red Persian carpets, which made me want to visit the beautiful places I assumed they came from. Instead, my mother would take me downtown on the electric street cars that everyone used back then. The cars ran on metal rails and had clanging bells and buzzer-pulls you used to let the conductor know when you wanted to get off. We would go to visit my grandmother, who worked in the children's department at the fancy Block's Department Store downtown, which was built and furnished to resemble Neiman-Marcus in Dallas, a fact of which my mother always reminded me. She used to let me wander the store while she fantasized in the pattern department about going to Paris to fashion shows.

My mother, alas, never made it to Paris, but later insisted—over my father's objections—on sending me on what ended up as a *two*-year Junior Year Abroad, the 1960s version of the old nineteenth-century Grand Tour of Europe. The only things I remember liking about Block's were the endless fresh-squeezed lemonades and peanut-butter-and-jelly sandwiches, which she claimed gave me that taste for fine food and wine which later drove me to faraway Morocco and Indonesia, not to mention France.

My serious travels began in first grade when my father pulled me out of school for two months, with teacher approval, for a sort of home-school trip to central Florida. My mother was seriously ill with pneumonia, and her doctor said she would not live unless my father got her to a warm, dry climate totally different from the damp, frozen plains of northern Indiana. My father chose Lake Wales, in central Florida, which was the highest, driest place in the state. Perhaps not coincidentally, the then–Milwaukee Braves were having spring training nearby while we stayed at Lake Wales. I still have a baseball my father got all the Braves, from Billy Bruton and Johnny Logan to Eddie Mathews and Andy Pafko to sign. In our ample spare time we rode around in glass-bottom boats looking at all the aquatic life under the clear lakes. That long stay opened my eyes for the first time to the idea that there were places where the weather was always good and people had a good time every day.

My small-town school was a good one, but fourth grade was best. That year our wonderful teacher, Mrs. Edwards, was a fervent lover of history and of adventurous travelers. I still have my big, handwritten notebook detailing all the adventures of everyone from Marco Polo and Captain Cook to Columbus and Vasco da Gama. But these were just dreams, however vivid. It was in fifth grade when my father again pulled me out for home-schooling (done mostly by my mother). We took our longest trip, a monster train voyage all the way to California and back. From Lafayette we went to Chicago and Minneapolis, then west on the Burlington Northern & Santa Fe, and several other trains whose names I've since forgotten.

From our little five hundred-person town of Linden I'd already gotten some romantic ideas of train travel. Back then two old railroad companies, The Monon [MOH-nahn] and the Nickel Plate, crossed at our little train depot on the north end of town near our beautiful little city park. There was then, in the 1950s, what they still called a "hobo park" where "tramps" and "bums," as my father called them, sat around campfires cooking open tin cans of beans and swapping colorful stories about the best trains to "hop," or board illegally for free. Chicago was a favorite destination, as was New Orleans. These grubby-looking but fascinating men, still hanging out since the Depression fifteen years earlier, were always bearded and not very clean, but told great scary stories. They often dared us to climb to the top of the nearby city water tower. A few of my friends did, but I was always too scared to climb past halfway. They said we could see the trains and the tracks for many miles in all directions. They offered to help us if we wanted to "hop a fast freight" and see the wide world. I was never tempted.

Unfortunately, one of my classmates, Paul Snyder, took them up on it. Paul was always daring and had been to "Reform School," as they called them back then, and never followed many rules. One night Paul, with the help of the hoboes, got into a freight car when a train had stopped to deliver something in Linden. Usually the trains just slowed down and then kept going after the stationmaster held out a big hook and grabbed a canvas sack full of the day's mail. When one stopped, Paul got on and the hoboes closed the doors behind him. In their hurry in the dark they failed to notice that on one side of the car was a tall stack of long, heavy iron reinforcing rods. When the train got to St. Louis and men began unloading the rods, which had shifted, they found the badly crushed body of Paul. None of us was ever tempted again to try that little train-hopping adventure. The local town marshal, Mr. Harshman, promptly ran the hoboes out of town.

First See the USA: By Car, Bus, and Old-Time Train

The "California trip" was (and is) our most unforgettable. When we crossed from frozen Minnesota into even more frozen North Dakota, the snow was the deepest I'd ever seen. On an isolated farm I saw a man checking his cows while holding a rope and walking on snowshoes held up by the layer of ice created over the deep snow by alternate thawing of the snow on sunny days and refreezing during the long, cold nights. Most amazing were some North Dakota farmers' early efforts at insulation against the freezing winds: the little wooden farmhouses had bales of hay stacked up as high as the eaves with only their doors left uncovered. It was a real testament to the hardy courage of those northern wheat farmers. My father said he wished we could stop and talk to some of them, but we had to keep rolling.

I remember the vast mountains and broad valleys of Montana. The train had to stop fairly frequently during the trip to take on water or coal or to fix the frequent "hot-boxes," which occurred when the train's brakes would overheat from constant use, and the brakemen (for the first time I understood what their name meant) would grease and otherwise somehow cool down the metal brakes. During those stops in Montana I always got out and bundled up to pick up broken stones along the tracks. They were several colors based on the color of the mountains through which the trains' routes had been cut and/ or dynamited.

My favorite stones were little purple ones from the "Purple Hills." For years I kept a big cigar box full of them. When my parents died, they were somehow lost during the sale of their home, along with my huge collection of arrowheads collected at the old primeval Native American burial grounds, then called "The Shades of Death," near our home, which was also only a few miles from the battlefield at Tippecanoe, where General and future President William Henry Harrison ("Tippecanoe and Tyler too") defeated Chief Tecumseh and his brother "The Prophet." Years later, in the early 1960s when I was a student in Paris, I drove slowly across Yugoslavia, from Austria to Greece. The mountains there strongly reminded me of Montana and rekindled many vivid memories.

Our train trip to California was unique, a life in a now-long-gone world. We slept in Pullman car sleepers, comfortable metal bunk beds with thick, soft, luxurious cotton mattresses and sheets and pillow-covers changed daily by neatly dressed Pullman porters, distinguished-looking black men in all-white uniforms whose responsible jobs and contact with well-educated and prosperous white travelers gave them valuable experiences in how America really worked. Those jobs eventually led the porters to be among the very first organizers and leaders of the civil rights movement. With their starched white uniforms and impeccable manners these black men—they were all men on that trip, even the cooks—invoked great respect among the all-white, often otherwise prejudiced train travelers.

We ate three ample, tasty meals each day on the train; there was really very little else to do except look out the window at the endlessly changing landscapes. These delicious meals, I'm sure, helped form me into the food-and-wine writer I later became. My only negative culinary experience of the trip came from my early dislike of green vegetables, especially broccoli and even lettuce. Then one evening my father laid down the law: "Eat your salad first or you don't eat at all." Trying to reduce the dreaded taste, I drenched one giant lettuce leaf with tasty, thick blue cheese dressing, then folded and wadded the entire huge leaf into a ball and stabbed it with my fork and tried to eat it all in one mouthful. Unfortunately for me, but hilariously to everyone else at the surrounding tables, the big leaf popped off my fork and spread out wide open like a flower blooming, covering me from chin to forehead and ear to ear with dripping blue cheese dressing. My father laughed so hard he cried and turned red and had to leave the table. My mother was afraid he would have a stroke. Fortunately, the subject of salad never came up again on the trip. Now I love it, especially with blue cheese dressing, an old-fashioned, out-of-style, unhealthy taste I enjoy often.

We listened every day to the constant, distinct sounds of the coal-burning train, as it moaned warnings to railroad crossings and small towns along the tracks. Although called "whistles," their sounds were not really like whistles at all. They were much more like musical calliopes that made tremendous blasts if you were standing outside—or even inside—your house, along the tracks. My children and grandchildren unfortunately will probably never know the clickety-clack of a train's metal wheels as they cross the rails or how lonesome a sound a train's warning "whistle" makes. The closest we can come now is by listening to old songs by Hank Williams or Jimmie Rodgers, Mississippi's "singing brakeman." All I have to do to re-create that vanished world in my mind is to hear one bar of the old song "All around the water tank, Waitin' for a train; A thousand miles away from home, Sleepin' in the rain. Went up to the conductor, Just to give him a line of talk. He said, 'If you've got money, Boy, I'll see that you don't walk.' I didn't have a nickel, Not a penny could I show. 'Get off! Get off! You railroad bum,' And he slammed that boxcar door."

It was only much later, on the way home, crossing New Mexico, that I saw something else to collect that reminded me of Montana and its colorful stones. When we crossed the famed Painted Desert, we stopped at a little station where they sold small glass-colored dome-like things filled with six or seven colorful levels of bright, shining sands. Sadly, those sands also disappeared during the short-notice auction of the contents of my parents' home in 1992. But the memories remain.

Even better than the Painted Desert was the old, unspoiled Grand Canyon, where my father and I rented mules and a guide to descend all the way down into the Canyon. But after less than an hour riding carefully down the slippery trail, with no guard rails at all, we decided at the last possible turnaround to go back up. It was tiring and scary. I sort of regret we did not go all the way to the bottom and spend the night, but my father was probably right for us to turn back. Back then there were too many people who never made it. I never climbed any real mountains either, but that's another story.

The next year, when I was in sixth grade in 1954, my father was invited to a big conference in Miami. I can't remember Miami at all, but I remember with great clarity our long side trip to Havana, Cuba. There are still two old black-and-white pictures, one of us boarding an Aero Cubana plane and the other of us eating dinner at the Hilton Sevilla in Havana. I recall clearly going to a cigar factory where they gave me a puff of some very expensive Cuban cigar, a Monte Cristo I believe. It made me cough, and except for a time in law school when I thought smoking Monte Cristos was really cool, I've never smoked again. The reason I quit was my daughter Allison. One night she looked up at me as I took a drag on my after-dinner cigar, which I used to compare to a good steak. When I saw a big tear roll down her cheek, I paused. She looked up at me and said, "Are you going to die, Papa?" That night I smoked my last cigar.

Our next visit in Havana was to a rum factory, which smelled very strong and very sweet. They gave me a sip, which was bitter and fiery and terrible

11

despite its sweet smell, and I spat it out and have never drunk rum again. My one experience with tequila was even worse. While in college, after several margaritas, we started driving around Jackson, Mississippi, shooting out street lights. We didn't get caught, but I never drank tequila again.

Our last visit in Havana was to a big, dark, stone fort called the Morro ("Moor") Castle where they showed us horrible instruments of torture featuring boiling oil, hot irons, and wrist and ankle shackles. I never wanted to go there again either. The Cubans serenaded us several times, clicking castanets and shaking carved maracas filled with little seeds to make them rattle. They even gave me a pair of red and green ones with my name carved into them. On the streets of Havana there were soldiers on every corner, all wearing light gray uniforms with white leather straps across the chest. Apparently Fidel Castro and his revolutionary followers were already up in the mountains preparing to overthrow the pro-American government of brutal dictator Fulgencio Batista. I've never been back to Cuba since, although now it is at last a possibility. Being "Back Home Again in Indiana," as the state song said, for another winter of ice and long underwear, did not sound like anything I wanted for my future life, whatever else I might be able to do. I wanted weather more like Cuba.

During our California trip we made lengthy stops at several national parks including Yellowstone and Yosemite. We also visited, inside and out, several gigantic hydroelectric dams like the Hoover and one on Snake River, which my father the electrical engineer really loved. We returned down along the California coast, then back by the southern route east across Arizona, New Mexico, and Texas, stopping at every National Park plus a brief foray into Mexico and Baja California down to Ensenada, where I ate my first lobster. A day trip to Tijuana was more of a mixed pleasure. A beautiful "silver" ring I bought turned my finger green within a week. A beautiful carved turtle I bought from a little Mexican boy was better, however. It was made from deep-brown, shiny, *palo fierro*, or ironwood. I still use it as a paperweight in my study today.

In the evenings everyone on the train played cards. At first we played euchre, a fast German game featuring an abbreviated deck with face cards only, also known as "one-eyed jacks." Euchre apparently derives from the German word for "knave" or "jack." As time went by, a then-famous movie actress named Ilona Massey joined the train. My father decided I was old enough to learn to play bridge as his partner against her. My mother hated all card games, so my father and I often teamed up against Ms. Massey and members of her entourage, which was on its way to Hollywood. I had to go to bed before my father's late-night, smoke-filled poker games, but often saw the green baize tables stacked high with both chips and paper money before turning in.

Ironically, it was not until much later, in 1984, that I began my frequent return trips to California. In that year, as explained in my 2014 book, *The Search for Good Wine*, my good friend John Grisanti, the Tuscan chef who had a wonderful north-Italian restaurant in Memphis, got me an invitation to be a wine judge at the Los Angeles County Fair, then and now the world's largest and best. From then on for the next twenty-five years, I traveled yearly to Los Angeles, San Francisco, Monterey, and San Diego to taste and vote on gold, silver, and bronze medals for the world's greatest wines. My invitation was largely based on my fluent French, gained as explained later in this book, which gave me a big hand up because I could pronounce all those trendy French labels and wine terms. In addition to my judging, from 1984 to 2005 I also wrote a nationally syndicated column on wine, food, and travel, taking me to Napa, Sonoma, Monterey, and Temecula several times a year as well.

After a few years of writing and wine judging, I began judging extra-virgin olive oils at the Los Angeles Fair as well, which can have interesting effects on your digestion. Then on a whim, another wine judge and I began judging pork barbecue cooking contests around the Deep South, as part of the MBN, Memphis Barbecue Network. My preference was strongly for "wet" ribs, never the dry rubbed kind often associated with Memphis. What a different world. Those rowdy contests, where the cooks often drank whiskey all night while basting ribs for eighteen hours, do not allow wine during the judging, a circumstance which finally persuaded me to retire from it after five years, even before I could graduate to my favorite: long-simmered beef ribs.

My favorite ribs of all-time were at Mama Romanov's, an old shanty restaurant just outside Jackson, Mississippi, when I was a student at Millsaps College there in the early 1960s. It was run by an unusual couple from New York City, with appropriate accents. The husband was a retired gymnast and professional boxer with the busted, crooked nose, cauliflower ears, and bad memory to match. The incomparable hostess was a long-retired dancer from the Ziegfeld Follies. She always met us with the same greeting: "Good evening, my children." In a huge iron pot on a back porch, whose rich, years-old sauce was never changed, just occasionally refreshed, they made the best barbecue I ever tasted. Today I suppose it would be called "Texas-style," but whatever you called it, for richness and long-lasting, intense flavor in moist and tender meat, it was the best barbecue of my long life. Better even than Kansas City, where my daughter went to medical school. But whatever the course of my culinary travels, I always knew that the thousands of miles I logged on my palate (and my liver) all led back eventually and inevitably to that first unforgettable train trip to California and back with its white tablecloths and long, leisurely, delicious dinners.

The Ole Miss Blues: Was "Ole Miss" Originally a Train?

My favorite train story of all involves the University of Mississippi and a key part of its colorful past, not to mention its present. Recently, it has been rumored—and by some people accepted—that the phrase "Ole Miss" was a bad mark on the university's history. That story, which I'm firmly convinced is false, involves the origin of the phrase "Ole Miss." A group of largely anti–Ole Miss people now allege that the phrase was originally used by black slaves to refer to white mistresses of plantations. All along, some tiny voice in the back of my mind has always told me that story did not ring true. Attributing a hostile and derogatory tone to that phrase has just never sounded right to me. Then in 2014 I received in the mail a big package of sheet music from my old friend the late Dr. Albert Earl "A. E." Elmore, an English professor and ardent historian, who then taught in Alabama.

The first thing I saw in the package was a big yellow-orange picture of an old-time black steam engine pulling a train from Memphis to New Orleans. The title was "Ole Miss Blues, Words and Music by W. C. Handy," famed Father of the Blues. The subtitle called the train, which was trailing a big plume of white smoke, "The Fastest Thing out of Memphis." The lyrics were vivid and explicit:

> Talk about your fast express,
> There's one train that I love best—
> I just want to tell you this—
> 'Bout an engine called "Ole Miss."

The most obvious interpretation of the phrase "Ole Miss" in the song is that it refers simply and with nostalgia to Mississippi as a place and to a specific train that runs through it. The date on the back of the sheet music, published in New York City by The Handy Brothers Music Co., Inc., is 1920.

A second copy of sheet music in the packet, also by The W. C. Handy Co. of New York City, shows a dark blue train trailing gray smoke with the headline "instrumental blues," copyright renewed in 1944 by W. C. Handy with rights reserved to European representatives in London. Clearly it was not an obscure work then, although it now seems to be largely forgotten. Dr. Elmore also included with the package a lengthy and persuasive essay describing the close relationship between blues great W. C. Handy and the University of Mississippi in Oxford.

Mr. Handy, whose famous band was based in Memphis, often played for University of Mississippi dances. William Faulkner sometimes led the dancing when Mr. Handy was playing at the university between 1912 and 1914, as cited in works by UM Professors Adam Gussow and Clifton Bondurant Webb. In 1916 Handy wrote, published, and recorded a second, related song called "Ole Miss Rag." On the sheet music of that Handy song was another engine, this time with a dramatic red and green background. On the front of the speeding black engine, again trailing white smoke, was a big clear date: "1909." Underneath the engine on that sheet are the words "The Fastest Thing out of Memphis," making it clear beyond dispute that "Ole Miss" was the name of a train, not some fictional plantation mistress.

W. C. Handy was not the only famed black blues composer and musician to use the phrase. The great Scott Joplin later recorded his own version of the "Ole Miss Rag" as well, apparently the only song Joplin ever recorded that was not his own composition. Recordings of Joplin's session are still available. Still later, the inimitable Louis Armstrong also issued his own slightly revised version of "Ole Miss Blues," which is also still available. W. C. Handy allegedly stated that he personally preferred Armstrong's version to all others, including his own.

I searched for some proof of the story that "Ole Miss" was not a relic of slavery but rather an old blues song about a Mississippi train. About the only thing I found was in the book of my good friend, retired Ole Miss Professor David Sansing. At pages 168–69 of his fine and definitive history of the university, Dr. Sansing seems to adopt the "plantation mistress" theory, but in a single sentence, citing absolutely no authority for it. That history of course in no way detracts from the well-known history of how the term "Ole Miss," cited by annual editor Emma Meek, became the title of the university's annual, as well as its later use as a nickname for the football and other sports teams. Those are simply true, but entirely separate story lines.

When the former Public Relations Director Ed Meek (no relation to Emma) of the School of Journalism published in his "Hotty Toddy" blog two articles Dr. Elmore and I wrote in 2014 expounding on the Ole Miss/train history, we received quite a bit of incoherent, near-hysterical blowback. We decided the issue was simply too volatile and emotional and pursuing it further would do Ole Miss no good. But now that I am seventy-seven years old and should at least be considered a somewhat neutral observer as a Millsaps graduate and former civil rights lawyer for North Mississippi Rural Legal Services in the 1960s, I decided I could not let the issue die without putting it in what will no doubt be the last of my five published books. So here it is for what it's worth. Personally, I still wish they would bring back the Handy-Joplin-Armstrong song and play it at Ole Miss parties and ball games to make sure the name is not abolished, but I doubt I'll live to see it happen.

Other Train Songs

Of all US states, Mississippi seems to have had the deepest musical nostalgia for trains, not surprising since we're the "Home of the Blues." I sometimes get the blues myself, thinking not only of the California trip and my frequent trips from Oxford to New Orleans on the old Crescent City Limited. Now I sometimes get the "Guntown Blues" when I realize this book will probably be my last. The first Elvis Presley song I ever heard was the haunting "Mystery Train," about a "long black train, sixteen coaches long." The best biography of Elvis was aptly named *Last Train to Memphis*.

Much earlier there had been Jimmie Rodgers's classic mournful ballad that began "All around the water tank, waitin' for a train," and several train songs by Mississippi John Hurt from the Delta, Fred McDowell from Como, and Huddy "Leadbelly" Ledbetter, whose "Midnight Special" allegedly shined its headlight on prison inmates, promising an early release to inmates from prisons like Angola in Louisiana and Parchman in Mississippi.

No Saturday television baseball game in my childhood would have been complete without the late Dizzy Dean of Wiggins belting out "The Wabash Cannonball" during the seventh inning stretch. By a happy coincidence, I happened to grow up on the Wabash River in rural Indiana. There is even another little-known train song about a freight train that ran through my old hometown called "The Nickel Plate #7-6-9." Even football had its own train song about the hard-hitting linebacker Dick "Night Train" Lane.

Most train songs are country, but Hank Snow and Jim Reeves did classic Western versions as well, and there is at least one well-known New York train song "The 'A' Train," and even Europe had its Orient Express. Perhaps my favorite train song name of all time is "3:10 to Yuma."

If someone wanted to write "The Guntown Blues," the subject could be the legend, accepted by many there, that the assassin John Wilkes Booth did not die in the famous barn fire where his body supposedly burned up, but escaped to faraway Guntown, Mississippi, where he allegedly lived out his life and was buried in the Guntown cemetery. Several locals have offered to show me his grave. Since my mother had several Booth relatives in the Shenandoah Valley near Front Royal, where I used to spend my summers, I really should investigate that legend I suppose, but maybe I'm afraid of what I might find.

Ruminating on all these train songs drove me to Wikipedia, where I found many a trove of them, dating from the 1920s. Skimming over six hundred of them, I found that their titles give a powerful impression of the romance of old trains and train travel: "Last Train Home," "Big Wheels," "Long Black Train," "Down by the Station," "Non-Stop to Nowhere," "Slow Train," and "Lonesome Whistle," not to mention the classics "Mystery Train" and "Midnight Special." Less romantic views are projected by songs like "Pullman Porter Blues," "Nine Pound Hammer," and "John Henry, The Steel-Drivin' Man." The latter song reminds me of high-school years when they used to hire us to drive big metal spikes into the hard wooden crossties under new tracks. We would even mockingly hum, "I've been working on the railroad, all the livelong day," a sort of American version of the old Russian serfs' work song "The Volga Boatman": "YOH-oh, Heave Ho, YOH-oh, Heave Ho, Toiling Weer-ill-lee, For-or-ward Go."

Train songs would of course not be complete without a few about the "Easy Riders" like "Box Car Willie," the "Hobo Jungle," the "Railroad Bums," and the classic "Ramblin' Man." Sadly, the most prescient of train-song singers was Merle Haggard, who wrote and recorded his little-known gem "No More Trains." Nowadays Europe has many fast trains, but no songs; in the US we have many good songs, but precious few trains.

A Long, Strange Road to Paris and the Wider World

I moved from the US to international travel by an unusually circuitous route. When in high school, like all teenagers, I had to have a car. My father said, "Fine, as soon as you can pay for it yourself." The quickest money around was baling hay. I leased a baler and custom-baled hay for farmers for two summers until I had the money for an old, rusted-out red Plymouth convertible with a cloth top. The first night I had it, I headed out some thirty-five miles south to an open-air dance with a live band. I asked a beautiful brunette to dance. We soon noticed a guy tapping dancers on the shoulder. I was afraid at first that he was cutting in but soon realized he was not cutting in, just removing couples from the dance, which turned out to be a dance *contest*. Before we knew it, we were alone before the band. We had won the dance contest—without even knowing each other's names.

I invited the girl out for the next weekend. She said I'd have to meet her mom first. I noticed her fancy new car and how it contrasted with my old, smoking Plymouth with its loud mufflers and period "fenderskirts." I should also have noticed that after baling hay all morning and practicing baseball all afternoon, then showering under a garden hose with my clothes on, and hay in my hair, I was not exactly presentable. But I was young, and after all, we had just won a dance contest together.

We pulled up before a big house with columns. Her mother met us on the broad porch, walking down a tall, curving staircase. When we chatted, I thought I did fine. I had blond hair, muscles and a suntan. What else did she need? Once back at home I called the girl. She was crying. "I'm so sorry, but I can't go out with you. My mother says you're too *countrified*." I was devastated.

When I told my mother what was wrong, she turned straight to my father and said firmly, "Dear, we're sending Johnny to Paris—to knock off his rough edges. Nobody calls *my* son 'countrified.'" After two intensive years of French classes at Millsaps College, summer school in 1961 in Aubigny in rural central France, and another in 1962 in Quebec, in northern Canada as preparation, I found myself headed for the famed Sorbonne for a classic Junior Year Abroad with Sweet Briar College. To help pay tuition, my father had sold my car. Little did I suspect that, being a perpetual student, living always in cities, from Paris to Quebec to New Orleans, it would be ten long years before I owned another car.

French Summers and My First Solo Travels Abroad

My wonderful Millsaps French professor, Bill Baskin, still a friend and now in his late eighties, told my parents I had promise in French but needed much more in-country experience. At first that sounded way too much like what the girl's mother had said. In any case, they shipped me off in the summer of 1961 to Aubigny in Berry, a rural province in central France that once belonged to Scotland and still has a real Scottish lord in residence. That summer we learned mostly grammar, the hard way, but the town had a good swimming pool, which I frequented every day to see the French girls at the pools wearing tiny bikinis, a pleasant new experience. I met my first French girlfriend, Gisele Berthelon, a dark, sultry beauty. The oddest thing about Aubigny was how "countrified" most of the people were. Some of the workmen still wore wooden shoes lined with heavy wool. Signs of World War II violence were still widespread. Most people there spoke with a strong regional accent, rolling their *r*'s in a way that would have horrified Bill Baskin. The organizer and lead professor for the summer was Dr. William Emile Strickland, Language Department Chairman at Ole Miss, a great man. His son William, who was five years old that summer, is now an optometrist in Oxford and a good friend and charter member of our wine-drinking group the OWLS, or Oxford Wine-Lovers Society.

My Aubigny summer exploded several myths I'd heard about France and the French. Somehow I had long imagined it was always warm in France in the summer. It was not. My mother, wiser than I was, had knitted me, by hand, a warm, thick, wool sweater, the only one I took with me. I ended up wearing it every morning and especially every evening, when you could sometimes see your breath. French housing was also a surprise. Dr. Strickland had me lodged in a beautiful eighteenth-century chateau just a couple of kilometers from La Chaumière, the cozy old inn, complete with shutters and boxes of flowers at the windows, where all the other American students stayed. There were nineteen of us in all: seventeen girls and two guys. The other guy was Watt Gregory from Arkansas, who later became a lawyer and a partner in the Rose Law Firm of Little Rock, later made famous by the Clintons.

My giant room in the chateau was beautiful, with shining parquet floors, velvet curtains, and a huge, high-to-climb-into four-poster bed. Although the place was stunningly beautiful, it did lack a few modern amenities, most notably running water, electricity, and an indoor toilet. The maid was dressed in a classic little black-and-white servant's costume with a really short skirt, high heels, sheer stockings, and a fancy apron. She always brought me a big, beautiful, empty bowl with a big, beautiful pitcher of fresh, cool water sitting in it. The first day I could not decide whether to brush my teeth first and my face second, using the toothpaste water, or wash first and be stuck with soapy water to brush my teeth. I also discovered that the French back then did not use washcloths, only hand towels. When I told Dr. Strickland of my dilemma, he told me to just wash my face in the cold water of the basin and leave my tooth brush and paste at the hotel to use after the delicious breakfast they served. He also gave me a cloth bath glove, which you put on your hand to replace our washcloth. It was handy. I still use one today. The breakfasts were the most pleasant surprise: flaky, buttery *croissants*, definitely not those doughy "crescent" rolls we still have in the US, slathered with apricot preserves.

The bathroom was a much less pleasant shock. Located just outside the elegant, carved wooden back door, it had a real marble seat, very handsome, over a plain, much-used hole in the ground. Beside the seat was a thick stock of neatly trimmed squares of old newspaper hanging from an antique brass hook. Someone had punched neat little round holes in the center of each piece and had strung a long piece of twine through all of them. A neat enough idea, but not tempting.

Once again I went to Dr. Strickland for an explanation. "Oh, of course. I'm sorry I forgot to tell you. You're to use Watt's bathroom. At least they didn't treat you to what they call here a Turkish toilet—no seat, just two places facing forward to put your feet on."

With those few exceptions, the chateau was delightful—chilly, but delightful. I even came to enjoy my cold morning walks across the little bridge over the peaceful Nère River (the town's full name being Aubigny-sur-Nère). I tried to chat with the workmen repairing the bridge and the walls along the river but found their French accents utterly different from the polished Parisian French Bill Baskin had tried to teach me. The classes, however, were in perfect French and fascinating. We studied France from the Middle Ages till the Revolution of 1789, plenty for the two months we were there.

At the end of classes, Dr. Strickland took us on a six-week tour around France, across Switzerland, Germany, and Austria and down into Italy. Our rickety bus was always breaking down, causing our elderly driver to intone in his best Berry peasant accent "Ça ne marshay pas." (It won't run). By the time we got to Venice, which was breathtaking at night, I had nearly forgotten the lovely Gisele and developed a huge crush on Nancy Buchanan, a classic Ole Miss sorority girl. When my attraction was not reciprocated, I became frustrated and decided to leave the tour. Despite Dr. Strickland's wonderful commentary and the company of his charming wife "Gigi," or Ginette, I also learned, on what was to be my very first package tour, that such travel would never be for me. Another day, another town, another hotel, another bus breakdown.

On our last night in Venice, I approached Dr. Strickland and told him I was leaving the tour and heading back for the Riviera, the Côte d'Azur (azure coast) as the French still call it. I had to get away from Nancy and had truly fond memories of the two nights we'd spent visiting Nice and Cannes, one night being at the summer solstice in June, when we spent a *Nuit Blanche* or "white night" (i.e., stayed up all night dancing and drinking champagne in the streets). To my surprise, Dr. Strickland agreed with me. "If I were your age and free, I'd do the very same thing." Not only did the kind professor agree to my leaving, he advanced me money for travel, which he said he would recoup by canceling my remaining hotel and meal bills. It was too good to believe.

I caught a train that evening for Nice, where I found a hotel/pension where I could get, for almost nothing, my breakfasts and dinners and a tiny room, which I shared with a French merchant marine, with the bathroom—and even a shower—down the hall. The food was more Italian than French and featured a kind of minestrone with every dinner, but it was hearty and delicious, and the place seemed pretty safe. As agreed with Dr. Strickland, we wrote separately to my parents, stressing that he thought my solo trip was not only safe, but a better way to improve my French than spending a month on a bus with other American students.

There was only one problem with going to the beach in Nice, which I had planned to do every day: Nice has no beaches, only steep hills of round, smooth black rocks. The real sand beaches were all at Cannes, five or ten miles to the west where the hotels were all way too expensive for my miniscule budget. My roommate told me the bus to Cannes cost only a nickel or so—roundtrip—so I took the bus and swam and sunned away the entire month at Cannes, turning the darkest tan I'd ever been in my life. My kit consisted of an extra pair of espadrilles, an extra pair of jeans, two blue cotton shirts, and a soft cotton sweater. All the rest of my gear stayed with the group. I was never cold, hungry, or lonesome but did develop a strong addiction to Orangina, a sparkly French drink I can still find in Oxford at Newk's Eatery.

I had zero money to travel to the Basque Country in the green Pyrenees, which I had most wanted to do (and did many times later), so I just toughed it out at the beach every day. One evening, sitting on the terrace of the hotel in Nice, an elderly couple came slowly strolling by. We struck up a conversation, and she invited me to her house for a drink. Her companion was a retired teacher. She was the widow of a famed (in France) *chansonnier* or nightclub singer named Mario Casarès. She and her companion were very worldly and told me amusing stories of their many travels. He explained how he had joined the Communist Party and was totally committed to its program to convert France to the Soviet bloc. I was shocked speechless, but it didn't matter since he loved to talk about it and explain it, over and over.

One evening my landlady reminded me of the date: my return flight to America was only two days away. I ran to the highway and started to hitchhike. I was picked up several times, once by an old couple who introduced me to chicory coffee, made entirely with milk, no water. I've drunk the same coffee ever since, now using 1% milk and Splenda sugar substitute with the Luzianne brand. Kept awake by the coffee, I arrived at our Paris hotel, the Hotel Cambon on the rue Cambon right beside the US Embassy. My comrades could hardly recognize me since I'd grown a long, bleached-blond, droopy, evil-looking Fu Manchu moustache. With my wild, uncut curly hair and deep tan, I think I worried Dr. Strickland for a moment, but he treated me to an immediate haircut and shave and all was quickly copacetic. The next morning we flew back to Mississippi.

For the summer of 1962 Bill Baskin got me a nice scholarship to Laval University in Quebec in northern Canada. My parents drove me there and stayed several days at the famous Château Frontenac, a massive hotel built high on a hill overlooking the St. Lawrence River. My father liked it so well in Quebec that he went fishing there every year for the rest of his life. I got friendly enough with the staff that they let me keep my books, even my tennis racket, under one of the big overstuffed chairs in the enormous lobby, which I used like a second home. I badly needed a place for studying and pit stops because my only real room was in a remote village outside Quebec City over an hour away by bus. The school allegedly put us there to make sure our Quebec family spoke no English. Unfortunately, their French was even more countrified than that spoken in Aubigny. Their accent had an ugly sort of burr sound like servants in a Molière comedy. But the classes were wonderful, transformative.

Classes went from 8:00 a.m. to 2:00 p.m., which meant my roommate Frank (from Saskatchewan) and I had to get up by 5:00 a.m. for the bus ride, which was usually spent standing up all the way. The mornings were remarkably cold for a boy used to Mississippi. It was on the bus that I saw the biggest difference between Quebec and Paris: It was loaded with priests and nuns. For most of my life till then I'd never been around Catholics, let alone nuns.

Some of their ways were a revelation. Frank and I always got up and gave our seats to the nuns, thinking that was normal. We quickly learned there was a much different rule for members of the monastic orders. I never saw one priest give up his seat to a nun; more shocking by far was seeing priests rushing forward in their black robes to beat the nuns to any available seats. Now that was another new world.

My favorite part about the priests was the way the mischievous little Quebecois boys would yell out "Madame" after a priest walked by, making fun of his long, black, dress-like robe. The boys of Quebec were especially fun. My Quebec family enlisted me to teach them the exotic, for them, art of baseball, everything from hook slides to bunting. They wanted to practice "beanballs," but I told them those were not tolerated. There were no protective helmets for young heads back then. There were not yet any Canadian big league teams like the Montreal Expos either, so they had made up all sorts of baseball franglais jargon based largely on American words with funny French accents. Hearing eight-year-olds speak French is a whole different school, full of useful slang.

I dated a very beautiful girl from Puerto Rico, who had been born and raised mainly in Spain, but her father had moved his business to Quebec. When we went out, even though she was already seventeen, she had to have her aunt as a chaperone at all times. She called her by an old Spanish term, a *duenna*. The aunt was good-natured and always looked the other way if we made out a little during our long evening carriage rides along the path above the St. Lawrence, the only thing we were allowed to do. Because it was so cold in the evenings, we were always under heavy wool blankets on the middle seats, behind the driver of the horse, and the aunt was in the back seat behind us, so she could not see much of what we were doing, but it was all quite innocent anyway; innocent, but great.

Our classes, which were mainly on phonetics and pronunciation, were difficult but highly effective. My best teacher was a grumpy fortyish redhead from Paris with a Parisian accent. The Quebecois called her a *métropole*, as being from mainland metropolitan France. The very first morning she called on me to pronounce *aujourd'hui*, French for "today." I confidently said it. She shook her head sadly, but kindly. "You have not pronounced one single sound correctly," she said. As my father had said already, "The French don't care what you say, just so you pronounce it right." They were both so right. There's a big difference to them between "oui" and "ui."

"Here are some rules," she said the first day. "In French, vowels always rule over consonants, which is the opposite of English, where your hard consonants control your speech." Eh? She went on to explain that you use fifty-eight more facial muscles in speaking French than you do in speaking like an American, where we speak with a more open mouth and a relaxed jaw.

She showed me how in French you always form your lips *first*, as if to speak the first vowel first in a word, even if the word begins with a consonant. That is probably too much explanation already, but I had to mention it because what she taught me explained all the future successes I had with my French, which were considerable and which opened the doors to all my future travels. Very few Americans ever seemed to care to go to the trouble of learning to do things the French way. To my surprise, it was worth it.

My favorite things about Laval were the Friday afternoons. Even though the food was not very good, the local idea of "haute cuisine" being pea soup and bean soup, the beer was for some reason all German and really good. Every Friday afternoon, with my student ID card, I went to the Dortmunder Rathskeller of the Laval Union, where from three to five o'clock all the beer you could drink was free. The only downside was its extreme popularity. You first stood in a long line in the brick-lined cellar to get a big, foamy stein of German beer. Then you walked straight to the back of the long line and steadily drank it standing up as you worked your way up the line again. By the time you got to the front of the line your stein was empty. Bathroom breaks had to wait till after five o'clock, when they were really crowded but really happy. I don't recall drinking a single glass of French wine while in Quebec. That had to wait for Paris.

After one year at the Sorbonne in Paris I was totally hooked on France and the French lifestyle. I called my father and told him I was staying for a second year. He said, "Fine—but you have to pay for it." I eventually landed a job with Air France as an interpreter and tour guide. Being fluent in French opened doors for me for the rest of my life. As for the girl's mother, I never saw her again. Too bad I never got to thank her. I don't even remember her name.

From Old Algiers to Marrakech

See the marketplace in old Algiers,
Send me photographs and souvenirs . . .
[From "You Belong to Me," by The Duprees, 1962]

My baby-blue 1961 US passport shows a naïve youth with wide round eyes. As copied in the endpapers here, its pages are covered with exotic entry and exit stamps from places like Yugoslavia, Istanbul, the Greek Islands, Indonesia, Russia, Mallorca, and Gibraltar. There is a student visa for the Sorbonne, a work permit for Air France, and a more unusual one for Algeria, partly handwritten, issued in Madrid on April 29, 1964, at the embassy of the new Democratic Republic of Algeria, and good for two months. An entry stamp, half in Arabic, shows I entered Algeria on May 11 and returned from there to the old Paris airport at Le Bourget on June 18. The intervening month was a fascinating, unforgettable one. How a young American ended up in wild and lawless Algeria less than two years after every last Frenchman was expelled in June 1962 on threat of death is an unusual tale.

One afternoon, in a Paris café, I noticed a beautiful young woman looking straight ahead with tears streaming down her face. She looked and dressed French, but with a tanned, exotic, athletic edge I could not quite identify. After a few moments of my staring at her, she turned and looked directly at me. Without thinking, I said, "I'm sorry to see you crying." She looked puzzled, then her eyes hardened. "It's you, the French, who caused it," she said. "You're cowards, afraid to defend your own country." Flattered that she thought I was French, I also wanted to get closer to her, so I said, "I'm *not* French. I'm from Mississippi."

I had long since learned that saying "American" opened a whole can of emotional and political worms that would just get in the way of any personal connection, while "Mississippi" always seemed to have an immediate positive impact of both mysterious and concrete visual associations for French people. I got right up and went over and sat down with her. She didn't object. Rather than doing something trite like offering to order her a drink, and risk breaking the energy that I felt we both sensed, I asked her again why she was crying. She seemed much more interested in what I'd said. "*How* are you from Mississippi? What is it like there? Violent and green and humid as our French writers say?"

A long conversation ensued in which I quickly disposed of my own rather mundane past and gently moved her into talking about hers, and why it made her cry in such a profound way. "I am a *pied noir*, a French Algerian," she began. "Or rather I was. Now I am *pied nu*" (barefoot). In French a *pied noir* is a French person, but native to Algeria, where multiple generations of French colonists had lived between the Mediterranean and the Sahara desert since the 1830s. French Algeria was a sort of wild California from the days of Zorro, a land warm year round, a land where poor French people with a sense of adventure went to improve their lives after times of trouble, sort of like Okies from Oklahoma went to California during the Great Depression.

Many *pied noirs* made their fortunes, amassing great wealth and vast plantations while constantly surrounded by resentful Arab-speaking Berbers, mixed-race Muslims brutally colonized against their culture by the French. In June 1962 the native Algerians finally won their long civil war of liberation as memorialized in the grimly accurate movie *The Battle of Algiers*. The Algerians gave the hundreds of thousands of French colonists just twenty-four hours to get on boats at the harbor and leave the country or be shot on sight. The French were allowed to carry with them only what they could put in one ordinary suitcase. The headlines in the papers called it "suitcase or coffin." Almost everyone chose the suitcase.

The young woman opened her purse, a sleek, expensive one. Inside, she showed me a slim black .32 caliber automatic. In my two years as a student in Paris, I'd never seen a woman with a gun. She began to tell me of her life in old Algiers, before the "great departure" of June 1962. She had been in her last year of high school, had tons of friends, and liked to swim and surf with them on Algeria's beautiful beaches and sit in the cafés, happy and healthy. Algeria was in so many ways France's California. The violence of the civil war had seemed to her for a long time to be just a nightmare that would pass. But the sight of Frenchmen with one arm blown off by a terror bomb was then common in Paris. More striking was someone with a black patch over one eye to cover the empty hole made by a favorite terrorist weapon: a raw potato with double-edged razor blades stuck in one side. Those were shoved into the faces of *pied noirs* strolling between the lovely classical pillars fronting the covered downtown walkways of Algiers built to shade people from the sun. The pillars also protected terrorists waiting to use their deadly weapons to terrorize the French to give up and leave "their" country. Even on the Paris métros there were corner seats with big signs noting they were reserved solely for the "mutilés de guerre," those crippled in war, from World War II through Indochina to Algeria. They were seldom empty.

The girl's name was Claude Achat [clode-ah-CHAT], one of those unisex French names applied equally to men and women and usually mispronounced in an ugly way by Americans as "clawed." She had lived in an eighteenth-century Turkish palace high above the crescent-shaped port, looking down on the deep-blue Bay of Algiers, which was always filled with colorful boats with white sails bobbing against blue water, as I'd seen in films and read about in Albert Camus, the classic *pied noir* writer. The young woman missed not only Algiers and her outdoor French life there but also the vast orange groves and cotton fields of her father's plantation farther inland. Strangely, she missed almost as much her Arab friends and playmates whom she'd known forever; she worried with nostalgia how they were getting along without what she saw as the paternal kindness of the French to protect them from their own worst impulses and from the strange, cruel lifestyle imposed by the barbaric premedieval rules of the Koran and the Sharia law about to be imposed on them.

As we talked and she described the beauty of the land and its peoples, the foolish idea formed in my mind that I would go there, photograph everything, talk to her friends, see and feel her lost country for her, and come back and report to her how things were. When I finally suggested it to her, she first looked moved, then laughed, calling me a childish American. She said I proved to her what Charles De Gaulle had once said, "Americans are brave fools; the French clever cowards." Her description about being "brave" appealed to me then, although I did not really agree about the French. Why I thought I could go there and survive I don't know. Certainly not from bravery. More like youthful ignorance. At some level I must have known the danger, because I misled my parents, writing to them that I was going to Spain and on to Morocco, carefully avoiding any mention of even the idea of going to Algeria.

Then Claude handed me a little bright-red hardback with gold lettering that said *Noces* and *l'Été*, two early groups of essays by Albert Camus, written in 1937, long before all the horrors he experienced, first in Paris under the Nazi occupation, then the loss of his homeland of Algeria to a pitiless Islamic/Communist revolution of the worst kind. Those bitter changes turned Camus from a lyrical writer of enthusiastic, hopeful energy to a burned-out "existentialist," a sort of highly talented nihilist who saw little hope for humanity's future. When I read his beautiful early essays, so different from his depressing later writings like *The Stranger*, I was hooked.

Some excerpts from the book of Camus essays may explain better my romantic motivations to travel to Algeria. Here, in my own amateur translation, is one of my favorites of Camus's youthful writings.

"Summer in Algiers"
One would no doubt have to live a long time in Algiers to understand how its excess of natural gifts can suck the life out of one. There is nothing here for those who want to learn or to improve themselves. This country teaches no lessons. Algeria neither promises nor delivers any philosophical insights. It is content simply to give, but in profusion. Its pleasures have no remedies and its joys remain without hope. It offers no consolations except the happy lassitude of days utterly married to the earth.

With the words of my hero Camus ringing in my ears, I headed for Algiers. Every last person I talked to begged me not to go, saying it was much too dangerous. Being young and foolish, I ignored them. Using my Air France travel pass, I flew to Madrid, where travel agents had told me I could obtain a visa for Algeria. There was no Algerian embassy there yet, the country still trying to establish a working government, let alone a working foreign service. But at a single desk in the Tunisian embassy I found an Algerian general, in uniform, who was acting as consul. Obviously puzzled at my request for a visa but pleased an American wanted to go to his new country, he filled it out, largely by hand, and put an inked stamp on it, in French and Arabic, which read "Visa Number One." That should have been a warning, but I of course thought it was cool.

With some Air France contacts, I got a flight on a Spanish plane that carried the mail to Morocco, via Gibraltar, where I managed to hitch onto another Spanish plane straight to Algiers. Arriving with just one small gym bag, I asked the customs officials about a hotel. Their welcome amazed me. The first one called the others over to show them my American passport with its "Visa Number One" stamp. First one, then another, started saying, "Kennedy, Kennedy." The first one explained they were saying that because President John Kennedy had been one of the very few leaders of any major nation to back the Algerians against the French in their revolution. The officials put me in a cab headed for town. As we drove along a sunny corniche under a searing blue sky, the driver showed me the bay, which was full of sailboats. Above it, laid out in a semicircle, was Algiers, which immediately reminded me strongly of San Francisco. Its tiered levels of houses, which artfully climbed the steep hillsides, were nearly all white, presenting a stunning sight, worthy of the French nickname for the city: "Alger La Blanche," Algiers the White.

When we pulled up to what had to have been a five-star hotel under the French, I told the driver I could never afford it. "Ah non, monsieur," he said. "You are our American guest," and refused to let me pay anything for the long ride from the airport. He escorted me inside and explained to everyone who and what I was. They seemed overjoyed I was there and took me up marble stairs to a beautiful room overlooking the spectacular bay. Tired from the flights, I decided to eat in the hotel restaurant. It was a magnificent meal of couscous with grilled baby goat. Once again my offer to pay was refused. But they gladly accepted tips.

I had noticed that I was the only diner in the restaurant. The next morning I learned I was also the hotel's only guest. Since the banishment of the French, almost no tourists came to Algiers, and the Algerians could not afford the hotels and restaurants abandoned to them by the French. That day I took another taxi up the steep hills to the former mansion of Claude's family. It had been built under the Turks and was lavish in its appearance, if a little run-down from being vacant. I began taking pictures when neighbors came up and warned me pictures were "not customary." They were very friendly, but became nervous and basically silent when I mentioned Claude and the Achat family. It was apparent that *pied noirs* were a taboo subject, and in all the rest of my stay there I was never able to ask about Claude and her family or their former Algerian friends.

For the next few days I simply wandered the streets, stopping in largely deserted cafés, eating great meals mostly for free in empty restaurants, talking to lonely waiters delighted to finally have a customer. I went to a few nearby villages, but can only remember one by name: Bab-el-Oued, nothing more. I avoided the city of Constantine, on the eastern coast by Tunisia, because it was the stronghold of militant Islamists and Communists, a strange mix. I was also told to avoid, much against my will, beautiful Kabylia, the wild mountainous home of the tribal Berbers, given that name by the Romans, who called them "Barbarians." I met several in Algiers and disagreed with that characterization, and still do, but avoided Kabylia and the High Atlas Mountains. At the suggestion of one waiter, I went to the public swimming pool, a former private club open only to the French. Algerians had been barred, except as servants. People again were friendly but reserved and this time a little nervous. The pool was filled with happy, splashing Algerians.

The lifeguard, a gorgeous blond Berber woman with a great tan and an utterly un-Islamic bikini, was pointed out to me as also the "speakerine," an interesting Franglais word for the local nightly news anchor on Algerian television. I swam up to talk to her. She got down from her perch and we had a long talk. She asked if I wanted to appear on television. My instinct to be open had by then been tempered. I felt that I was too prominent already and politely declined. She understood and readily agreed that I had made the right choice. Her offer was apparently just hospitality and good manners. With total inconsistency, I could not resist inviting her to dinner. The cold look on her face immediately told me I had crossed another invisible line. This was the new Algeria, and no matter how she was dressed and how happy people were to have an American visitor, there would definitely be no fraternization of that kind.

After my experience at the pool, I continued for a week or so exploring Algiers without incident, but somewhat as Camus had warned, the country was in a strange way beautiful but empty. I felt odd sitting in cafés alone, reading. There was really nothing else to do. And, to my surprise for that time of year, it was fearfully hot, although pleasantly dry. It did not seem to cool down much at night and I found it hard to sleep, which was totally unusual for me. The concierge at the hotel suggested I do what the French used to do (an unusual mention of their existence): fill the tub with cold water and lie in it for a couple of minutes every hour or so to cool down. It worked. He even suggested he would put a plastic sheet on my bed and I could wet my cotton sheets in the bathtub and lie with them under me and over me to cool off. I didn't go that far, but did enjoy the frequent dips in the tub.

After a couple of weeks, to my surprise I felt that odd sadness Camus had predicted. I was well fed mostly for free, and flattered and pampered everywhere, but lonelier than I'd been in years. Feeling guilty at my lack of gratitude, I nevertheless hailed a rare taxi to the train station and took a train west to see the city of Oran. There was an American Consul there who offered to help me call my parents, but I declined, explaining I did not want to scare them. The consul gave me a surprising sum in cash and also bought me a first-class train ticket to Tangier, Morocco, and from there on to Casablanca, where

I caught the worst bronchitis of my life sleeping on the beach, but a local Arab pharmacist gave me, without even a prescription, a box of Néo-Codéions, narcotic pills that cured it fast, through heavy coughing.

With my Air France pass, I bought a reduced-price, first-class night-train ticket south to Marrakech, sharing a luxurious sleeping cabin with a Belgian businessman who wore one of the fanciest suits, complete with shiny silk socks, I'd ever seen. When I told him I'd been in Algeria, he was shocked and told me some really scary stories and encouraged me not to go back.

After several days in Marrakech, eating like a king and exploring the maze of souks and the massive, magnificent central market, the Djemaa el Fna, with its fortune-tellers, snake charmers, and amazing array of grilled meats, all things I had failed to find in Algiers. But of course they were not free. I reluctantly got an Air Maroc flight back to Algiers and on to Paris. My head still spins when I reminisce about the trip. Ironically, when I got back to Paris, Claude and her family had moved to Nice. I never saw her again, but we wrote back and forth for months, even after I returned to the US. I still have her beautifully written letters, among the few physical souvenirs I retained of a most amazing travel experience. My other souvenir, much cherished, is a big Berber blanket, woven in rough, heavy wool, which I purchased in some souk in Marrakech and shipped home. I had doubted it would ever arrive, but when I got home it was waiting for me. So much for the famous anti-Arab French proverb about dishonest *marchands de tapis* (rug merchants). It was beautifully woven of heavy beige and white threads with bright-red central medallions. As I write this, the rug sits folded upon the couch in my study, waiting for winter.

Two Years of Really Parisian Life

Certainly the most powerful formative experiences of travel during my youth, legal and otherwise, came during those two years as a student at the Sorbonne in Paris. My first year I spent as a semiserious student, going occasionally to class but mainly reading voraciously on my own in heated cafés, studying French novels and poems, practicing my accent, and pretending unsuccessfully to be French. Then my luck ran out. The academic year ended and my father and my draft board—the Vietnam War was cranking up—told me to come home. But I was not ready. I asked my father to finance a second "wander-year," as the Germans call it. He refused, but the draft board relented. "You can stay on if you like, but only if you pay for it yourself." I of course went for it.

My French friends at the fairly expensive *pension* (boardinghouse) where I lived were sympathetic. "We'll find you a really cheap hotel, and you can live less high. Maybe we'll even find you a job." I believed them and moved into a fifth-floor walk-up in the old Hotel Napoleon on the rue Bonaparte, an easy walk down to the Seine. But I had no luck finding a job, and my money was running out fast. One night a friend invited me to a party and introduced me to a pretty, if somewhat chubby, blond Frenchwoman. To my surprise (but not my friends'), *she* invited *me* out, apparently knowing I was broke. We went to dinner and dancing and then walked along the quais of the Seine. But somehow there was zero chemistry, or at least not that I noticed.

The next day my French friends said, "You fool. That was one of the richest young women in Paris. Her father owns a department store. And she *likes* you in spite of your attitude. The idea of a naïve American who speaks French intrigues her."

"But I'm uncomfortable with her," I said. "She doesn't attract me."

They were astonished: "What a fool! What an American! You need to eat, my friend, and worry less about attraction." Then they paused. "But you're still our friend. We just need to look out for you better."

I had no idea what they were talking about. And I could never have told the stories which follow if my parents were still alive. My wife, surprisingly, agreed to most of them, but my daughter Allison managed to talk me out of the most annoying ones. She was probably right, and this way we at least have some of the story.

One day a rough-looking guy we'll call "Jean-Pierre," who played on a friend's local rugby team, called me. "They tell me you are their friend and badly need some work to make money. Are you free for a glass of wine at the Corsican café, the Ajaccio, around 5 p.m.?" I was nothing if not free, especially for free wine. Jean-Pierre told me politely that I'd been foolish not to pursue the pudgy blonde, but he admired my spirit. "She told a friend of hers about you. That is unusual. The friend is a brunette, dark. Maybe she is more to your taste." I asked what he meant. "She too is *intrigued* by the idea of a young American man. None of them ever speak French like you do. It seems for some reason Americans are just not interested in speaking French."

I was puzzled. "So what's the *work*?" I asked.

"This girl knows you're broke and so you can't ask anyone out. She will pay for the evening if you like." Some instinct told me "No," but my young ego said, "Hell, yes, let her pay." So I agreed.

The next weekend I met the stunning brunette at the Corsican café, with Jean-Pierre making the introductions. She was obviously not exactly a "girl" and was at least ten years older than I was, thirty-something to my twenty-two. Jean-Pierre told me before she arrived, rather bluntly I thought, the ground rules. She was married. The name she would give me would not be hers. I would go out with her one time only and never see her again. "Do you accept?" he asked. I was slightly shocked but flattered at the same time. How French was this? She arrived shortly after Jean-Pierre explained the rules. We got into her expensive little sports car and headed for the country, stopping at a remote little roadhouse several miles outside Paris. We hit it off immediately. She had a soft, throaty voice and was dressed expensively and perfectly suiting her looks. It surprised both of us I think that we were both so at ease.

We had a long, slow dinner in a tiny private room in a discreet restaurant attached to the little country inn. We did, without the slightest hesitation or embarrassment, what every teenage boy imagines he would do with a beautiful woman if life were just a beautiful dream. Nothing really new, but all slow and perfect. In the morning they brought us breakfast in bed. Around noon she gave me the cash to check us out and drove me back to the Left Bank, where she let me out several blocks from the café where she picked me up.

"I wish I could see you again, but that is not possible. It would not be wise. My husband is a very jealous man. You will understand?" I sort of understood but did not want to accept it, yet what could I say? I did remember to offer her the envelope full of change from the large multi-franc notes she'd given me. She just laughed a little tinkling laugh and waved at me as she drove off. The money was more than my hotel and meals would cost for a month.

That evening I stopped by the Corsican café for a glass of wine with Jean-Pierre. "I hear it went well," he said. "Too well," I said. "She was perfect. I want to see her again. Surely you know how to contact her."

He cut me short. "You Americans. So naïve. You'll never understand French women. She can't afford to see you again. Besides, neither of you would enjoy it in the same way again. It would become complicated." I began to wonder. Maybe French women really were as different as people said.

Jean-Pierre asked me what I was doing the following weekend. "There is another woman, another brunette since that is what you seem to prefer. You are interested, I presume?"

I didn't know what to say—where was this going? I had a little money for once, but still no prospects of a job, not even a work permit. I sort of didn't want to, but sort of did. Looking at it in the abstract, it was kind of an adventure. I told Jean-Pierre I had a problem. "I felt something for that woman, and whatever she says, I think she felt it for me too."

He shook his head slowly: "Perhaps it is as my friends said. You may just be *too American* for Paris." That comment stung my pride. "Ok," I said. "We're on for next weekend."

When the time came, at a different café, equally anonymous on the Place de l'Acadie, a dark convertible pulled up. The woman did not get out. Jean-Pierre nodded to the car. "There she is."

I walked over and got in. She drove off. After giving me a name, she drove out east along the Seine toward Meaux, where the famous brie cheese is made. She pulled over and asked me to drive, which made me feel really good and much more confident. She no doubt knew that. This time was even better. Never had I felt a faster connection, and I was sure she did too. This time she paid for the dinner and the room, but as she dropped me off the next morning, without a word, she slipped me a scented envelope which I did not look at until after she drove away. It had even more money than the first woman had given me.

With mixed emotions I told Jean-Pierre the next time I saw him that this "deal" was getting to me. I loved it and I hated it. He said, "Take some time off. Now you have money." But it wasn't the money. I had started loving the excitement, was hooked on the intrigue, the mystery, and the ego satisfaction of it all—not to mention the lovemaking. The atmosphere was just so unique. It was like living in a strange, foreign novel. I finally told Jean-Pierre I was not going to do it again. By that time I had enough money to last me for a month or two with my cheap lifestyle, enough even to ask a French woman out and pay for it myself. But I couldn't keep doing it.

I had taken their money gladly enough but told myself it was over. It had just become too uncomfortable for me, like what those women they call "courtesans" must feel. Luckily, I could walk away, and I did. I didn't tell Jean-Pierre exactly what happened, but I'm sure he understood, probably better than I did. He later asked me to meet a couple of other women, but I declined.

Françoise

A couple of weeks after my experiences with Jean-Pierre, I got a call at my hotel from Madame Annie, the proprietor of the wonderful, homey pension where I'd lived during my first year in Paris. It was just two blocks from the beautiful Luxemburg Gardens, through which I ambled to my Sorbonne classes every day—when I went at all. Madame Annie was a fantastic cook and a real second mother to all of us students, especially the foreign ones. That night she told me she had a "lost sheep," a new American student who really needed help, and she thought I could provide it. His name was Rhett Symonds. He was a Sweet Briar junior-year student and a wealthy banker's son from Charleston, South Carolina. His parents had sent him to Paris, sort of like mine had, to "knock off his rough edges" and learn a new world. I had loved it, but Rhett hated it. Madame Annie said he'd started drinking heavily and was so depressed she feared he was suicidal.

When I met Rhett, he said all he wanted was to go home and relax on his sailboat in Charleston harbor. When I told him his father said he had to stick it out a little longer, he said he'd settle short-term for two things Paris had so far failed to provide: an endless supply of Budweiser and a Zippo cigarette lighter. We stopped at the big Bon Marché department store, and I found him what the French call a "zee-poh." I promised to find him a Budweiser source the next day. When I asked if he would like female companionship, he cheered up considerably. I took him to the Coupole, a huge café where it was easy to meet women, French and otherwise, especially from 11:00 p.m. on.

We got a table and I foolishly tried to interest him in raw oysters. Absolutely no dice. Way too French. Sauerkraut and Alsatian Riesling went better. I introduced him to a tableful of lovely young women from the Canary Islands who looked friendly. One rubbed his cheek. When they looked the other way, he whispered in my ear: "They're mulattoes! What if my father found out?" I couldn't believe it. "You're in Paris. My god, look at them. They're gorgeous— and they speak English." Rhett was unmoved, so I gave up. The girls finished their meal and left, looking puzzled. I tried to explain to them that they were really beautiful, but Rhett was a "head case." Unfortunately I think he overheard and understood me better than they did.

Rhett finally settled into his sauerkraut and ordered a pitcher of beer while I tackled a few dozen oysters with some more Alsatian Riesling. Around 2:00 a.m. our waiter told us his section was closing and he had to move us. He put us at a table beside an elegant, striking young Frenchwoman and a fidgety, effeminate man who turned out to be American. He was a fashion photographer and had a stunning book of glossy photos of her he was pitching to her, trying to convince her to become a client. "Not interested," she said coldly. I'd seen plenty of cold, snobby Parisian women, but she stood out. His pictures were good, but she was obviously bored stiff. After a few minutes, Rhett and I started talking to him in English, which seemed to annoy both of them. Her face looked even more bored. She was such a showoff about it that she finally succeeded in annoying me, beautiful as she was. I asked her in French if she did not understand simple English. She said she "didn't understand it and didn't want to," especially not the "nasal" version spoken by Americans. She said we sounded like we were talking with a hot potato in our mouths. I thought that was funny. When I translated for Rhett, he was much less amused than I was.

The photographer went back to showing her pictures while she took long, bored drags on one strong Russian cigarette after another. "Sobranies," she called them. They were obviously expensive and smelled good, even to a nonsmoker like me. I had just about forgotten about her when Rhett cheered up, ordered himself another pitcher of beer and me another bottle of Riesling. As I turned to watch the beer arrive, I caught her staring at us. For once not bored, her face looked animated, interested even. Insulting us had apparently turned her on. I suspect it may do that with the French.

As the waiter set the beer down, the photographer told her it was time to go. I didn't want her to leave. On a sudden impulse I reached over and knocked the whole pitcher of beer all over him and his photos, catching her eye. She was smiling broadly, but quickly tried to avert her eyes. He started screaming and cursing. Then they both giggled like girls. While he went to get a waiter with a towel, I asked her if she'd give me one of her pictures. She looked puzzled. "What kind of Americans are these?" her face seemed to say. "They are not my pictures. They are *his* pictures," she said.

"Well he's certainly not going to give *me* one after I sloshed beer on them. What should I do?"

She surprised me: "Give me your address and I'll send you one," she said.

"Where will I send the thank-you note?" I asked her.

"You don't get my address so easily. You are obviously a very impetuous man. Who knows what you are capable of? You cannot have my address—or my phone number," thinking ahead of me. But I absolutely could not let her just slip away.

"Alright, I understand completely. What if I meet you here tomorrow night, ten o'clock, out in public, and you bring me the pictures? Ok? Perfectly safe?"

She smiled. "Okay."

Then I asked her name. She said, "I know yours is John from hearing your friend say it. Very ordinary name. His is much better; I like *Rhett*, very 'old South,'" she tried to say in English, but it came out old "souse."

I persisted: "And your name?"

She actually smiled again. "My name too is very ordinary. It is Françoise, which means "French girl" in French. My last name is a little better, it is Fersancourt [fehr-saw-COOR]." It was musical to the ear. Roughly translated it means "to flirt with." Appropriate and promising.

Later I found a steady supply of Budweiser for Rhett, Madame Annie found him an American girlfriend, and he enjoyed Paris just fine, although he never learned to like the French or their ways.

Françoise and I met as agreed, and after a few days of preliminary sparring she asked me to move in with her in a beautiful little apartment her father paid for on the rue St. Sulpice, right behind the interesting old Eglise St. Sulpice, which was later featured in the famous novel by Dan Brown about the search for the Holy Grail. Years later it was featured in the award-winning movie *The Da Vinci Code* with Tom Hanks. When we lived there, the church was black with soot and leaked heavily because part of its roof was missing. By the time the movie was made and I was back in America, the old church had been beautifully restored and looks as it does now.

One reason Françoise agreed for me to move in with her was because I'd found a job, thanks to a friend of my old college roommate Christian Garrison.

The friend worked for Air France and called in a couple of favors to help a stranded American. The job was easy, as I describe later on, and led to plenty of interesting travel. In the meantime, my life with Françoise was Paris at its best. She worked part time as a freelance model, specializing in sweaters and hats, while working half time in a fancy boutique on the elegant Boulevard St. Germain, in the heart of the Latin Quarter. Her father supported her in high style but was eager for her to get married. At twenty-seven, she was well past the right French age but liked her life so well she had no desire whatsoever to marry, which was fine for me. Beautiful as she was, I was beginning to miss America and knew I had to go home for the fall semester of 1964 and had no desire to *be* French, although, like so many Americans before and after me, I liked pretending.

After several weeks together, Françoise finally told her parents that she had a live-in boyfriend. Her father was delighted, but suspicious, and when he heard I was American, he was highly suspicious. He invited us to a typically lavish French Sunday dinner outside Paris where we ate and drank richly all afternoon. At the end of the evening, he invited me to lunch the following week. We met at a fine bistro near the Palais Royal, where my Air Tour France office was on the rue Ste. Anne. Apparently we hit it off well, because he asked if I'd ever thought of becoming a French citizen. I told him definitely not, that America was my country, but that I had begun to dream of one day having a second home in France, though first I had to find a way to make a good living, perhaps as a lawyer. I went to the Palais de Justice a lot to fantasize what it would be like. We left it at that.

A couple of weeks later M. Fersancourt invited me to lunch again. This time he closed the lunch with a proposition: Would I be interested in learning to manage one of his several restaurants in Paris? He badly needed a fluent English speaker who understood American customers and who knew at least a little about food and wine, which he figured I must know from the many fine meals he'd been buying Françoise and me. I knew I had to say no, but stalled. It was obvious that marrying Françoise and probably giving up my US citizenship would eventually be part of the deal, and I knew I'd never do that, but did not want to give up Françoise and our life together any sooner than I had to. We agreed to talk more about it later.

In another month or so, we had another long, leisurely French lunch one Sunday in the country. For the first time I noticed tension and anger between Françoise's mother and father. She was angry; he was silent. Back at our apartment, I asked Françoise what was up. "It's my father's mistress. She's my age. My mother is furious."

Once again M. Fersancourt had invited me to lunch the next week. When I arrived, beside him was a beautiful, young *pied noir*, a Frenchwoman from

Algeria, recently run out of the country after the Algerian Revolution. We had a pleasant lunch. Toward the end, when she excused herself for a moment, he asked me a stunning question: "Would you like to have lunch again next week? I can have Chantal invite a friend to keep you company. Obviously, Françoise must know nothing about it." I didn't know how to reply. Thinking as an American, I immediately assumed he was testing me to see if I would cheat so openly on his daughter, which would surely disqualify me as a husband. But that seemed too obvious, too clumsy. So once again I stalled, claiming I was going out of the country on a trip for Air France and would call him when I got back.

Going straight home, I told Françoise exactly what he said. "Oh, *pauvre John*. You are still so American. My father is testing you in the *opposite* sense; he wants to be sure you are discreet and trustworthy. He knows most French husbands cheat on their wives. He just wants to see if you can do it *properly*." I thought "Nice use of the word," but "wow, I really *do* think like an American." Françoise and I saw then and there that things would never work out, but that we would string her father along as long as we needed to while we stayed together. And we did.

Probably the most pleasantly amazing Parisian experience happened sometime in 1963 just after the movie *The Great Escape* came out. It starred several famous British actors playing English pilots trying to escape from a high-security Nazi prison camp. The movie was a huge hit in Paris, especially its one American star, Steve McQueen, who played a classic American-looking guy in a baseball jacket and cap who spent his time bouncing a baseball off a concrete prison wall and catching it in a real baseball glove he had somehow managed to hold onto. One afternoon we were at my favorite Parisian café, the Dome in Montparnasse, where an English friend and I were debating the relative merits of English cricket and American baseball. I had with me my old fielder's glove, which closely resembled Steve McQueen's. My English friend had a big cricket bat and a shiny, single-seamed red cricket ball.

The next thing I knew a couple of giggling teenage French girls approached us and nervously asked me for my autograph. I was nonplussed. "Pourquoi moi?" I asked, wondering why in the world me of all people. "Oh, Monsieur McQueen, of course you know why," they gushed. The word must have gotten around because for the next week or so young women kept coming up to me at the Dome for "my" autograph. To me, I looked nothing like Steve McQueen, but even some of my French male friends claimed they saw a resemblance beyond the baseball glove. Maybe it was my build or my round Germanic head, or just our American look. I don't know. But rather than offer the women any further arguments (some got huffy when I at first refused to sign), I finally started signing autographs as "Steve." One day the real Steve McQueen showed up on the covers of several French magazines during a visit to Paris to promote the movie. My cover was blown and there were no more autograph requests, but it was definitely fun while it lasted.

After those several early flirtations with marriage, I remained single until I was twenty-seven and have since remained a remarkably faithful husband, despite my earlier proclivities. According to two old gentlemen I saw outside of our old apartment by St. Sulpice, Françoise managed and later owned the entire building, living in a penthouse on the top floor. They said she always went for her daily cup of hot chocolate at the Café Flore and her usual six-week French vacation at St. Tropez every summer. I later learned from neighbors that Françoise Fersancourt never married.

A Little Bit of Sorbonne

Lest I leave the impression that my time in Paris was totally social and frivolous, it should be noted just how much we seriously studied the origins of words we have in common with other cultures. My professors even gave me books about where words in French came from. One of the books has disappeared with the passage of time, but an updated version of one of them is still in my library: *French Words of Arabic Origin*, or *Mots Français d'Origine Arabe* by Nas E. Boutammina. Nearly all our modern words beginning with "al," Arabic for "the," whether French or English, are of Arabic origin, such as "alcohol" and "algebra." More surprising are words like "amen" and "antique," not to mention everything from "cotton" to "sugar."

Even more interesting to me than our Arabic connections were the remarkable number of words in English borrowed from French, and although the French hate to admit it, the vast number of French words borrowed wholesale from English, as follows:

French Words Common in English and American
à la carte * à la mode * à propos * Art Deco * avant-garde * bon appétit *
bourgeois * carte blanche * c'est la vie * chic * cliché * crème brûlée * cuisine *
debutante * décolleté * encore * ennui * femme fatale * fiancé * folie-a-deux *
hors d'oeuvre * lingerie * Mardi Gras * ménage à trois * négligée * papier-maché *
petite * protégé * RSVP * sabotage * savoir-faire * souvenir * tête-à-tête * trompe
l'oeil * vis-à-vis * voilà

Often shocking to American eyes and ears are the vast array of trendy English words you see and hear everywhere in Paris, from shopfront names to café gossip, for example:

English Words Common in French

babysitter * best seller * blackout * boss * brainstorming * break * briefing *
business * camping * checkup * chewing gum * coach * cool * crash * design *
discount * dry martini * duty-free * fair play * fast food * has-been * hobby *
holdup * interview * kidnapping * leader * lobby * look * must-have * nonstop
* one-man show * overbooking * overdose * pacemaker * package * parking *
penalty * planning * pool * puzzle * racket * remake * rock * rush * scoop * self-
control * sexy * shopping * show * skateboard * skinhead * sponsor * stress *
striptease * talk show * timing * weekend

So there: Proof that not all my time in Paris was spent on night life. One
nostalgic update about the evolution of our cultures: using French words
in English, which once seemed "cool," now sounds more old fashioned than
sophisticated. The English words borrowed by the French, by contrast, sound
modern, rushed, and often full of "stress," as the French now constantly say.
Perhaps it's still not too late to just say, "C'est la vie."

Tending Bar on the Island of Mallorca, Then to London with a Beautiful Parsee, and on Again to the Greek Islands for One Last Summer of Freedom

My job at Air France began as a sort of all-purpose gofer position doing
whatever the executives needed done. Working daily in a French office was
a real eye-opener. Employees, male and female, had sex together a lot, most
often during lunch. The guys told me that a couple of the hotter young
secretaries put moleskin, like you use on corns on your feet, in their bras to
stimulate their nipples. Now that was French. Pretty young girls from the
country who worked as clerks in nearby shops often had "nooners" with older
men with money, meeting in *hotels particuliers*, elegant, high-end Parisian
"no-tell hotels." The girls were called "midinettes" after the French word for
noon. As I was the lone American, my role there was unique, but that's a story
for another day.

My first job, other than running errands, was to attend long evening
cocktail parties for our English-speaking clients, most of whom were from
Asia. Our office, which was actually a subsidiary of Air France called AirTour
France, handled package tours for international clients. Most of the ones I
dealt with were from India and seeing Europe for the first time. All drinks and
hors d'oeuvres were free. After a week of hangovers, I learned never to drink
alcohol on those evenings. I drank only tonic water with lots of ice, pretending
they were gin and tonics.

One side benefit of my modest job as a gofer was getting two free Air France tickets for a weekend on the Island of Corsica, of Napoleonic fame, with my then-fiancée (I hoped) Dorothy Kalins, known on her personal calling cards as "Bunny" (seemed appropriate at the time). We took a quick trip to what the French call the Île de Beauté (Isle of Beauty), rented a nice little Citroen Deux Chevaux two-seater and made the circuit of the entire island, hugging the coast. In the spring of 1963, there were virtually *no* tourists, only us *travelers*. The interior was a wild country of gorse-like maquis, for which the French Resistance was named, since it was a land of rugged bushes somewhat like parts of the old West Texas Panhandle where it's easy to hide, a fact of which Corsican bandits supposedly took full advantage.

Our only scare was one night when we stayed too long on the road, almost failing entirely to find a hotel. At last in the small village of Erbalunga, we found a tiny hotel-restaurant called *Le Pirate*, the name indicating proudly its shady past. The "dining" room was lighted only by a big fireplace. The food was delicious wild game in a rich sauce. The heavy red local wine had no label that I recall, but the rich, viscous, light-brown moscato aperitif they offered us stranded Americans was called Cap Corse and has been one of my favorites ever since. We fell asleep pretty quickly to the peaceful sound of the sea—we thought. To our shock, when we awoke, we found that the sea, which fortunately was calm, there being virtually no tide in the Mediterranean, was only several inches below our open window.

After a hearty Corsican breakfast, more Italian than French, we drove back southeast and on to Paris, talking of what other exotic parts of France we would explore next. My ideas were two regions which later became my favorite places in France outside Paris, both deeply green and relatively unspoiled: Alsace in the northeast and the Basque Country in the Pyrenees in the deep southwest. Sadly, we never made it together to either one, but there is an outstanding book on the latter, which I recommend highly: *The Basque History of the World* by Mark Kurlansky.

In the meantime, my mother and Bunny (can't stop using it) became friends and my mother, for the first and only time in her life, actually lobbied me to persuade her to marry me, a frivolous young student with (at the time) no serious prospects. But her father put the quietus on that idea quickly. "He absolutely insists I marry an 'NJB.'" "What is that?" I asked. "Nice Jewish Boy." Little did I suspect what she would go on to do: edit *Metropolitan Home*, found and edit *Saveur*, serve as *Newsweek*'s executive editor under John Meacham, and write several books. I probably could never have kept up with her brilliant, high-octane life, but for a few wonderful weeks it was fun imagining.

After a few weeks it became apparent that most of my days at Air France were being spent in taxis traveling around to various embassies and consulates straightening out paperwork like visas and vaccinations for Indians, Indonesians, Malaysians, and the occasional Australian or New Zealander. One day Monsieur Joudon, the *patron*, or boss, said, "John, you're spending way too much on taxis riding around Paris. If you can put up with him, I'm going to give you your own driver, an old, worn-out, retired Foreign Legionnaire named Sergeant Emile. He will chauffeur you wherever you need to go. We have given him an old beat-up Deux Chevaux (two-horse) Citroen to use. It's not sleek, but it will get you around."

M. Joudon was so right. Emile was burned out and cynical, but good company and a great storyteller of scabrous Foreign Legion adventures he'd had from Algeria to Indo-China, as the French then called Vietnam, Laos, and Cambodia. Emile's dangerous life of adventure had left him missing a couple of finger joints and parts of his nose and upper lip, but he was a surprisingly careful driver—for a Frenchman. For weeks we drove around Paris and were so successful with that and with my cocktail party schmoozing that M. Joudon gave me a sort of promotion: no more pay, still minimum wage, but a much more interesting and pleasurable task, accompanying package tour groups on weekends to the Spanish Island of Mallorca in the Mediterranean off Barcelona. I would fly every Friday morning with a planeload of fifty or so two-week tourists to Palma, Mallorca, and return on Sunday evening with a different group who'd already been there for two weeks. I could spend all my free weekend time at the beach and sleep for free in one of the cozy bedrooms at the Air France office in Palma. This idyll lasted until May, when I began to think about my return to school in the US. I wanted to travel and see as much of Europe as possible before my return; I especially wanted to see the Greek Islands.

M. Joudon kindly let me use my Air France ID card as a free pass on any Air France flight with room. Empty seats were way more available back then. I headed first to Madrid to see the Prado Museum and attend a classical Spanish play by Lope de Vega, thinking my Spanish was much better than it was. It was a time of youthful romantic notions on my part. I loved the saying *La vida es sueño, y sueños sueños son* ("Life is a dream, even *dreams* are dreams"). From Madrid I went on south to Andalusia, the romantic land once ruled by the Moors, most artistic and sophisticated of all Muslim cultures, which they still proclaim whenever we Westerners ask them what Islam ever did for civilization.

At Granada I visited the magnificent Alhambra and bought an intricately woven Andalusian blanket with golden threads on a red and blue background which still hangs on the wall in my study sixty years later. I heard there was a famous fiesta in Málaga on the coast and spent a week of nights there in candle-lit caves watching and listening to gypsies sing Flamenco songs in piercing voices while stomping their feet to Flamenco guitars. Two rich young bankers' sons from El Salvador, who were homesick for their Ivy League colleges in the US, took me along in their new black Mercedes and showed me the inside view of a classic Spanish Fiesta. When they went home, I was broke again. Using my last card, my Air France pass, I flew back over to Mallorca, planning to sleep in the office. It was, alas, full of vacationing Air France employees. Even my beautiful friend Danielle Desjardins, the local Air France manager, had taken her red convertible off on a tour somewhere, so I was stranded with no money and nowhere to sleep. So I just slept on the beach and swam and sunbathed all day, thinking of how to raise some cash.

I had somehow kept just enough money to afford one solid meal a day, a three-egg Spanish potato omelet which I washed down with a rich, delicious chocolate milkshake. One afternoon, with my entire body and long, unkempt hair covered with sea salt from swimming all day, I sat in a beachside café slowly chewing my omelet to make it last. There being no other free tables, a young Englishman my age asked to join me. When I told him of my plight, he immediately had an idea. His mother owned and ran a private English guesthouse, *not* a hotel he stressed, on the north end of the island. She badly needed a good bartender but insisted he be French. I told the guy, whose name was Louie, that I spoke fluent French and had been an interpreter for Air France. "Not a chance. She would spot you for an American in a minute," he said. As we talked, I told him of my summer in Quebec studying at Laval University. "That's it," Louie said. "You're French Canadian but spent lots of time in English Canada, which explains your accent."

We got on Louie's motorcycle and headed out. I had no luggage but a tiny gym bag with an extra pair of jeans and espadrilles, and definitely no hotel to check out of, so we wandered north across Mallorca. On our way we stopped for Louie to pay homage to one of his favorite characters, Father Junípero Serra, the Franciscan scholar and missionary who introduced Spanish grapes and wine to California while supervising construction of the great Spanish Missions along the California coast from the Baja and San Diego to Monterey and San Francisco, planting grapes as he went.

After several hours, we arrived at the guesthouse, which was named Casa Cumberledge for his deceased father, a retired British admiral. As we practiced my story about being French Canadian and an experienced bartender and waiter, Louie told me about the colorful assortment of British aristocrats who spent their summers at Casa Cumberledge, which was located near a fishing village named Cala Ratjada. He warned me that some pretty scandalous love affairs and other louche behavior went on and that I should not appear too shocked at the salty language of some of the aristocratic women.

Louie also explained the other language challenge of Mallorca. Legally it was part of Catalonia, whose capital is Barcelona. The people there, especially poor people, do not speak Spanish but Catalan, a dialect somewhat like Provençal in deep southern France. The language explains why there are the two spellings of the island's name: Mallorca, the Spanish one, and Majorca, the Catalonian one. Since both double "ll" in Spanish and "j" in Catalan are pronounced like an English "y," pronunciation is no problem. Louie also explained how strangers always said they were *on* the Island of Mallorca, while locals and veteran ex-pats who lived there always said they were "in" Mallorca, considering the exclusive little island to be a world of its own.

Madame Cumberledge bought Louie's story about my being French Canadian and hired me on the spot to be a sort of combination bartender/ waiter. The guesthouse had a huge stone terrace facing the Mediterranean with dozens of well-spaced tables. The guests never bothered to go in the bar; it was too beautiful and comfortable outside. So I did more waiting than bartending, first taking orders and mixing their drinks, mostly gin and tonics and local wines or simple *Cuba Libres*, rum and cokes, drunk to protest dictators, especially "Generalissimo" Francisco Franco, the long-time Fascist dictator who still ruled Spain back then. Such simple drinks made it easy for me to pose as a knowledgeable bartender, which I certainly was not.

In contrast with their simple tastes in drinks, the guests were a complex and remarkable group. Several had titles like "Lord This" and "Lady That," which everyone used freely. They argued loud and long. To me it was like a home for unhappy married couples who, for the sake of appearances and financial reasons, would not divorce, but made it clear they hated each other thoroughly. In many cases the women wanted to dance, but the husbands usually did not, which led to the second, more unpleasant part of my job. If a woman wanted to dance, I was to accommodate her. There was a handsome but sleazy Spanish piano player with the French name René who wore white shorts, had shaved legs, and favored shiny white patent leather sandals with no socks. The British guests said he gave gigolos a bad name. René was even said by some to be Madame Cumberledge's lover (among others), but I doubted that. He actually seemed to enjoy dancing with those bitter, grumpy thirty-something women, perhaps expecting return favors from them later.

The most colorful character there was a handsome, athletic-looking horseman with gray hair and a rough Cockney accent. I can't recall his name or find it in my old address books or the letters to my parents, all of which my mother kept and later gave to me, but he was the national Steeplechase champion of England and a big favorite of the ladies despite his out-of-place accent.

The next most colorful character was a tall, lean, sunburned Englishman with an American girlfriend who never took her nose out of a book. They would arrive each afternoon in a little red two-seater convertible and stay all evening. The first day he came, the assembled lords and ladies applauded. I asked Louie what the big deal was. "He's a sort of local hero, a well-known gun smuggler for the anti-Franco rebels." I was impressed, but became much more so one evening when I saw him in action. His girlfriend always had a medium-sized English bulldog with her. On that evening a new guest brought her own bulldog. When the two dogs sniffed each other's rears and apparently didn't like what they smelled, they started a huge, snarling, roaring fight, slinging bulldog slobber in all directions. The gun smuggler, looking even taller and leaner than before, calmly snatched up his girlfriend's bulldog, which probably weighed fifty pounds, in one hand, and the other fifty-pound bulldog in the other and did a remarkable thing: he slowly eased them forward as they snarled and tried unsuccessfully to bite him and gradually placed them nose to nose.

This maneuver somehow intimidated both of them. They turned their muzzles away from each other and began to whimper. The tall man forced their noses together over and over, then rubbed them on each other briefly, and slowly placed them both on the ground far apart, causing them to slink quickly off in opposite directions. This time the guests really applauded. The tall man, rather than seeming to enjoy his notoriety, told his girlfriend "let's go," and they abruptly left. Louie explained to me later that the gunrunner came to Casa Cumberledge, like the others, because it was quiet and discreet; people there knew how to keep secrets. He obviously did not want it widely known, because of his gun smuggling, where he could be found.

While at the Casa I was allowed to drive the Cumberledge's big, old 1940s Citroen DS, and I found time to visit sites all over the island, including the famous bullfighting ring in an abandoned limestone quarry at Múro, where El Cordobés often performed. I also visited the beautiful, terraced seaside vineyards where the Mallorcans made a wonderful Muscat wine, like a Malmsey Madeira, and visited by small rowboat some spectacular seaside grottoes which became important to me fifty years later, long after I'd forgotten ever seeing them, as explained in the Epilogue.

I was probably lucky to miss the one sordid story to strike a glancing blow at the secretive reputation of Casa Cumberledge. One of the biggest British government scandals of the era had broken not long before I arrived. A senior member of the cabinet, War Secretary John Profumo, was caught going with, and perhaps discreetly pimping for, two high-end call girls named Christine Keeler and Mandy Rice-Davies. The sticky part was that while Profumo was "keeping" Christine, she was also being shared, as it were, unbeknownst to Profumo, with a Russian spy, the Soviet naval attaché in London. There was no proof that any secrets were ever revealed to him, but the revelation of the matter itself caused a huge brouhaha in the press. John Profumo's brother had for many years been a regular summer houseguest at Casa Cumberledge.

Luckily for Madame and Louie, the Profumo brother had already been there and left before the spy scandal broke, and no Mallorcan connection to John Profumo ever appeared in the press.

The bad odor that entire episode gave to the otherwise distinguished administration of Prime Minister Harold Macmillan nearly brought down his government. He resigned a few months later, claiming acute ill health. The British still laugh about it. Later, on a visit to Oxford, I met and befriended Macmillan's interesting grandson Joshua, a tall, dark, dashing character who usually wore a long, black cape and tended to (or tried to) resemble Lord Byron. Sadly, before I got to know Joshua better, he died of an accidental heroin overdose after a Rolling Stones concert we attended.

My favorite customer at Casa Cumberledge was the great British writer Robert Graves, who lived most of his life in a village on the southwest side of the island called Deià. He came to Cala Ratjada for privacy for several weeks that summer to escape a constant stream of famous visitors to his own home. Alec Guinness, Ava Gardner, and Peter Ustinov were just a few of the celebrities who constantly sought him out there. Mr. Graves walked with a cane and had a huge halo of long, curly, white hair, which on breezy days he covered with one of those flat-brimmed, round, black Spanish hats. He was always accompanied by a beautiful Spanish-looking girl who wore a similar type of flat hat. She asked that he not be disturbed, and I honored the request, sort of, but sent him questions sometimes through the girl, whose name was Pilar [PEE-lahr]. I assumed she was his daughter, but did not ask. I asked her to tell him first how much I loved his classic memoir of World War I *Goodbye to All That*. When he did not object, I had her tell him I thought his book *The Greek Myths* was by far the finest book I'd ever read on one of my favorite subjects. His response through Pilar was "Try my poetry; I am a poet; I write those other books only for money, so I can live freely like this in this beautiful place." That was our only real "conversation," but it was an inspiration to me for the rest of my life.

My own modest life there was just about perfect. Although I was not paid anything at all, my meals and drinks were all free, and I was given a beautiful cozy room with French doors, always open, looking out on the beach and the Mediterranean. I usually only worked from 4:00 p.m. or so to 3:00 or 4:00 a.m., bartending the endless beach parties. All the rest of the day I was free to swim or lie on our private beach. Next door was a public beach hidden behind a tall tourist hotel, which was much more unusual then than now. That hotel was always crowded with blond stewardesses from Lufthansa and the old Swedish SAS Airlines. I never got to enjoy their company, however. Then someone far more interesting suddenly appeared.

One calm, peaceful evening a lovely woman with shining silver hair, probably in her fifties but looking more like twenty-five, summoned me to dance. She was the only person there with an American accent. She was a great dancer. Then there was a tap on *her* shoulder, not mine, a sign someone wanted to "cut in." The hand was a light golden brown and smooth, with fingernails a cream color, a strong contrast to her golden arm. When I looked up, I saw almond-shaped eyes in a face so exotic it reminded me of one of those old Persian miniature paintings. I could not believe it was the daughter of the American woman I was dancing with, but they were quickly sparring verbally. "To think my own daughter would cut in on me." The girl, who was my height, was dressed in a long diaphanous gown-like silk dress which made her look still more exotic and Eurasian and totally unlike her mother.

As we began a slow dance, I listened to her whispery voice, delivered in a beautiful, educated Oxbridge accent as unlike her mother's as her appearance. She held me close during our first slow dance, saying little. When the music stopped, she took my shoulders and whispered in my ear, "You are the biggest phony here and this place is full of them." When I stumbled to ask what she meant, she whispered more assertively, but still so softly no one else could hear, "You are no more French Canadian than I am, and that is saying something. You are a pure American. Well maybe not so pure, but who are you trying to fool—and why?"

I quickly asked her not to give away my little secret, and she just as quickly agreed if I would just answer *all* her questions. My answers were simple and easy for her to accept. My questions to her, however, were much longer and more complicated because she was so much more complicated, and we ended up in long, whispered conversations over several slow dances. When we continued to slow-dance during a fast number her mother returned. "You two have got to stop this. Your dancing is so heated the whole crowd is whispering about you, and this is a hard crowd to shock. Let me have him for a little while." As I fast-danced with the mother, whose name I've long since forgotten, I kept turning my head to stare at the daughter, whom we will call "Z." She still called me "Jean" [zhaw].

She had told me briefly a little of her complex background, which expanded, if not exploded, my mind. Her mother was a wealthy American who had married a rich UN diplomat with several children and a complicated past. Z was born the same year as me, 1942, in British India. Her father was a member of the elite Parsee sect, a unique society within British India. Being neither Hindu nor Muslim, the Parsees served as the primary civil servants and professionals under the British Raj. Their origins were well known to the English, but not to me. When the Muslims conquered Persia, now called Iran, many of the Parsees fled to India. The origin of their name is easy enough to figure, but just about everything else about the Parsees is complex: their origins, for example. Known in Persia as Zoroastrians, the Parsees in India continued their ancient practice of "honoring" fire in their ceremonies in tall fire towers. Most Christians and Muslims mistakenly called them "fire-worshippers," but the Parsees strongly deny that, insisting that their great towers of flames were built to honor their god and that although fire was indeed sacred to them as a symbol of the power and beauty of the universe, they certainly did not worship it. Their monotheistic religion allegedly predates both Christianity and even Judaism. To me they sounded much more like pantheists, who worshipped the earth and life itself. But that was probably just me.

Z explained to me that many people had never heard of Zoroaster or Zoroastrians until the powerful German writer Friedrich Nietzsche wrote his influential work *Thus Spake Zarathustra*, the German spelling of the name of their powerful god. Nietzsche got a bad name, like the composer Richard Wagner, when Adolf Hitler claimed his heroic Zoroastrian philosophy as part of the basis for his Nazi "Will to Power," Hitler's insane vision of establishing world domination. After that brief episode of bad publicity, the Zoroastrians again quietly fell out of the public consciousness outside India.

Her brief history hardly satisfied my intense curiosity about her, and Z and I spent the rest of our time together at the Casa talking personally and intimately. She explained to me that she was born a Parsee in the sophisticated ancient city of Lahore. When the British left India, the Parsees lost most of their privileged official positions under the British. Some, including her father, reluctantly claimed to convert to Islam, at least on the surface. Although most Parsees, including her father, retained their immense wealth, her father's conversion would have dramatically lowered her own status and possibilities for education and all other freedoms she would have had as a Parsee princess rather than a sequestered, veiled Muslim woman.

Her father took several actions to protect her. First, he successfully demanded that she continue to be considered a *begum* [BAY-goom], a sort of princess-like status (like a Bey in Turkey where the word originated), even while posing as a Muslim. When the violent Hindu vs. Muslim religious wars broke out, her father sent her to England for school. While she was in England, her home country of India was divided into Hindu India and a new Muslim country, Pakistan, whose name was an acronym of the names of its peoples: Pashtuns, Afghans, Kashmiris, and their common religion, Islam: "PAKIS-stan,"—*stan* meaning "land of." Her home in the ancient city of Lahore, capital of the old Punjab region, was on the border and just barely became part of the new country, Pakistan.

Outside of my bartender duties, Z and I were inseparable. At her suggestion, I told Madame Cumberledge who I really was: an American student on his own, totally broke, fluent in French and delighted with my no-pay job and ample free time, both of which I hoped to keep. Madame C. then totally blew my plans away: "You know, Jean (she kept the French name part), I've been talking to Louie. We are all just here to have fun; no one wants to do any work, but someone has to manage this place and although you're young, you seem like the only responsible one around." I couldn't believe it. Manage Casa Cumberledge? At age twenty-two I knew nothing about such a task. Then she added, "What salary would you like?" Again I was speechless. It was like one of those confusing good/bad dreams I've had most of my life: part pleasure, part disaster. I told Mrs. C. I'd have to sleep on it.

That night I told Z about it, and even wrote my parents to tell them I had at last the offer of a good-paying job. I thought I would have to take it. Then Z dropped some more news on me: her mother didn't like the elegant but raunchy crowd at Cala Ratjada, adding kindly that she *did* like "Jean," her new American boyfriend, "who is the only decent person here." She and her mother would be leaving for London the following Monday. There was a silver lining, however. "Thanks to my father, I have my own independent income, and it is substantial. Please don't be offended and think it's charity. I want to spend my time with you in London. If you'll come, I'll pay for everything."

Suddenly I did not need to sleep on it. "I've still got my Air France pass. Let's do it." I told Mrs. Cumberledge and Louie our plan. They said they'd miss me but that no one could compete with Z, so beautiful, so charming and talented, everyone's favorite at the Casa. Of course I never told them she was paying. I probably didn't need to.

The next week we met in London and stayed at various little West End hotels as we tried all the best Parsee-influenced Indian and Pakistani restaurants for every meal. We went to concerts and plays every night, partied late and slept late every morning. Z had an unusual way of checking out Indian restaurants. We would go in first and she would discreetly sniff the aromas of the curries. When the curry was really rich and aromatic, her forehead would bead slightly with sweat. After a few tries, where she said little beyond encouraging me to experiment widely, we soon learned that we both liked the same curry: highly aromatic to the nose, but not burningly spicy on the tongue. She told me that the mother cuisine of India was Persian, just as French cuisine was originally based on Italian, brought to France by the French Kings' Medici queens.

After two weeks we decided that we both preferred food from the Punjab region, with its strong Parsee influence, meaning that both the Hindu prejudice against beef and the Muslim prejudice against pork did not apply. We loved mostly delicate lamb and young goat, but why skip beautiful pork loins and beef ribs? We formed the habit of having one huge meal around three in the afternoon in a modest but wonderful little place called the Star of India near the Earl's Court tube station in an ethnic neighborhood that has since gone downhill. So few restaurants anywhere stay the course long term.

One day, while browsing side-by-side in a London bookstore, our eyes fell upon a copy of the *Kama Sutra*, which I had always assumed, from looking at some of the kinkier pictures, was a sort of Indian sex manual. Z picked it up and asked me if I knew the book. Embarrassed, I semi-lied and claimed I'd only heard about it. "Well, what you heard is not true," she said. I hoped she would stop there, but she went on. "Westerners never bother to look past the erotic pictures, but the book is actually pretty boring, written for parents to use in instructing their children on how to have a happy marriage. The imaginative sex is only a *very* small part, which could easily have been left out." That was a relief.

"The ancient *Kama Sutra* assumes arranged marriages, but it does have a few practical parts and there are some useful ideas in it."

With some hesitation, I popped the question she obviously was soliciting: "For example?"

She laughed. "Well, men's personal hygiene for one thing." I shuddered, hoping we were not going to begin discussing French bidets, which I knew were not for washing your socks. I strongly preferred not to go into such topics. I should have known she wouldn't. "Just for one example," she said, "a gentleman should trim his fingernails once a week." Well. Practical. I didn't reply, but I followed that practical advice ever since, and as far as I can recall, no woman has ever criticized my fingernails. I think we were both relieved when she put the *Kama Sutra* back on the shelf. It was never mentioned between us again.

While we were in London, Z did undertake to instruct me, at my request, about the Parsees' history and culture, explaining that their founder, Zoroaster, was said to have lived in the time of our prophet Abraham. She said Herodotus mentioned them and that Cyrus "the Persian" was said to be a practicing Parsee. From the beginning, they always believed in one god and an afterlife. It was their culture which interested me most. As I have since confirmed by a little research, the Parsees were indeed the elite of Indian society under the British Raj. They filled the most important positions in the empire as diplomats, lawyers, and famous personalities, like actress Vivien Leigh. Because they had no caste system and none of the severe dietary and social restrictions of either the Hindus or Muslims, they moved freely in all societies and were highly esteemed by the English. Surprisingly, they even dominated sports, particularly cricket, Parsee men being known as just as athletic as the sports-mad English.

The philanthropist Andrew Carnegie, during a visit to India, was especially impressed by Parsee women, who were liberated and educated far beyond any other women in India, including in some cases Englishwomen. Carnegie called Parsees "the most handsome race of all Hindoostan." Many had English governesses, and others were sent to England to school. The Parsees' idea was that educated women made better and more useful and enjoyable wives, and educated Parsee women were said to be "powerful" within the family and were sometimes compared to Jewish mothers. They wore both beautiful silk saris and European dresses, both sandals and high heels.

Interestingly, the Parsees condemned the smoking of tobacco as a "defilement of fire." Being paler than Indian Hindus, Parsee women were easy to spot in a crowd as Eurasian beauties. Despite their attractiveness, however, they rarely married outside their faith. It was obvious to me that Z was sensitive about her father's alleged "conversion" to Islam. She told me then, and I have since confirmed, that most Parsees reluctantly had to take their wealth and emigrate to England and other parts of the British Commonwealth, as well as to the United States, where they have quietly retained their culture in small groups in cities from Los Angeles and Boston to Chicago and Houston. But only a very few words of their language have made it into English, one notable exception being "toddy" for a cocktail, which is from the Parsee word for "palm wine." Our "Hotty Toddy" chant at Ole Miss is therefore more exotic than we ever imagined.

At the end of two glorious weeks, Z suddenly told me it was over. She had not wanted to tell me earlier and spoil our glorious time with news that she had to leave. The professional string quartet in which she played viola was going on tour, playing elegant country-house parties in Buckinghamshire. Obviously I could not tag along. She gave me a choice. I could stay all summer in London with the same lifestyle, but without her, with her older sister looking out for me. In the alternative, she had two friends who would be driving across Europe to Greece the day after she was leaving: Manuel, son of a wealthy Greek ship owner, and Michael, an English friend of Manuel, who was teaching him English. Manuel had a big comfy Fiat ready for the trip. All I needed were visas for Yugoslavia and Greece. I did not hesitate. Staying in London without Z would have been one long, sad summer. A month in the Greek Islands was the obvious choice.

Exploring the Balkans

In a London bookstore I found to my surprise a current guide, in French, to traveling in Yugoslavia in 1963. We crossed the English Channel by boat train and sped through France and Austria, eager to see Yugoslavia, which was the only Communist country you could visit back then. We stopped first in Ljubljana [lee-OOB-lee-AH-nuh], Slovenia, for two days of testing some really fine, really cheap wines, then down the Dalmatian coast of Croatia to Split (what a name). From Split we crossed the mountains, which reminded me of Montana, to beautiful, peaceful Sarajevo, capital of Bosnia, and later the scene of a terrible civil war when United Yugoslavia was divided into warring ethnic enclaves. Still curious, we crossed over to Belgrade, capital of Serbia, where we had some great, hearty stews of lamb and beef with really rich red wines. Our waiters seemed amazed to see their "first American," US tourists not yet being willing, apparently, to explore there. We finally decided to speed on to Greece.

Somehow, not knowing any local language, we knew nothing of the massive 7.0 earthquake that had leveled Skopje, the capital of our next destination, Macedonia. One morning, as we topped a tall rise, we saw below us a vast city of white refugee tents standing beside a large, ruined city, reduced to rubble as if it had been bombed. The city of white tents looked like a picture from Ken Burns's later film of the American Civil War. Barred from entering Skopje, and unable to offer the citizens any help, we drove quickly on to the Greek border.

We arrived our first night in Greece at the beautiful port of Thessalonica, where we had dinner under the stars with Manuel's family on a balcony overlooking the Aegean. They introduced me to my first taste of calamari, which was delicious and sounded a lot tastier than "fried squid." The next day we drove on to Athens, where I stayed for a few days under sweltering heat until Manuel took me to the port of Piraeus to catch a ride with some Greek fishermen friends who had a boat that carried day laborers from island to island. We spent a month together, living on bread, cheese, fruit, and fresh Greek wine. Each day I would sail with a new group to a different little island, all beautiful and unspoiled in those days. I never made it to either Rhodes or Crete, but vividly recall Chios and Mykonos and similar-looking islands and especially the sacred Sanctuary of the Goddess Athena and the Temple of Apollo at Delphi, which we visited several times. Each time I had my fortune told and it was always positive. I was deep into both the *Iliad* and the *Odyssey* at the time, and those stops were like a dream.

The Aegean was not exactly, to me, wine dark, but had a unique blue-green caste I hadn't seen before. The sun was so bright and the sky so blue and the little stone houses on the brown island hills so vivid that it was like I'd always needed glasses and had just put them on for the first time. I slept at night mostly on straw mats in the whitewashed little houses, paying either a pittance for my keep or helping with little chores for the islanders, most of whom seemed elderly but happy. We sailed on again every morning. The only Greek words I knew (or can recall at least) were parakalo [pah-rah-kah-LOH] for "please," epharesto [eff-fahr-ess-TOH] for "Thank you," and the beautiful-sounding kalenichta [kah-lay-NEEK-tah] for "good night," but those words and a few hand gestures seemed to suffice.

Never having been a strong swimmer (my parents wouldn't let me swim till I was fifteen from fear of polio), one day I nearly drowned after being left accidently behind the boat. Full of good wine and truly immature, I thought what a romantic death it would have been and how people would say "he died young, swimming in the Aegean." Then I thought of my parents and how they would feel and swam strongly back to the boat.

◆ ◆ ◆

Unfortunately, after checking all my old, voluminous photo albums of those days, I have found no picture of the incomparable Z. My old address book did list an apartment for her father on the upper east side of New York, but I've hesitated to check it further. It is often better not to disturb one's most personal memories after so many years.

So I went back and finished my BA in French at Millsaps College. Broke and dependent on the kindness of strangers, I got a Woodrow Wilson Fellowship and an MA in French at Tulane in New Orleans, then a three-year Ford Foundation Fellowship to the Ole Miss Law School followed by a clerkship for famed Chief Judge William C. Keady, who helped me get a Prettyman Fellowship at Georgetown Law. I then spent three years in an intense private trial practice with a litigation firm and serving as legal counsel to US Senator John C. Stennis, during Watergate, after which I finally moved back to Oxford to litigate as an assistant US district attorney. I had been too busy to notice I had not traveled outside the United States in over a decade.

But my travels within the US continued to get more interesting. My good friend John Grisanti, who had a great Tuscan restaurant in Memphis, invited me to join him in judging wines every year at the Los Angeles County Fair, the largest such judging in the world. (You put the judgings where the consumers are, not where the wines are made.) On my four-person panel were Max Lake, an Australian winemaker, and David Lake, the only US winemaker to be a member of, as well as president of, The Order of the Masters of Wine, an ancient guild. My fellow panel members, due to their names, were called "The Great Lakes."

We began our judging by awarding gold, silver, and bronze medals to California wines only, but Oregon pinots and Washington State Rieslings were soon added. Within five years the best French, Italian, Spanish, and German vintners joined the competition. Among my favorite discoveries were the great cab francs and late-harvest dessert wines from the Okanagan Valley of Canada's mild, coastal British Columbia. We also discovered the wonderful port-style dessert wines of Don Galleano from hot, dry southern California, especially his Aleatico, a red muscat wine praised long ago by Thomas Jefferson, and his Angelica, a unique wine and the only fine wine still made from the first European wine grape brought to the US, the Mission grape of Spain. Galleano, uniformly referred to because of his big 6'4" frame and dominant, hospitable personality as "The Don," became, and remains, one of my closest and most cherished friends.

The most knowledgeable and distinguished member of our panel, year after year, was the eminent Peter M. F. Sichel, a German from an old wine-making family, who fled the Nazis in the 1930s, settling in England for "public" school and acquiring a classic Oxbridge accent with a Germanic lilt, which gives him an elegant air of striking authority and distinction. Upon leaving England, Peter came to America in the early 1940s to join the US Army to "kill Nazis." His astonishingly high score on his entrance exam IQ test caused "Wild Bill" Donovan, head of the OSS spy network, to invite Peter to join, which he did. When the OSS became the CIA, Peter was named CIA station chief for Berlin, where he stayed for a remarkable eight years, followed by several more years as CIA station chief in Hong Kong. He married a beautiful soft-spoken Greek woman named Stella. They are still together over fifty years later.

One evening the fair was presenting Peter with the Wineman of the Year Award, but everyone they asked to be the presenter of it begged off, saying his height, accent, and intimidating demeanor (to them) scared them off. As an old friend, I was drafted to do the job. Not wanting to look overwhelmed, which I actually should have been, I made an atrocious pun on Peter's middle initials, M.F., noting he was "one M.F.ing" good winemaker. Don Galleano liked the pun so much he came up to us, and we became close friends ever after. Wine puns are a sort of cottage industry in California. A big sign in front of the popular Napa Valley restaurant Mustard's Grill used to reserve the prime parking spot by the front door for the person who made the "Wine Pun of the Month." Unfortunately I never won that one.

Peter Sichel led a life of high adventure unlike anyone else I've ever met, or for that matter ever read about. After escaping from the Nazis in Germany, he was imprisoned for several months by the Vichy government in southern France along the Spanish border as an "enemy alien," ironically being held along with some German Nazis. Peter finally escaped again across the Pyrenees and on to the US via Portugal. His memoir, which I personally hounded him for several years to write, as eloquently as his natural modesty allowed, tells his story. The title succinctly sums up his remarkable history of professions: *Secrets of My Life: Vintner, Prisoner, Soldier, Spy.* A real-life Le Carré character, Peter spent World War II parachuting into occupied France behind Nazi lines to deliver radios and other critical contraband to French resistance fighters. Later, while serving undercover as our consul in Algiers, he also landed alone several times, in tiny rubber boats, all along the coast to collect hoards of gold coins hidden from the Nazis by local Jews and loyal French citizens of Algeria known as *pieds noirs*.

A more swashbuckling life than Peter's is hard to imagine. Fortunately, although he is now ninety-six, Peter is reluctantly collaborating in the making of a feature movie of his adventurous life. A publisher in Germany is also translating his memoirs into German.

After the war Peter, a nonsmoker, was offered all the cartons of free cigarettes he could carry away as a bonus for his services to France, which was too broke to offer him cash. Peter took the cigarettes and, in a rare moment of commendable wisdom if slightly dubious ethics, sold them on the black market for a huge profit. With the proceeds, Peter rebuilt the demolished and bankrupt Sichel & Sons wine business in Germany and began producing wonderful Rieslings. The first I tasted, a trockenbeerenauslese from the Rhine was at John Grisanti's in Memphis. Although John sadly succumbed to cancer a few years ago, Peter and I remain the same close friends as ever. Too old now to travel far, we share our wine experiences by phone just as well and happily as ever.

A Memorable Trip to the Famed Chateau Biltmore—With Wine

Nearly all of my most interesting trips inside the US have been, in one way or another, inspired (and financed) by my twenty-five years of writing a wine, food, and travel column which was nationally syndicated to over a hundred daily newspapers by the Gannett News Service. One of the best trips of all began with a modest little story about the new wines being made at the famous Chateau Biltmore in Asheville, North Carolina. At the time, Mississippi State University had its own winemaking school, said to be the finest one east of the Mississippi. Sadly, it failed due to our humid climate, which allowed vine lice to spread the dreaded Pierce's disease killing all our vines. There was, and is, no cure. Excited by our school, I was constantly writing about and eagerly encouraging winemaking across the South, especially in Virginia and North Carolina.

Every summer my wife Regan and I would drive our younger daughter Lydia to Camp Hollymont, stopping en route at the famed Chateau Biltmore, which had been built, after six years of construction, in 1895. Still the largest private house in the United States, it had over 200 bedrooms, 43 bathrooms, 65 fireplaces and covered over 62,000 square feet. Biltmore has been privately owned ever since it was built by the fantastically wealthy George Washington Vanderbilt, great-grandson of the shipping and railroad magnate, iron-fisted capitalist Cornelius Vanderbilt. Although easier to build before the infernal federal income tax was enacted, it was and always has been highly expensive to maintain. Various Vanderbilts have paid for its upkeep by a number of schemes from managed forestry (successful) to growing and selling vast crops of tomatoes (unsuccessful—too perishable) to a "piggery" (successful but closed because it smelled too bad).

In the 1980s, William Cecil, the husband of the last Vanderbilt daughter, decided to turn the estate's mildly successful dairy farm into a successful winery. During an early visit to the estate in 1988 after dropping off Lydia at camp, I tested some of its new sparkling "champagnes," pinot noirs, and chenin blancs, and liked them so much I wrote a long column about them. The estate's publicity director, Elizabeth Sims, whom I'd known ever since she was a reporter for the now-defunct *Memphis Press-Scimitar* newspaper, invited me to bring the family for a longer visit to taste all the winery's new wines and meet its new French winemaker, Philippe Jourdain. It was probably our best family vacation ever.

Elizabeth introduced us to owner William Cecil [pronounced SEH-sull, not SEE-sull], a direct descendant of the first Queen Elizabeth's prime minister and principal advisor, who put us up gratis at the new Biltmore Estate guesthouse right on the grounds. The place was like a miniature Biltmore, complete with its own butler, who was also an excellent chef. Each day he cooked our breakfasts. Our older daughter Allison still remembers his homemade blueberry muffins. All our other lavish meals were taken at one of the three restaurants on the estate. In return, my only task was to study, and in some cases translate from French, three years' worth of G. W. Vanderbilt's leather-bound menus and wine lists from the turn of the twentieth century, and to recommend new menus and wine lists in line with the founder's preferences.

My "only" pay was to be endless meals and free wines. At the time I was still serving as a federal prosecutor and chief of the Criminal Division of the US Attorney's Office in Oxford, Mississippi, and strictly forbidden by law from holding any outside job or receiving a salary. A gilded junket of free travel, meals, wines, and lavish accommodation was probably also against the rules technically, but the offer was too tempting, especially since it included my wife Regan and daughters Allison, age twelve and Lydia, age seven. Anyway, I'm retired now and the statute of limitations on my peccadilloes surely ran out years ago.

We rented a big, heavy, long-distance car, a Chrysler I think, rather than try to cram the four of us into our old Volkswagen Beetle. The visit, even beyond the meals and the butler, was a huge success. I reveled in Mr. Vanderbilt's menus and wine lists and submitted updated, modern versions, which Elizabeth Sims recommended and Mr. Cecil adopted. The details of the wines are given in the seven books listed in the Further Readings at the end of this book. My favorite Biltmore wine is still the pinot noir which, sadly, is not available to me now under Mississippi's crazy wine laws. The outstanding Sangiovese is legal and on our table nearly every day, however. As a matter of fact, I'm drinking a glass of Biltmore Estate Sangiovese ($18) as I write these words.

My only failure on our big Biltmore trip was our attempt to rebuild and refurnish the old concrete wine bins in the cellars. Our plan had been to make them available for the hundreds of thousands of annual visitors to the chateau to inspect in person. Sadly, the engineers ruled that the two ancient Biltmore elevators were too decrepit to use for tourists and could not be repaired well enough to accommodate the hordes of annual visitors, which often exceeded 700,000. We did succeed, however, in having a beautiful, Biltmore-styled tasting room built for the wines. As of my last visit, the Biltmore winery was the most-visited winery in the United States, including those in California's Napa Valley. A worthy outcome for the trip of a lifetime.

FOREIGN
LEGAL
MISSIONS

The Glamour of Strangeness

MY FIRST FOREIGN MISSION
AS A PROSECUTOR: TESTING A
NEW TREATY IN GENEVA (1979)

One day in late 1978, US Attorney H. M. Ray called me into his office and made me an offer I couldn't refuse: How would I like to go to Geneva, Switzerland, for a couple of days to gather evidence of a fraud against some Swiss bankers? The bankers, having heard horror stories about the weirdness of the US justice system, had invoked their right under a US-Swiss treaty to testify by sworn deposition and only in their own country. My fluent French was the main factor that caused me to be selected for the trip.

The defendant was Bobby Gerald Culpepper, a convicted bank robber, who posed in the United States as a suave businessman "Robert O'Neal." Although he only went through the sixth grade, Culpepper was clever. He managed to present himself, in writing and on the phone, as a rich investment banker who put together deals with major international corporations. In a scam known as a "bust-out," he managed to buy on credit many thousands of dollars' worth of industrial aluminum from Reynolds, then resold it, pocketed the profit, and skipped town before the law got there. In our case he failed to skip town quickly enough. He first flew to Geneva and somehow got an actual check on a Swiss bank in Geneva and took it to a printer in the US and had him make books of such checks, adding the word "Certified," a nonlegal term which made them sound legit.

In January 1979, I boarded a plane in sunny Memphis and headed for Geneva. When I arrived, there was a foot of snow on the ground. At the airport a Swiss policeman, a detective named Hayoz [HIGH-oh], picked me up and drove me to the Hôtel d'Allèves, a cozy, old-style small hotel much favored by the Geneva police and an easy walk from the courthouse. Behind the concierge desk was a round table reserved for drinking Swiss wine. It was known as the "table maudite" (accursed table), because it was said that no one had ever gotten up from it sober.

Somehow I'd always thought of the Swiss as either beer drinkers or sober-sided Calvinists, but these were southern, French-speaking Swiss, not the

Germanic variety. And they did know how to party. My favorite wine was a white called Ermitage, which came in tall, brown, fluted bottles. It was named for the great French Rhone wine of the Hermitage hill, where the ice-cold Rhone River flows down from the Swiss glaciers. Made from the Roussanne grape, I learned much later that it was Thomas Jefferson's favorite white wine during his retirement. It is now grown in California and winning gold medals.

My first night in Geneva, Detective Hayoz and others walked me around the old part of town. To my surprise they knew everyone from shopkeepers to prostitutes, who, just as in the US, are reliable police informants having, as it were, a very wide "acquaintance" with all levels of society. The next morning I met Inspector Brillant, chief of the judicial police, (called the "fraud squad"), and he was indeed brilliant.

Their squad room looked like an old FBI or NYPD office with gray tables, cheap chairs, and gray metal filing cabinets. But this was Geneva. When lunch time came, they opened the gray cabinets to reveal hidden refrigerators filled with cold cuts, fresh bread, and plenty of Swiss wine, red and white. They produced bright-colored tablecloths, wine glasses and cutlery, and every day we had a tasty lunch. The fun over, they brushed the crumbs into a wastebasket and carried them out with the empty wine bottles. In five minutes the squad room was as dull and drab as ever, and no one would have dreamed such a pleasant lunch had just been had there. It was a perfect portrait of the French Swiss character: Stiff on the outside, warm and pleasure-loving on the inside.

That first afternoon we went for a visit with the judge, which I tried to think of as a proper courtesy visit from a foreign prosecutor and not as a seriously unethical ex parte ear-wigging session as it might have been considered in the US. The judge, who stood over six feet tall and had a strong Geneva accent, was delighted we could converse entirely in French. She'd always been curious about the justice system in the US, which she'd never visited. We spent a pleasant hour swapping stories and were both careful never to talk about the merits of the case other than for her to explain local procedures to me. They were a shock.

First of all, court reporters and verbatim transcripts, like we have in the US, were forbidden. The judge and not the attorneys was to ask all the questions. She would then dictate a short summary or *procès-verbal* to her clerk, much like an FBI "302" report. I politely explained to her that this would never work, that our US Constitution required that the defense attorney be allowed full cross-examination of every witness. Questions by the judge and mere summaries of testimony were inadmissible and useless. "I had heard your system was strange. Our system goes back to the Romans. Since you are in Switzerland, you must follow Swiss law."

The next morning the defense counsel and I appeared before Judge Hurni to proceed with the depositions, planning to do them all in a couple of long days, then head back to the US. No dice. Each of the three depos would be on a separate day, for which she'd set aside just thirty minutes for each witness out of her busy schedule. We tried to explain American depositions to her and how each would take at least a whole day under the American way of doing it. "Wasteful and childish," was her reaction. Mark Kadish, the Atlanta-based defense attorney, danced around the point, claiming rightly that different legal systems had different ways of getting to the truth, which she sort of accepted.

Then she set forth another problem. The court clerks were on strike, and our case was a new bone of contention. They insisted we follow Swiss rules strictly, with no American exceptions, or the clerks union would not allow the proceedings to be taken down at all. In a miracle of judicious and lawyerly reasoning, the judge resolved all our problems. To satisfy Swiss law, we would officially follow Swiss procedures to the letter: she would ask all questions, dictate a summary to her clerk, and only that document would go in the official Swiss file. To comply with a US-Swiss treaty, however, after she finished we would be allowed to question the witnesses under our rules, tape-recorded, and full transcripts would be prepared by a bilingual translator. The judge would even, somewhat extra-judicially, sign certificates verifying that the results were accurate as required by US law. She was a genius.

The first day of depositions started off strangely. The first banker, a very proper gentleman, was very cordial out in the hallway. Once in the judge's chamber, however, problems developed. When she asked him to state his name, he refused, stating, "I decline to answer on the grounds of Swiss bank secrecy laws."

Unperturbed, the judge stated, "I hereby release you from the strictures of Swiss bank secrecy because the US indictment establishes that a crime was likely committed and in that case under the treaty you must answer." Unabashed, he replied, "I respectfully decline." Her eyes flashed briefly and she turned to the bailiff and said, "Put the cuffs on him." Shocked, the banker began to shake. "May I call my lawyer?" The judge said, "I will dial him for you. What is the number?"

When his lawyer answered, the banker held the judge's phone in his handcuffed hands, turned his back on all of us, and began to whisper to his lawyer. After a few minutes he turned back from the phone and said he would answer questions. The cuffs were removed.

To dispel the judge's notion that we were querulous school boys, I cut to the chase with questions right on point. After the banker had verified that an American calling himself "Robert O'Neal" had opened an account with his bank, I engaged in a little US-style courtroom drama, walking over to the judge's outer door and knocking loudly three times. Detective Hayoz stepped in carrying a framed photospread of eight similar-looking males, one of them the defendant Culpepper. The other seven photos were of Swiss policemen. Without hesitation he picked out Culpepper as the man calling himself O'Neal who opened the account in his bank with a check which later bounced. It was all recorded properly under US law.

The last day was almost a disaster, if not an international incident. We went by the judge's chambers with three volumes of thick, completed transcripts. Each was accompanied by several certificates necessary to comply with both the Swiss treaty and US rules. As we were leaving, the judge motioned to me to stick around. When Mark and the police were gone, she reminded me of what I'd said offhandedly that first day about US lawyers and judges having a meal together after a big case was over. Since it would be improper for a lawyer to pay for a judge's lunch, she would act as host and was inviting me to lunch. In a cozy Swiss restaurant across from the courtroom we ordered a multicourse meal. I introduced her to Allève Ermitage. She introduced me to Italian-Swiss lamb shanks. About 3:00 p.m. she said, "Oh, mon Dieu. I had a séance at 1:00 p.m." Too mellow to be aware of our happily intoxicated condition, we went back to her chambers where the unhappy Swiss lawyers were still waiting. As I exited down the hall, I heard a male voice say "Americans" in a negative tone. Judge Hurni's voice responded, "They are not bad at all. Much better than I expected."

Unknown Switzerland

My practice has always been to read a variety of books on a country and its people and cultures before a visit. For Switzerland, it was not so easy. I had only a brief time for study and quickly discovered there were virtually *no* good books on the subject. Most of what was written was in shallow, glossy magazines on skiing and ski resorts. I did grab a copy of one excellent, short but in-depth book on Switzerland by one of our best writers, John McPhee, whose book features this striking statement: "Switzerland does not *have* an army. Switzerland *is* an army." Obviously there must be more to the Swiss Army than knives. McPhee began his excellent book by explaining that the vaunted Israeli Army was based mainly on and trained mainly by the Swiss Army. McPhee explained how every Swiss male (women were not even granted the vote until the 1970s) is by law *in* the army from age twenty to age fifty and must serve thirty days a year on active duty, plus one weekend of training a month, and keep his Swiss Army machine gun at his residence oiled and ready for use at all times. Quite a contrast with our gun laws, but it did sound eerily like the language of our own Second Amendment with its "well-regulated militia" language.

McPhee recounts interesting stories of judges, bank presidents, and other wealthy and powerful Swiss leaders, all of whom serve enthusiastically in the military and how almost no one ever tries to buy or otherwise weasel his way out of active service. The backbone of McPhee's story of Swiss life follows the career of one Luc Massy [mah-SEE], a happy-go-lucky French Swiss winemaker from one of the cantons overlooking Lake Geneva. So taken was I with Massy's story that when my daughter Lydia received a prestigious year-long Rotary Club Ambassadorial Scholarship to the University of Lausanne, I persuaded her to sacrifice one of her precious weekends to visit Luc Massy at his winery to check out McPhee's story. She brought me back a bottle of Massy's excellent white wine (much Swiss wine is white despite the cold weather) along with a magnificent selection of Switzerland's beautifully designed, totally unknown wine labels.

McPhee had great early success with in-depth books of fascinating essays on popular subjects from professional tennis (*Levels of the Game*, 1969) and the commerce of New Jersey truck-farm goods in New York (he lives in Princeton, New Jersey). He later delved deeper into more esoteric subjects, especially geology, a subject I always wanted to know more about after suffering through a wretched class on the subject at Millsaps College in the 1960s. I wanted to know *more* about the subject, but perhaps not quite as much as McPhee devoted to it in four excruciatingly long and detailed, but beautifully written books.

The same problem, either his or his editors', no doubt powerfully affected the relatively small sales and readership of this great *New Yorker* writer's unique book on Switzerland. After describing at decent length the little-known, highly skilled, and technologically advanced Swiss Air Force planes and how they are deftly hidden in huge hangers inside the Alps, which open up via vast stone gates, McPhee tells how one of the world's best air forces fly out of its mountain hideouts. McPhee was especially taken, as I was, by the Swiss practice of flying, Blue Angels style, in intricate formations over the top peaks of the Alps, synchronized wing-to-wing, daringly crossing paths, sometimes while flying upside down. Then, unfortunately, either McPhee or his editors, or both, decided to make that fact the title of the book calling it *La Place de la Concorde Suisse* (Farrar, Strauss, Giroux). Boldly ignoring most American readers' mistrust of French, McPhee chose that phrase as the title of his fine book, focusing on the highest point in the Alps, where the Swiss Air Force does its fanciest crossover maneuvers. Drawing on the image of heavy, closely packed traffic, the Swiss Army does call that dangerous spot "Concordplatz," or the "Place de La Concorde," after the biggest, most congested and dangerous traffic circle in Paris, the same place where King Louis XVI and Marie Antoinette were beheaded after the French Revolution. That is all interesting as history of course but to my mind no way to title a book for even the most francophile of Americans. Although the title turned me off, it was the only book I found on short notice, and it does have an excellent cover, silver with a big red cross in a vivid reproduction of a classic Swiss Army knife. For that reason, I take up here, dear reader, the flag that I feel was dropped by McPhee's title. Read this book, regardless of its title. It is better on the Swiss and their culture than any other book I've seen. There is one other book on the subject, called *Swisswatching*, but it pales in comparison.

McPhee relates how Switzerland survived a bitter civil war between its German- and French-speaking cantons just before our own Civil War and then added the charming little Italian-speaking canton at its foot, Ticino [tee-CHEE-no], as its last canton. We seldom hear now of "Italian Swiss Colony" wine, it having descended to jug-wine level, but that canton still borders fashionable, lovely Lake Garda and the spectacular Italian Lake Country while remaining a legal and integral part of Switzerland.

Riding by car through Switzerland, you can listen on your radio to fine music in all three languages. Although sometimes criticized by both the Germans and the French for producing too few great writers or musicians of their own, the Swiss have long been a haven for great writers, in exile or otherwise. Englishman Edward Gibbon, author of the masterpiece *The History of the Decline and Fall of the Roman Empire*, chose to be educated in Switzerland rather than at Oxford or Cambridge. More recently, the great literary stylist and author of classic literature in the form of spy novels, former British spy David Cornwell, who writes under the pseudonym "John Le Carré," chose the university in the Swiss capital of Bern (a renowned city of spies) for his own education and has since lived much of his life at his isolated chalet in the Alps.

Other less flattering things have also been said of the Swiss, accusing them of furnishing haven not only for writers but for international money launderers and even Nazis seeking to hide, in its famous numbered bank accounts, like the one I cracked in Geneva, money and property stolen from Europe's Jews during World War II. Others say a few Swiss bankers profited by financing *both* sides in World War II. Still others, on the contrary, note how courageously the Swiss furnished safe haven for many thousands wishing to avoid the horrors of World War I as shown in the great movie *Grand Illusions*, by Jean Renoir.

My own two weeks in Switzerland were probably most memorable for the several days I spent in their deliberately simple, primitive mountain dwellings in the Alps in January with Inspector Brillant and his detectives, where the only heat was from wood-burning fireplaces and where we drank fine, clear, icy water from snow-melt. Those were no fancy ski lodges but rustic retreats where we had simple but magnificent meals from local sheep, goats, and cattle:

dried beef with white gravy, pots of delicious cheese fondue, and raclette with simple Swiss bread and wine. I'll never forget the warmth of those long, cold, bright nights deep in the snow of the Alps.

Nor will I forget the splendid three-story chalet of Inspector Brillant, who lodged me there during the celebration of the wedding of his daughter. It was he who taught me to build long rows of shelves along the walls leading down to the wine cellar and to line them with favorite empty bottles, the ones with the most beautiful and colorful labels and memories, a practice I've followed for over forty years in my own cellar.

Perhaps a good place to stop this praise of the unknown sides of beautiful Switzerland would be to note that the late famed chef, world traveler, and student of foreign cultures Anthony Bourdain recently devoted one entire segment of his lengthy television series to the same subject I describe here. In *Parts Unknown*, Bourdain details his love of the Swiss life I've just tried to describe. It seems that, despite a fast-changing world, lovely Switzerland has changed very little and is still a warm home in an otherwise cold world.

A NEW VOYAGE TO ITHACA
(BY WAY OF TUNISIA)

When you start your journey,
Pray that the road is long,
Full of adventures and knowledge.
—Translated and excerpted by Lawrence Durrell from
Constantine Cavafy, the Greek poet of Alexandria

Ithaca was the home of Ulysses (called Odysseus by the Greeks) who sailed for nine long years to reunite with his family following the Trojan War. As noted by sixteenth-century French poet Joachim du Bellay: *"Heureux qui, comme Ulysse, a fait un beau voyage."*

If there was ever an island paradise, it is spectacular Djerba, my favorite island in the Mediterranean, just off the coast of Tunisia. Djerba is generally accepted as the island where Ulysses was "held" for years, supposedly against his will, by a beautiful, love-crazed nymph. Several of his "wandering" years thus may not have been that painful after all. Not even a recent terrorist bombing on Djerba of the last great Jewish synagogue of North Africa has dimmed its appeal as one of the earth's last unspoiled paradises.

A Human Rights Mission to Tunisia (1992)

After my trip to Geneva, it seemed for a while as if my foreign travels as a federal prosecutor were going to be limited. Then one morning in late December 1991 I sat in my office, mildly bored, thinking of drug deals and healthcare fraud cases I was investigating, and sick of interruptions by endless phone calls. The receptionist rang once again and said, "There's a Miss Fragos on the line." She spelled out the name and pronounced it for me, "fray as in fight and gos as in ghost but without the t." She said the lady was from the Office of International Affairs. That was good enough for me. Fran Fragos later became famous as Fran Fragos Townsend, George W. Bush's international security advisor during the terrorist years. She is now a frequent television commentator on terrorism and other subjects and was briefly a candidate for FBI Director under Donald Trump. But in 1991 her name was not yet a household word, even in Washington. Her first words to me quickly stated her request: "John, I've got a great mission for you. Unfortunately, it's on very short notice. We need you to go to Geneva next week."

It had been nearly a decade since the Swiss banker depositions, but the memory was fresh and pleasant. "I'm your guy," I said. "My French is ready to go."

She didn't dawdle. "Good. I'll call you back after lunch with details." I immediately called my wife Regan and my parents with the good news and suggested they go with me.

After lunch, reality set in. Fran called back and said she'd made a terrible mistake. She was covered up with assignments and had confused the old Geneva reference in my file with the new case. This time they wanted me to go on an open-ended, fact-finding mission on conditions in Tunisia, a French-speaking country on the Mediterranean coast of North Africa with beautiful beaches and delicious food. My previous travels as a student in Algeria and Morocco in the 1960s had been exciting and fun. "Count me in anyway" I said without thinking.

When I called my father to tell him we would not be going to Geneva, he said skeptically, "Tunisia. Isn't that where that ugly guy Arafat is hiding out? Didn't they just burn the place during anti-American riots there protesting the Gulf War?"

My father never suggested I consider not going; he was too patriotic for that, and he probably didn't want to worry me—or my mother—with his apprehensions. But unbeknownst to either of us, our trip to Tunisia would have been our last one together. He died of a totally unexpected heart attack just after a long day of deep-sea fishing on the Gulf of Mexico at the age of eighty-four in late February 1992. My mother died of cancer later that same year.

My flight touched down in Tunis on January 23, 1992, two hours late. The taxi rushed me to my hotel, the towering Meridien, which looked out over the Mediterranean, and then on to a banquet given in our honor. In my box at the hotel was a cryptic, handwritten note in English in the style of something from a bathroom wall: "For a good time, call" and a telephone number. Thinking it was a prank, I went on to the banquet.

When I arrived, a dozen North African men awaited, all distinguished lawyers, prosecutors, and professors. Oddly, there were no other Americans. They had finished dinner and gone on to another meeting. Since they'd been keeping dinner warm for me for nearly an hour, we were seated quickly. When I asked about the other two Americans, a judge and a professor, the Tunisians said they'd entertained them the night before and did not want me to feel slighted, so they were holding a separate banquet just for me.

The food was delicious and the hospitality warm. They even relaxed enough for some good-natured ragging on each other about the supposed differences of their national characters, which to me had seemed extremely similar. Not so to them. The Tunisians occupied what once was ancient Carthage, the warlike mortal enemy of the Romans, which the Romans finally destroyed stone by stone before supposedly sowing the whole land with salt at the urging of senator and historian Cato the Elder (whom I'd had to study in junior high), who said *Carthago delenda est*, "Carthage must be destroyed."

Tunisia had been settled much earlier by Phoenicians who sailed from what is now Lebanon and are known today mainly as peaceable merchants and traders who were for centuries subjects of the Turkish Sultans. Tunisians had always been a moderate, commerce-oriented people unlike the more warlike Algerians and Moroccans. Since the inaptly titled "Arab Spring," with its region-wide violence, that has changed somewhat.

Algerians, on the other hand, had been totally and brutally colonized and ruled with an iron fist by the French from the 1830s until 1962 when, in a bloody revolution, the Algerians ordered every last Frenchman out of the country in twenty-four hours with the famous choice: "You can leave carrying one suitcase or lying in one coffin." Ever since the French left, Algeria has been racked by internal violence as described in the Prologue about my one early visit there.

The Moroccans see themselves very differently. Never totally conquered by the Turks, the Moroccans also resisted colonization by the French, barely tolerated a mild "protectorate" by the French for a few years late in the colonial period, and now carry much less bitterness toward France as a result. A Moroccan privately described the national characters of those three North Africans to me this way: "The Tunisian is a lamb, the Algerian a wolf. The Moroccan is a lion."

"What about the Mauritanians?" I asked. I hate to repeat it, but he said, "They are slaves and the sons of slaves. In their deserts, they still keep slaves."

The original dinner meeting with all conference participants had been organized by Rachid Driss, the former Tunisian ambassador to the United States, who sat beside me. Across from me were a Moroccan judge, two Tunisian diplomats, an Egyptian law professor, a defense attorney from Mauritania, and the dean of the Law School at the University of Tclemcen [KLEM-son] in Algeria.

Our conversations were uninhibited and interesting. The Maghreb participants were all very courteous toward me while needling each other good-naturedly. The president of Algeria had just resigned and the army had taken over the government the previous weekend, so the Moroccan kept asking the Algerian with mock seriousness if they wanted to "seek asylum" in Tunisia. They harassed the Mauritanian attorney about alleged slavery in the southern part of his country. He replied they couldn't change customs overnight and that the entrenched Saharan caste system was actually *more* of a problem than slavery. A client of his was recently beaten up by family members for letting his daughter marry a low-caste blacksmith.

This conversation brought home to me just how far from Mississippi I really was. I had had a similar impression at the airport when a large crowd of approximately five hundred people had waited behind a tall chain-link fence, with dark sullen appearances, averting their eyes from me, the only occidental in sight. The Tunisian driver who picked me up said it was considered bad manners to stare at someone directly and that's why they were not looking at me the way Americans would have. He said they were just curious to see an American and looked sullen because all the flights were very late, like mine. That made me feel better.

As I told the dinner participants about my background and what I did for a living, they volunteered how their roles in their legal systems compared to my own. Dean Mekamcha of Tclemcen spoke impeccable French and had a doctorate in law from Aix-en-Provence. He said he envied American professors for their ability to publish, saying he and his colleagues had no money or publishing outlets.

They wanted to share their experiences of undergoing an anticolonial revolution, a socialist economic disaster, and now the threat of an elected Islamist government which would likely take away the democratic freedoms they were elected to preserve, possibly leaving Algerians even worse off than under the French. Dean Mekamcha expressed interest in my suggestion that I send him the names and addresses of some American law reviews, particularly our local *Mississippi Law Journal*, and I offered to have his articles translated into English for publication. I had to follow up on our conversations discreetly due to the volatile political situation and personal risk to him for even communicating with an American.

The most striking cross-cultural event of our first dinner meeting was the waiter's request for wine orders. Since I was then writing a nationally syndicated wine column, I had researched Tunisian wines, but did not tell my hosts and deferred to them for recommendations. After some squirming, a couple of recommendations were made, but not one person would join me in drinking wine. The Moroccan joked that they must all be *intégristes*, the French Arab term for fundamentalist Muslims who strictly interpret the Koran and will drink no wine and punish severely those who do. Interestingly, the term *intégriste* supposedly comes from a former Catholic movement which wanted to overthrow the French government, *intégriste* religion with politics, and run the country as a theocratic state under an extremist interpretation of the Bible.

When one Tunisian kindly said he hoped I did not feel uncomfortable drinking wine alone, I replied that on the contrary it made me feel right at home, being similar to having dinner with a group of teetotaling Mississippi Baptists. They seemed considerably relaxed by this unexpected common experience, which contradicted their assumptions about that area of difference in our countries. When the waiter asked if I wanted red, white, or rosé wine, I replied, "All three." The rosé was best, as it is in all North African countries. It goes well with all their excellent food, not to mention their hot steamy climates.

On Friday morning, January 24, I spoke for an hour in French based on a paper I'd written in French entitled *Human Rights in American Courts: Personal Experiences of a Veteran Prosecutor.* The audience consisted of fifty participants plus another dozen or so guests including at least two reporters, one of whom tried to interview me but was not successful because my schedule was so tight and I was a little wary of his intentions. The speech seemed well received and provoked numerous friendly questions. Several people asked me to recommend books on our American courts and legal history.

One of the points that most intrigued the Tunisians and other Arab participants was the continued existence of a chancery court in Mississippi, which has its roots in early English church law and is heavily dependent on our poetic-sounding maxims of equity, which correspond strikingly to passages in the Islamic Sharia. They were also interested in the alleged influence of certain American Indian customs on our system of federalism and the separation of powers. I wasn't so sure about that point but told the group what a modern Choctaw trial is like in Mississippi and promised to send to the embassy copies of books on the subject, including *Indian Givers*, on contributions of American Indian cultures, and the *Cheyenne Way*, which describes an Indian legal culture, which I taught in my Ole Miss law course Law and Literature.

One goal of our visit was to inquire discreetly into human rights in Tunisian courts, which were alleged to be suffering from instances of torture, coerced confessions, and summary executions. Realizing that overt preaching from a foreigner would not be well received, I took the approach of explaining our own problems with beatings of prisoners and police brutality, stressing convictions I had obtained from all-white juries in instances where blacks were beaten. The Maghreb participants were intrigued with a brief history of the Ku Klux Klan in our district and my recent conviction of Dale Walton, Grand Dragon of the Knights of the Green Forest. They seemed reassured to know that we had terrorist problems in America not so unlike their own problems with Iranian infiltrators, their crazy neighbor Colonel Khadafy, and the Muslim brotherhoods, or "Islamists," as the Tunisians call them.

As background I had read a two-page article in the French magazine *L'Express* describing how the Tunisian government claimed to have crushed the Islamist leaders in Tunisia. The article had appeared the very day I arrived in Tunis. I had already read two articles with diametrically opposite viewpoints on the situation in Algeria, one from my own local paper, the *Jackson Clarion-Ledger*, naïvely deploring the "undemocratic" suppression of Islamists by the Algerian army. The other, a column by Richard Cohen of the *Washington Post*, had argued that it was suicide to allow the election of Hitler-like parties whose platform was to abolish democracy and impose a totalitarian theocratic state. Whatever the government's official position really was, I strongly agreed in my own mind with Mr. Cohen. I also wondered whether any of them, due to my name, suspected I was Jewish, but no one asked.

The participants, to my surprise, had few questions about our role in the Gulf War, perhaps considering the topic too "hot"; they were much more interested in what President Bush's "New World Order" would mean for the Maghreb. Their general view was that with only one superpower left, the United States planned to abandon the Third World since it will no longer be an arena for competition with the former Soviet Union. They admitted having been successful in obtaining financial and other help from both sides by pitting the superpowers against each other. They feared we would retrench and deal mainly with the newly rich Pacific-rim and European-community blocs, leaving potentially friendly developing nations in North Africa at the mercy of rich Gulf States like Saudi Arabia and the militant Islamists, between whom they would be torn.

One surprising element I observed was the great freedom of speech and opinion among Tunisian and Moroccan women. There were several women attorneys and professors in the group, all of whom dressed and looked totally Europeanized. According to articles furnished me previously by the State Department, 25 percent of Tunisian magistrates are now women. Women employees of the Tunisian government are not only *not required* to wear veils, they are *forbidden* to wear them on the job. Ironically, in the streets of Tunis the most conservatively dressed women I observed were European women married to Tunisian husbands. Women in the more rural parts were of course veiled and totally covered.

The next morning I talked at breakfast to the other Americans in our group. They regretted I didn't call the number they left. They had surreptitiously met with the PLO and some of Yasser Arafat's people, strictly against instructions. The next day some went home early, whether banished as the Tunisians claimed or because their seminars were completed as they said, I never knew. My days and evenings were rounds of Arab-style dining, tea drinking, and sitting on verandas overlooking the sky-blue Mediterranean mixed with visits to the homes of my hosts, rightly known for their hospitality.

After being there a few days, one of my embassy handlers said I'd received an unusually flattering invitation to teach a criminal law class at the elite Tunis I Law School with Sassi ben Halima, a famous Tunis defense attorney and the only trial practitioner allowed to teach as an adjunct at the Law School. An embassy driver took me there alone, my first time without a handler. I had noticed in a secure room at the embassy a huge map of the country with various colored pins stuck in it. The colors, I was told, represented danger levels. Every American in the country had his own pin, in all only a dozen or so. Having neither relatives in the country nor any substantial knowledge of Arabic, I was assigned a red pin, indicating the most endangered species.

Tunis I Law School was a handsome group of pure white buildings, marred by large black splotches on the walls. "Fire-bombs," my Tunisian driver told me. "The students tried to burn the school in a riot because our government sided with America during the Gulf War." Somewhat surprised, I asked the driver why no one from the embassy was with me. "Dr. Halima said you were coming as his guest and personal friend, not as a representative of your government. That way you will be safer." He was right. Everyone was friendly and open and eager to learn about criminal trials in the US. The one-hour criminal law class expanded to three hours. Tired but satisfied, I returned to the Meridien Hotel where, for once, there was no banquet, and I dined alone and grateful, beginning with lovely local olives and specialty *brik*, an egg cooked in phylo pastry. I tried every Tunisian wine I could find to accompany my lamb couscous and small crockpot of *tagine*, a Tunisian stew.

Later presentations by Arab speakers followed the practice of making Sorbonne-style "interventions," which are self-serving speeches by audience members disagreeing with the speaker, a practice that resembles the rambling diatribes of US senators who interrupt witnesses at committee hearings. Interestingly, when I spoke, the Arab participants took a totally different tack, respectfully asking brief, fair and honest questions rather than abusing me with counter-speeches as they did to each other. Perhaps this was just standard Arab courtesy, but it certainly showed commendable sensitivity and respect for our customs.

From the hotel, where a tall black man in a red fez served me delicious Turkish coffee, Arab mint tea, and fresh squeezed orange juice whenever I asked all day long, our group went to Ambassador John McCarthy's residence out beyond Carthage. Security was tight, as the driver noted to us when we passed Yasser Arafat's alleged office. Throughout my stay I noticed clusters of national police in their grey uniforms with white leather straps, all carrying machine guns and many wearing long black leather coats. The overall impression reminded me of a long-ago trip to Cuba when I was a little boy just before the dictator Batista was overthrown by Castro. I hoped the parallel would end there.

At the ambassador's residence we were treated royally and introduced to the Tunisian minister of justice and prominent local attorneys and judges whose business cards I still have in a box. The talk was all social, politics seeming to be a topic the Tunisians did not consider appropriate for the occasion. I met several Tunisians with either relatives in the US or whose children were studying in the US. Ambassador McCarthy asked some good questions about my speech and how it was received and what I had learned to date.

On Saturday morning, the conference started with more lengthy speeches on international law and the New World Order. It appeared there were two agendas, one for the Maghreb speakers and a different one for the Americans. Everyone seemed to accept that the Arab speakers would not address human rights, which might have caused rancor. When the dean of the Cairo Law School spoke, he said that Coptic Christians in his country, 15 percent of the population, had never been interfered with. Arab participants laughed openly and slapped each other on the shoulder in apparent disbelief.

A Japanese prosecutor once spent a sixth-month tour in our office. At the end he told us: "You Americans never seem to accomplish much in your meetings; all your serious business is conducted during the breaks and at dinner." In many ways, the Tunis conference operated similarly, the formal meetings being cautiously formal (not one person removed his coat), but the receptions were extremely productive in personal contacts and candor.

The most impressive presentations of the conference were by Ambassador Driss and Dr. Cherif Bassiouni, who now teaches in the United States. Mr. Driss is a polished, elegant, and enjoyable speaker and moderator, well respected by the other participants. Tunisia looks to be very much a top-down political society where a handful of people control things, but has been lucky ever since Mr. Bourguiba took office to have had good, sophisticated leaders at the top, as exemplified by Ambassador Driss, as well as a professional, largely uncorrupt civil service and growing middle class.

From scuttlebutt I had heard varying reports on Dr. Bassiouni. My own impression was favorable. He gave a masterful summation of the importance of the conference as a beginning. He pulled together, in a way I thought nobody could, its disparate elements, praising Maghreb countries for their progress, but encouraging them to take more responsibility in ensuring stability, prosperity, and the perception of fairness in their countries.

Dr. Bassiouni's summation gave me a good, positive feeling about the conference and a hope that there would be others in the future leading to further, deeper contacts. This impression was reinforced when I read, after my return to the US, the speeches from the third summit meeting of the Arab Maghreb Union, in April 1991, published in English by the Association for International Studies. In it were papers and speeches by several participants from our conference which indicated deep divisions among member nations despite their formal treaty in which aggression against one member was to be considered aggression against all. This point was particularly striking since the 1991 summit was held, incredibly, in Libya and presided over by none other than the unstable Colonel Khadafy.

Saturday afternoon we spent shopping in the souks, where it was evident how deeply the Arab culture underlies the Tunisian veneer of Europeanism. When an American professor with our group asked a shopkeeper about a pair of gazelle horns above the door inside his shop, the owner, after invoking the name of Allah several times, explained that he needed them to keep away the Evil Eye, which his neighbors had put on him due to jealousy over his success in business. This Western-appearing businessman was not just putting on a folklore show for us; he strongly believed in the efficacy of his juju. It reminded me of the story I told one evening at dinner about voodoo hexes certain defendants recently tried to place on judges and juries in our district. No wonder my audience did not seem as surprised as I'd expected. Nevertheless, I bought a beautiful pair of "lucky" carved wooden gazelle horns which now hang above the entrance to my library at home, just in case there really is an Evil Eye.

Returning to the Hotel Meridien after midnight one night, I saw a small sign indicating a famous Syrian singer was appearing on the twentieth floor nightclub. The crowd was upper-middle-class Tunisian couples from about twenty-five to forty-five with no occidentals present but me. The singer was very good, but it was the dancing that surprised me. The women were conservatively dressed, but four or five at a time would take the floor and dance with scarves wrapped around their hips and undulate alluringly like belly dancers with their clothes on. They were obviously teasing their husbands or boyfriends by dancing in front of them and their friends, which they all seemed to enjoy. No men danced at all. It was a fairly electric scene, unlike anything I had seen before. I stayed till "last call" at 3:30 a.m.

Tunisian television, which I watched for at least an hour each evening, was interesting. There was one Italian channel, three French channels, and the international version of CNN in English. The schedule showed a Tunisian channel for a few hours a day in Arabic, but I was never able to watch it. There is no cable, and only institutions with satellite dishes have the television access we had at my hotel. The Tunisians I met who regularly watched European or American television had a very different idea of Saddam Hussein and the Gulf War from those who did not. It would be a useful expenditure of our foreign-aid resources to make CNN and European television as widely available in Tunisia as possible, especially to the young.

The Tunisian day of rest is Sunday rather than Friday as in the rest of the Islamic world, thanks again to former strongman President Habib Bourguiba.

The embassy treated me to a tour of Carthage and Sidi Bou Said, the old Andalusian settlement on a beautiful whitewashed hillside village all trimmed in blue. They spent the day teaching me Arab phrases such as "keef-keef" (weed, weed) which means "ok, whatever you say," and "feel mish-mish," which means "when the apricots ripen" (which they rarely do in Tunisia), signifying "never." We visited the incredible Bardo museum of Roman artifacts, the Roman theatre, and the American military cemetery from World War II. My impression after those visits was that some rural Tunisians are nearly as poor as some of the Mexicans you see along our border, and there are not as many signs of ostentatious wealth, at least not around Tunis, as you see in too many otherwise underdeveloped countries. The Tunisian temperament seems down-to-earth, friendly, and polite, although less elegant and laden with reciprocal obligations as the Gulf Arabs I am more familiar with. They are much less excitable and voluble than either the Italians or the French, and seem to be hard workers despite the number of unemployed young men you see in the streets all day.

On Sunday night, after dinner, I had my first contact with what the French would call *la Tunisie profonde*. Wary of wandering too far alone among the glum-looking crowds of young Tunisian males, I sat on the brightly lit terrace bar of the Meridien with a beer. Seeing my *Herald Tribune*, a young Tunisian about twenty-five years old asked to join me. He said he had an English girlfriend and wanted to practice his English. He told me he had a high school degree and wanted to go into business, but had lost his job at a hotel when Western tourists stopped coming after the riots following the first Gulf War.

My visitor, Youssef, at first said that Tunisians had no interest in the Gulf War. After we chatted for a while about conditions in our respective countries, we soon shifted to French, his English being inadequate. Shortly thereafter he apologized, shook my hand profusely, and said he had not been truthful in what he said about the Gulf War and that my candor had made him embarrassed for his dissembling. He said that in truth he thought Saddam Hussein was a very intelligent man, a great hero, and a true Arab. Youssef said that the Kuwaitis were snobs who would not even visit Tunisia, a country they felt was beneath them. He thought the Saudis were even worse, saying they invested only 4 percent of their vast wealth in "brother Arab" states and all the rest in the US and Europe.

Youssef said that the previous evening a Saudi had called to him from a limousine offering large sums for whiskey and prostitutes. He said this common occurrence caused Tunisians great anger toward the rich Gulf Arabs who treated the Tunisians like poor relations, if not pimps. I asked him what all the young unemployed Tunisians were thinking about the US. Youssef said he thought it was natural for the US to protect its interests by preventing

Saddam from seizing the oil we need, but they could not figure out why we let him live. He said, perhaps out of Arab politeness, that Americans were less to blame than the French because Americans knew little about Arabs while the French knew better.

Youssef wondered why Americans seemed to stay home; they looked friendly, but Tunisians never got to meet them. He said he and his friends could care less if we had totally taken over both Kuwait and Saudi Arabia. Despite his good intelligence and obvious interest in the outside world, he said he had no access to CNN or other television during the Gulf War. Most surprisingly, he said that since the Soviet Union was "dead," the United States was now the "Mother of the World," a choice of words I'd never heard before. He said we needed to be the "world's soldier," but also needed to "know a lot more about other countries." He apologized for drinking beer, saying that he and most of his friends were more religious than their fathers, who came from a secular generation. He said his grandfather had made the Haj, the sacred pilgrimage to Mecca, and that he intended to also. He began to say that Islam was not a threat like Americans thought it was, but then changed the subject as if he had gotten into something he should not pursue.

While riding the elevator up to my room, three young Tunisians got on. One said hello in French and thanked me for "returning." I told him I was not French but American, upon which his two friends rolled their eyes and said, "Oh no, here we go." The first young man began telling me that he had spent six months in New Orleans in 1990 learning the seafood export business. He wouldn't stop talking about his good experiences in America, just as his friends had warned. Interestingly, this young Tunisian, like Youssef, asked if I was a believer in the Book, seeming to put great store in our common religious roots.

The three young men asked if Americans were afraid of Islam after the bad experience of having our diplomats kidnapped in Iran. I told him we did not understand it because no one had really explained it to us. They seemed to accept this, nodding a lot. They said they were proud of Arab history, but not optimistic about the future. When I told them Tunisia was a beautiful country with good people and that America was once a poor frontier country, they seemed surprised but willing to agree, at least out of politeness. They said what they liked most about Americans was their equality and candor, which was unlike Europeans. The other two finally said they had to meet their girlfriends, and he needed to stop going on about America. I told them they should find a way to visit us, and they could then persuade Americans to come to Tunisia for vacations on the beautiful beaches if the politics ever settled down. They responded that they doubted that could happen anytime soon. It gave me the feeling of being the classic naïve, unduly optimistic American, but then maybe that's just the way it is.

Upon returning from my first mission to Tunisia, I received a small, unusual pair of letters from the US ambassador. When you do a job for Justice, they always politely thank you and your boss, but Ambassador McCarthy's very personal letters were far more than routine "bread and butter" thank you letters. Even more encouraging than the letters from the ambassador was a lengthy editorial on the front page of our local paper, the *Oxford Eagle*, right after my return home, which swelled me with pride:

> I've known John Hailman professionally since the early 1980s as a result of covering federal courts and I was always impressed by his professionalism and strong sense of justice and fair play. I've also had occasion to enjoy his sense of humor, his friendly, informal manner and witty conversation that caused me to leave interviews with him wondering if I had actually been talking with a hard-nosed prosecutor who is the scourge of crooks and dishonest politicians. (David Rushing, "John Hailman's Selection Was a Good One," 21 February 1992)

Follow-Up Mission to Tunisia

One fine evening early in a hastily convened return mission to Tunisia the following June, US Consul Greta Holtz, former Ambassador Charlie Dunbar, and I met with Salah Essersi, the president of the Council of Magistrates, and two of its members. This meeting, which had sounded like a boring official function, turned out to be the most profitable of all our encounters regarding human rights. Mr. Essersi, another magistrate, and a young prosecutor were interested in how our system worked and how our ideas could be incorporated into their system to make it work better. Mr. Essersi was the only official who really opened up about problems of police brutality in Tunisia, and I believed in his truthfulness.

He said that the problem was not one coming down from the top; no one was telling anyone to mistreat prisoners to get confessions or information, but it was simply the classic overbearing attitude that some policemen "worldwide" tend to have. Education of police, he said, is a long, slow process. We agreed the most important element to progress in the area is proper screening *before* hiring and a clear message that officers will be fired and prosecuted like anyone else for violations of law.

Tunisia does not have functioning internal affairs units in its police jurisdictions, nor does it have any specialized prosecutors like we have to devote full time to investigating and prosecuting human/civil rights abuses. It was only under President Kennedy that the Civil Rights Division was finally established in our own country, but every administration since then has strongly supported at least the part of that division which prosecutes police officers for brutality. Mr. Essersi agreed Tunisia needed such an institution with strong support from the president and the Ministry of Justice.

Mr. Essersi was pleased to hear of other programs we have such as the FBI Academy, where assistant US attorneys like me teach agents not only how to draft search warrants and withstand cross-examination, but also how to socialize with prosecutors and gain their trust. He said there was a huge social and salary gulf between police officers and prosecutors. I told him the same situation existed in our country to a lesser extent, especially between local officers and district attorneys, but that on the federal level the agents were paid as much as the attorneys and that we communicate pretty easily and as partners. The Tunisians seemed amazed at that idea but were certainly not at all opposed to it, even though they doubted it would be possible in their country any time soon.

I was surprised to learn that the Council of Magistrates is not at an official organization, but a private, unofficial group interested in improving its system of justice, including human rights, by its own efforts. A sense of dedication and professionalism was palpable. Several spoke good enough English. I informally invited them to the US, especially to Mississippi, stressing it would be important to get them out of New York and other large cities into university towns like Oxford and the "real America." Mr. Essersi and several others later visited us, touring both large cities, including Washington and New York, and one small one, Oxford, staying in our home and at our farm in the county outside of Oxford. They could not believe my wife bred horses and cows.

When I told the magistrates about Aminncourt (American Inns of Court), our system of nationwide clubs begun by retired Chief Justice Warren Burger, they said that was something else they thought was needed. An Aminncourt chapter consists of twenty permanent members, ten of them experienced, full-time trial attorneys, both civil and criminal, including federal and state prosecutors, as well as five law professors and five judges, both federal and state. Each club is usually attached to both a law school and a US District Court, thereby providing administrative support and places to meet. We have met nearly every month since 1999. It is a great forum to exchange ideas. We also discussed with the magistrates our LECCs, or Law Enforcement Coordinating Committees, which have joint conferences for federal and state prosecutors and investigators and contribute enormously to camaraderie and cooperation. The Tunisians asked for suggestions and our participation in a trial run at such an event in Tunis. So far no one has followed up from our end.

It is important to understand how the Tunisian-French court system is constructed, because it is so radically different from ours. The differences are

The author (right) with high school baseball and basketball coach Bill Springer and teammate John Childress (left), who went on to the US Air Force Academy.

The author sailing for France at age twenty on the old ship *Mauretania*, identical twin of the ill-fated luxury passenger liner *Lusitania*, which was sunk by a German submarine at the start of World War I.

Hailman honored

Assistant U.S. District Attorney Al Moreton (left) and U.S. District Attorney Robert Q. Whitwell present longtime Assitant U.S. District Attorney John *Hailman with a plaque signifying Hailman's promotion to Senior Litigation Counsel.*
—EAGLE Staff Photo by Bruce Newman

Hailman joins elite nationwide group

John R. Hailman of Oxford is among 20 Assistant U.S. District Attorneys nationwide who were recently nominated to serve as senior government litigation counsels.

The announcement was made by William P. Tyson, director of the Justice Department's Executive Office for U.S. Attorneys. The Senior Litigation Councel Program was created to recognize outstanding U.S. attorneys based on their litigation careers, their performance and their commitment. Nationwide, only 63 of the more than 2,450 assistant U.S. District Attorneys have achieved this career honor.

To be eligible a federal prosecutor must have at least five years of experience, most of it in litigation, hold a GS-15 employee rating equivalent and have commendations for their courtroom performance. A recipient also must be available to serve on a rotating basis as a faculty member of the Attorney General's Advocacy Institute.

Hailman has served as an Assistant U.S. District Attorney here for more than 12 years, nearly all of which has been the preparation and trial of government cases. He has been especially active in bringing to justice complex and lengthy public cor-

ruption, white collar and drug cases, as well as cases dealing with bank robbery, murder and kidnapping. Throughout his tenure with the Northern District federal courts he has handled all civil rights cases and numerous class action lawsuits.

Included in his litigation are several precedent-setting cases and has been very active in the area of public corruption and narcotics litigation. Hailman is the supervisory attorney for the FBI's statewide Pretense undercover investigation which revealed widespread corruption on the county level.

Hailman holds a Master's Degree from Tulane and a fellowship in trial advocacy at Georgetown University. He also spent two years at the Sorbonne in Paris, where he served as an interpreter. His legal skills and command of French led him to handle the first case under a treaty with Switzerland involving mutal assistance in criminal proceedings which resulted in a guilty plea from a Swiss banker accused of fraud in the Northern District.

Hailman served as a law clerk under U.S. District Court Judge Willaim C. Keady, was a legal counsel to Sen. John Stennis and was in private practice in Washington D.C.

Author honored in 1987.

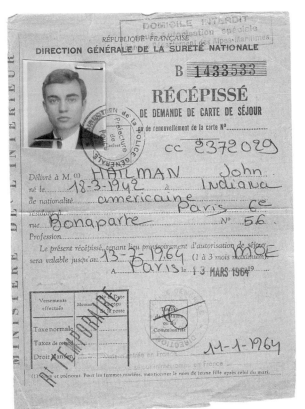

The author's temporary work permit allowing him to serve as an interpreter for Air France in Paris. The permit was later denied, *two years* after he returned to the US, a typically French way to deal with unwanted bureaucratic regulations.

The author as a student at the Sorbonne in Paris in 1964. His daughters call it the "German Officer" picture.

The author's beautiful wife, Regan, shortly after their marriage in June 1969.

The author's first French girl-friend, Gisele Berthelon, in 1961. An entirely new experience.

Parisian model Françoise Fersancourt, whom the author dated for six months in 1964. Her apartment was behind the St. Sulpice Church, said to be the hiding place of the Holy Grail as depicted in the Dan Brown book *The Da Vinci Code* and the movie starring Tom Hanks.

A veiled Omani Bedouin woman with her very unusual blond-haired, blue-eyed son. She lives in the desert while her husband works in a nearby market village.

The author with friend Saïd al-Harthy before a swim in the Indian Ocean, which abuts Oman on the south.

The author walks a *falaj*, an ancient stone irrigation canal built by the Persians to bring melted mountain snow to the desert seashore below.

The beach in Bali that suffered a terrorist bombing that killed dozens. The lone bomber was tried and executed. It was a most unusual happening for one of the most spiritual and peaceful places on earth.

A Balinese temple shaped to resemble a mountain considered holy by the Balinese, who fear the ocean surrounding their magical island, considering it the "domain of evil."

ჯონ ჰეილმანი

The author's name rendered in the ancient Georgian alphabet, which dates to the second century.

The author in snowy Istanbul, headed for the Republic of Georgia.

The author with guide Temo beside the statue of the ancient King Vakhtang overlooking Tbilisi, Georgia.

The author in an old bear-fur cap from Iceland on a windy hilltop high above the Georgian capital, Tbilisi, with interpreter and guide Nino.

even greater than they appear because their system uses some of the same words, but those words describe enormously different functions and are thus doubly confusing. Such words, which sound and look the same, but may have nearly opposite meanings are called "false friends" in French. For example, the French have a so-called jury system for criminal cases in which the punishment is more than five years. Since judges sit in with the jurors and dominate them, however, most French people have little faith in the idea of true juries. Our system, with its near-total juror control, has always seemed too revolutionary and Anglo-Saxon to the French, who passed their ideas on to the Tunisians. Both seem to prefer a tightly controlled bureaucratic system with specialized training for judges and prosecutors, believing jurors too subject to passion and prejudice. After independence in 1956, the Tunisians briefly tried the French jury system, but abolished it in 1966 and now have no juries at all, and no Tunisian I spoke to was at all receptive to the idea of having juries. They have enough trouble adapting Islamic values to a French system without trying our Anglo-Saxon notions, whose populist, ad hoc, case-by-case nature seems to unsettle them.

The most different part of the French-Tunisian system involves the "examining magistrates," a position copied from the French system. These lawyer-judges actually perform nearly the same functions as a one-man federal grand jury under the direction of prosecutors. They issue search warrants, compel witnesses to testify, subpoena and examine documents, and receive reports from the police. Interestingly, confessions obtained by the police are not admissible evidence in Tunisia unless the examining magistrate personally questions the defendant again and obtains a new confession.

The magistrate makes a written report called an accusation, the equivalent of our indictment. If the defendant challenges it or the method by which it was obtained, he may appeal pretrial to what is called the Court of Appeals, which may send it back for reinvestigation, assign a new magistrate, or even dismiss the charges entirely. Such a procedure would probably be disastrous in our already over-complex appellate system, but is needed for Tunisia because of its system's lack of other safeguards like the grand jury and our practice of allowing suppression of illegally obtained evidence.

At a Tunisian trial the defendant can be compelled to testify, and his silence may be held against him. He has no effective right of silence during the investigative phase. Much of the evidence at trial is presented in the form of hearsay and most questioning is conducted by the judge rather than by the prosecutor. The defense attorney is given some latitude, but the judges prefer asking most questions themselves, totally unlike our system.

The defense attorney's role seems to be primarily in making closing legal arguments to the judges. The role of the prosecutor is odd. Referred to as

Le Parquet (the "floor" from which they speak), the prosecutor's office seems mainly to supervise and guide the examining judges, a strange set of affairs to an American. Prosecutors even have a voice in which judges will be promoted, assess the judges' job performance and assignments, and are usually paid *more* than the judges. They are feared but not necessarily respected, more like prosecutors on *Perry Mason* than more recent and accurate television shows like *Law and Order*. After the three-judge trial court makes its decision, an appeal may be taken to what they call the "Cour de Cassation," or "breaking" court, which corresponds to our Supreme Court and considers only questions of law.

Time prevented me from visiting a Tunisian jail, but Consul Greta Holtz had recently interviewed an American who had served time in both American and Tunisian jails for drug crimes of which he was guilty, and he said, somewhat surprisingly, that conditions were about the same, although Tunisian convicts were much less violent. Food is provided not by the state but by inmates' families. The only real complaint I heard from conference attendees about judicial abuses was from some professors who said that civilians who conspired with military officers were tried in military courts. Since the Tunisian Courts of Appeal have no right of constitutional judicial review like our Supreme Court, there is nowhere to go to challenge usurpation of civilian rights by military tribunals which decide the extent of their own jurisdiction and cannot be overturned. The one institution which it seems to me could "hear" such a case is the Tunisian Administrative Tribunal, discussed later, but international human rights activists have been complaining that it is one of the institutions most abusive of citizen rights. My visit was too brief and superficial to plumb these allegations, but further time in the future could probably determine the truth. Making changes would be another matter.

On Monday, I had lunch with Dr. Habib Slim, [sleem], dean of the Law and Political Science faculty at the University of Tunis, the second tier law school, and several colleagues. The lunch took place in the beautiful Kuwaiti-financed hotel Abu Nawas. Named for the ancient Arab poet, the Abu Nawas is the most luxurious hotel in Tunis. Over an elegant, elaborate outdoor buffet luncheon overlooking Tunis we had a very pleasant discussion between DCM Shaun Donnelly and USIS Chief Dick Undeland, both of whom seemed to have the respect of the Tunisians. The conversations were entirely in French and impressed me highly with the representation we were receiving in Tunis. Undeland spoke fluent Arabic, which was highly unusual in the modern US Foreign Service. After lunch we went back to Tunis I, where students came to discuss "common interests," including the similarities and differences in our legal systems. Unfortunately there were more professors than students present. The students seemed to be an older group and were not very willing to ask questions despite my frequent urging. I was told by another professor that no American had spoken to a class at that university since the Gulf War. I encountered no hostility on the campus, which was rather rundown with lots of uncollected debris, like on American highways.

After the meeting with the students, I spent another half hour or so with Dean Slim, during which he explained to me the law school's methods of teaching, which did not include any "clinical" education as we call it; i.e., Tunisian law students get no practical experience. My impression was that they are totally spoon fed. Oddly, their instruction is mainly in French; then their courtroom practice is required to be entirely in Arabic, a most unusual mix. Following my time with Dean Slim I also met one of the two most interesting characters of my visit, Maitre Sassi ben Halima, the only practicing defense attorney who also teaches a law class in Tunis. I taught his lively criminal law class again the next day.

From 6:30 to 11:00 p.m. on Monday, we had a long lovely buffet dinner at the residence of Consul Greta Holtz where several members of the Tunisian Bar Association were present. Their sophistication and knowledge of not only European legal systems but our own American system was quite surprising. Some had offices in Paris. On Tuesday morning I visited the faculty of Judicial Science at the other law school in Tunis. Dean Amour was obviously happy to have an American who could speak French with his students. His approach was very different from what I had seen the day before. I was told by knowledgeable embassy staff members that the students at the judicial school had to have much higher test scores than those at the law school. From their appearance and demeanor they were younger, more affluent, and more confident and outspoken.

After a brief meeting with the dean, I spoke again for two hours in French to the class of Maître Sassi. The group of approximately seventy students, arranged in theatre-like tiered seating just as in American law schools, was eager to hear from and question an American. At the end of the class they asked if I would return the following day for a second, unscheduled meeting. I could hardly refuse, especially since I was again the only American since the Gulf War to set foot in a classroom at any Tunis university. According to the embassy, it was off-limits to Americans for at least six months after the Gulf War, and there were some serious demonstrations on the campus. By the time I arrived, all was different, and the students seemed eager to meet and discuss any issue that might come up.

At noon on Tuesday I met with Mr. Bechir Tekkari, president of the Administrative Court. This institution was described in the book *Arab Voices* by Kenneth Dwyer (see Further Readings) as a "tool" of the Tunisian government used to repress political dissidents. The embassy referred to it more favorably as a puzzle and a wild card whose role was evolving and not unpromising. From my years on Capitol Hill as a legal counsel to former Senator John Stennis, the atmosphere of the Administrative Court was not unfamiliar. The members came in one or two at a time in a highly collegial atmosphere. Had I met them in the US, I would have said they were big campaign contributors and presidential advisors with a lot of private influence.

President Tekkari explained that his group had been founded based on an Italian model, but in its functions tended to work somewhat like the British Privy Council. The members explained their function as akin to that of facilitators or ombudsmen. Most were former or current judges on other courts. Their main function was to decide claims and complaints against the government, covering everything from citizens run over by a government truck to complaints of political corruption.

The members explained that under both traditional Islamic law and the vestiges of French law they had inherited, the government could not be sued unless it consented. It sounded just like our doctrine of sovereign immunity. I asked them about the complaints I had heard concerning the revocation of business licenses of persons expressing views contrary to those of the government. The allegations, I told them, sounded much like the type of political muscle used by American mayors and governors to handcuff their political opponents.

The judges replied that this was a misunderstanding, but that they did tend to be asked to handle the worst political hot potatoes that no one else knew how to handle institutionally. Overall they struck me as a sort of informal, collegial committee of wise men on the old Clark Clifford model (we know now where that can lead), but they by no means impressed me as repressive or passive tools of an overbearing administration. In their expressions at least they sounded flexible in attempting to make some sense out of their hybrid political/judicial system which has no traditional or historic basis for individual rights of the kind we expect.

At 3:30 that same afternoon I met with Mr. Saadallah Jemel, who had been described as the only Tunisian official I would meet who refused to speak anything but Arabic. I was told he had studied law "the old-fashioned way," at a mosque called El-Zitouna ("Olive Tree") University, where only the Sharia was taught. It was said to be the oldest mosque in Africa after Kairouan. Mr. Emir of the embassy was to accompany me as translator.

Mr. Jemel turned out to be a very dignified, scholarly gentleman of approximately sixty dressed in western clothes. He had the most meticulously organized office I saw in Tunis. His legal training was much more modern than I was told. His French title was "Avocat General," which sounds like attorney general, but had nothing to do with prosecutions; he was in charge of appeals.

From our discussions he appeared to be equivalent to our solicitor general, the Justice Department official who handles all appeals on behalf of the government in the Supreme Court, including criminal appeals.

After about three minutes of preliminaries, I respectfully addressed Mr. Jemel directly in French and suggested that since it was a foreign language for both of us we would be equals in using it and could communicate more spontaneously without an interpreter, who could remain there to help both of us with particular legal or other terms whose correct translation we did not know. He greeted this with enthusiasm and turned out to speak excellent French. He was no militant, but apparently a very precise man who just did not want to get anything wrong by mistranslation.

Mr. Jemel discussed some books I should read about the history of Islamic law and human rights under Islam and promised to try to find French translations for me. His most interesting point was that Napoleon got much of his famous legal code from the Sharia while he was in Egypt. A few concepts may have come to Egypt through the Romans, but Mr. Jemel explained several examples of supposedly French legal principles which really went back to Islamic and even Chinese roots, especially regarding property and personal rights. He cited the former French chief justice of Tunis, when Tunisia was a French protectorate, M. Dechezelle, as an authority on the matter of Islamic roots of the French code, saying he had returned to Tunis in 1965 and had at one time been a French cabinet minister. I have not had time or resources to check out this point. It sounds like at least partly wishful thinking, but good faith wishful thinking. Several books suggest Napoleon got most of his new ideas not only from Egypt, but from Confucian China, with its system of literate bureaucrats and professional mandarins.

Mr. Jemel seemed eager to explain his culture to an American. Sensitive to criticisms of his culture as backward and cruel, which he thought was the American perception of Arab justice, it was a view he admitted had some support based on the public hangings and mutilations still carried out in Iran and some Gulf kingdoms. Our discussion was eerily reminiscent of encounters I had read about between Crusaders and Saracens in the Middle Ages. We definitely need to get to know men like Mr. Jemel better, which would be a pleasure as well.

Late that afternoon US Consul Greta Holtz took me to the office of a fascinating character, Maître Ammar Dakhlaoui, a mature gentleman with an ancient, colorful, Arabian Nights office connected to the main tribunal by an old tiled underground tunnel from Turkish days. He took me to watch what he described as the first divorce case ever in Tunis in which all three judges on the panel were women. Everyone greeted him as we went through the courthouse. He was an old-time trial lawyer like we have in Mississippi, with an obvious gift of gab and flattery. The case was conducted entirely in Arabic, but Mr. Dakhlaoui whispered translations to me as a Bedouin couple hotly disputed their case before the three women judges in a scene not visually unlike our television program *People's Court*, but in different costume. The litigants slapped each other a few times as on *Jerry Springer*, but otherwise order was good.

Mr. Dakhlaoui handed me copies of "Overheard at the Palace of Justice," his satirical weekly columns on courtroom oddities and legal incidents, which he had written for over thirty years for the leading Tunis daily under the pseudonym "Adak." He told how President Bourguiba had first threatened to disbar him for his radical views, then later made him a cabinet minister. He was obviously a famous character and could get away with things ordinary Tunisians could not, such as a plaque on his wall, in French, which said with supreme political incorrectness: "Men lawyers win cases by putting on robes; women lawyers by taking them off." His age and status and the general climate of Islamic countries seemed to protect this sort of way out-of-date statement despite the fact that 25 percent of all Tunisian magistrates are now women: unveiled and outspoken.

My overall impression of the Tunisian court system from defense attorneys like Sassi Ben Halima and Mr. Dakhlaoui, and several other prosecutors and trial and appellate judges, was not at all that of a repressive or brutal regime. My impression was of a civilized society rendered unique by centuries of rule by conflicting cultures and legal systems, which now faced the prospect of living between Libya, ruled by a madman, and an unstable Algeria, whose people might elect, through frustration, a totalitarian government which would strip them of every personal right and privilege they had ever hoped to experience. This anomaly, which Tunisians likened to the Germans' choice of Hitler, was the heart of the Tunisian human rights and self-government issues.

The basic problem was thus a classic political one and not a problem of government-approved institutional violence. My personal suspicion is that many of the allegations of human rights abuses were mistargeted against the administration based upon prior experience with other regimes in the region. The freethinking Tunisians I met did not strike me as favoring the kind of police brutality I had witnessed in my two years in Paris nor what I have seen close-up at home. It is especially unfortunate that since the ill-fated "Arab Spring" and the overthrow of the Tunisian government, it now sends more militant volunteers to ISIS than any other country.

Ambassador McCarthy kindly followed up on my mission with a flattering letter to my DOJ supervisors thanking them for sending me back again. I wonder what it would be like to visit Tunisia now.

Follow-Up Mission to Tunisia

Embassy of the United States of America
June 30, 1992

The Honorable Drew Arena
Office of International Programs
U.S. Department of Justice
10th & Constitution Avenues, N.W.
Washington, DC 20530

Dear Mr. Arena,

I am writing to thank you for permitting John Hailman, Chief of the Criminal Division of the U.S. Attorney's Office for the Northern Division of Mississippi, to come to Tunisia for a second time this year. I also want to bring his outstanding performance to your attention.

Tunisia is a country with which the United States has traditionally had a warm and close relationship. Recently, human rights abuses here have clouded that relationship. During his January and June visits, Mr. Hailman has done much to enhance Tunisian-American relations by advancing the themes and understanding of the Rule of Law. With his excellent language skills, vast experience and personal charm and candor, Mr. Hailman has been warmly and respectfully welcomed into Tunisian circles.

I would point out that this society is not naturally open to foreigners. However, a few minutes with Mr. Hailman and Tunisians were discussing their work, professional concerns and even inviting him to their homes. He has an uncanny ability to entice people into dialogue and the experience to provide insights which have given much food for thought to his various interlocutors and audiences. As a result, we and the Tunisian government have successfully begun elaborating a program of exchanges and seminars which will help raise the level of individual freedom and respect for the law in this country.

I realize that Mr. Hailman's work in Oxford, Mississippi is very important. I very much appreciate your willingness, that of the U.S. Attorney for the Northern District of Mississippi and the Department of Justice in making Mr. Hailman available for this important program. His work in Tunisia has truly been in the U.S. national interest and he has performed superbly.

Sincerely,
John T. McCarthy
Ambassador

cc: Mr. Robert Q. Whitwell

OPDAT: THE JUSTICE DEPARTMENT GETS ITS OWN FOREIGN SERVICE

Shortly after my mission to Tunisia, the Justice Department announced a whole new, vastly expanded program for US prosecutors to train our foreign counterparts. Universally the program is called by its acronym, "OPDAT," which replaced its bureaucratic title, "Office of Overseas Prosecutorial Development and Training." Contrary to its intimidating official title, OPDAT is actually a small, informal, friendly unit in DOJ. Once OPDAT took over all foreign missions, I worked only with it. The new program worked so well and expanded so fast that our friendly rivals at the State Department were a little jealous, privately accusing DOJ of "running its own Foreign Service."

My missions with OPDAT were run by Jim Silverwood, a veteran prosecutor who in his "spare" time was also the ethics officer for the entire, massive Criminal Division of DOJ. Jim is the ultimate professional and quickly became not only a valued mentor but a close personal friend. Rather than trying to paraphrase its mission, I'm going to use an excerpt of OPDAT's website statement of that mission, its origins, its expansion and its considerable successes.

> OPDAT was established to provide assistance to enhance foreign justice institutions and their law enforcement officers so they could partner with the US DOJ in combating terrorism, organized crime, corruption, and financial crimes. The rule of law and the rights of individuals are the cornerstones of the OPDAT mission. Crime and the misuse of the public trust undermine confidence in government itself and discredit our free market economies. The fair administration of justice offers its citizens the greatest protection from lawlessness. When those goals are realities in foreign countries, the US has a stronger base of foreign cooperation to fight organized crime, illegal narcotics, and terrorism....
>
> OPDAT draws on DOJ resources and expertise to strengthen foreign criminal justice institutions and enhance the administration of justice abroad and encourage legislative and justice sector reform in countries with inadequate laws by improving the skills of foreign prosecutors, investigators and judges.

OPDAT also serves as the Justice Department's liaison with both private and public agencies to sponsor visits to the US by foreign officials interested in our legal system. Visitors come from a wide variety of backgrounds, including cabinet members, judges, and prosecutors seeking to improve democratic institutions in their own countries.

International visitors receive presentations about the US system in English, Spanish, and Russian from OPDAT attorneys. Visitors with specific interests meet with practitioners from specialized components of the department. Despite differences in culture and circumstances, visitors say they gain new insights from our institutions and practices which foster better international cooperation and help develop reform efforts in their own countries. In FY 2012 alone, OPDAT arranged meetings for 2,263 visitors with DOJ attorneys who invested thousands of hours of their time participating in these international visitor programs.

A Little History

First established within the Criminal Division of the Department of Justice in 1991 for the limited purpose of educating Criminal Division attorneys in complex legal developments such as money laundering and anticorruption strategies, OPDAT soon evolved into an important tool in developing more effective prosecutions. White-collar and organized-crime prosecutions began to focus on large international organizations, and OPDAT was called upon to share its abilities by developing programs to educate prosecutors and judges from other countries. In 1993 OPDAT began accepting funding from the State Department and USAID to develop programs of justice assistance in Bolivia, Colombia, Haiti, Poland, and Russia. Early programs involved drafting criminal procedure codes, prosecution manuals, and substantive laws against corruption, fraud, money laundering, and terrorism. By 2012 OPDAT had placed forty-eight resident legal advisors, or RLAs, in thirty-two countries. RLAs are experienced federal prosecutors stationed in a host country for at least one year to provide full-time advice and assistance in establishing professional justice sector institutions and practices.

OPDAT now also conducts short and midterm assistance programs, ranging from one week to six months, which focus on a specific aspect of criminal justice reform. Intermittent legal advisors, ILAs, like the RLAs are experienced federal prosecutors. By 2012 OPDAT had conducted 588 assistance programs in a remarkable ninety-two countries and managed over $72.9 million in State Department, USAID, and Department of Defense funding. OPDAT now acts as host to hundreds of international visitors each year who come to the US to gain an appreciation of our legal system through specially tailored training workshops supplemented by foreign language translation.

Why DOJ Chose Such an Obscure Prosecutor to Teach Law Internationally

Much later, over twenty years later actually, when I was already an unusually experienced jury-trial lawyer, DOJ selected me to teach trial practice internationally. Of course I'd already taught it for twenty years to American law students at Ole Miss and at DOJ's Advocacy Institute for new federal prosecutors. I'd been in the US Attorney's Office in Oxford for twenty years, since 1974, and before that had spent two years in an intense private trial practice in Washington, DC. Even earlier I had tried scores of nonjury misdemeanor cases in city court and domestic cases (by judge's permission) in Mississippi chancery courts throughout all three years of law school at Ole Miss.

My US attorney experiences were especially helpful because of the iron rule of veteran US Attorney H. M. Ray, who for seven years would allow *no* plea bargaining. A defendant had to plead guilty to our entire indictment or the case went to trial. With no chance for a deal predicting his client's punishment, defense attorneys nearly all chose to go to trial. It was not an efficient system financially, since jury cases cost thousands of dollars a day to try to a verdict, but it was a fantastic experience for a young trial lawyer. We were able to survive in such a system partly because we were a small rural district with a manageable load of cases. Later, when drug crimes exploded, we had to shift to plea bargaining, joining the rest of the country, with over 90 percent of all our cases *not* going to jury trial but being settled by plea agreements usually limiting the maximum sentence a defendant could receive.

Defendants in our district in the 1970s also went to trial a lot because of the rules and personalities of our two federal trial judges: William Keady of Greenville, for whom I had clerked for two years, the well-educated and colorful son of an Irish immigrant bar owner; and Orma (not Omar) "Hack" Smith, a judicious, grandfatherly former Ole Miss football star. Those judges had a fair, if unusual, rule: No defendant would ever be punished for exercising his right to submit his fate to a jury at a trial. In nearly every other court in the US, although it was never written down as a formal rule, the opposite practice was followed: If you put the judge and the taxpayers to the cost of a jury trial and were convicted, you would get a much stiffer sentence. On the other hand, if you helped the judge handle his heavy caseload by a speedy plea of guilty, you could count on a lighter sentence unless your crime was an unusually violent or otherwise heinous one. Our judges' fair, if idealistic, rule encouraged every defendant to take his chances on a trial before a jury. Despite their obvious sense of fair play, our judges were certainly not soft. In all my years before them, I only recall two cases when a defendant decided to "waive," or give up, their right to a jury trial and be tried by a judge alone. Both were quickly and decisively convicted and given stiff sentences by our judges.

AT INTERPOL IN LYON AND THE FRENCH
SCHOOL FOR MAGISTRATES IN PARIS (1994)

One of my favorite things to do in Paris, while skipping classes at the Sorbonne, was to attend French trials. Of course at the time (1962–64), I had no idea I would later spend forty years of my life as a courtroom lawyer in the US, but even back then I was fascinated by the drama of trials. My father always hated lawyers, calling them "parasites," so I never dreamed I'd one day be a lawyer myself. My father didn't care much for the French either, always saying, "If you have to use a French word to say it, it's probably *nasty.*"

Knowing very little of US laws or rules back then, I failed to notice how wildly different French courtrooms were from ours: The formal, authoritarian atmosphere of Paris courtrooms was of course noticeable but not out of place in a city filled with the magnificent old stone palaces that housed French government agencies. I did notice, however, quite a contrast with the many English trials I had witnessed at the Old Bailey during my numerous lengthy visits to London. In England the lawyers, whose subtleties of language I understood better, did most of the talking, with only occasional sarcastic and humorous interruptions from the be-robed and bewigged English judges. In England attorneys and judges frequently exchanged barbed, joking comments, something I never saw either the severe French judges or the rather subdued French lawyers do. In fact in Paris the judges seemed to do all the talking, questioning and cross-examining every witness with little input from the lawyers, whose main function, both prosecution and defense, was to make long, flowery closing arguments. Attending French trials was for me a good way to polish my French skills, since the judges and lawyers spoke clear, correct, and educated French, featuring rich vocabularies and well-pronounced phrases, much easier to follow than the rough, slangy language I knew from the streets and cafés. All in all, it never really occurred to me at the time to make a comparison of French and American trials: I clearly didn't know enough about American trials to consider it.

Then thirty years later, in 1994, I was not only allowed but required to make a serious professional comparison of the two systems as part of my role as the person in our US Attorney's Office responsible for all international matters, of which there were more than I expected. I had of course already taken depositions in French-speaking Switzerland and had tried to teach US law in French to Tunisian lawyers during two separate two-week stays there on American Bar missions in 1992.

Then, in the fall of 1994, Jim Silverwood of OPDAT asked me during a trip to Washington if I'd be interested in a two-week, expenses-paid trip to study French law in Paris. The offer nearly took my breath away. "There's a second part of the program at Interpol in Lyon, and after two weeks there you even get a French certificate saying you're an expert in international law." When Jim said that, I really did begin to stutter. I figured the idea of some kind of certificate, in French, wouldn't mean much in Oxford, Mississippi, but just *being* in Paris was a dream. Plus the word "Interpol" had always had for me a romantic connotation of adventures with flashy big-time crimes and criminals. Another plus, Lyon has been the center of French food ever since Julius Caesar made it the Roman capital of Gaul over two thousand years ago. I told Jim I thought I could somehow fit the time away from Oxford into my busy schedule.

I landed in Paris on a rainy day in early October with two other US prosecutors and two American judges. We went straight to our classroom, which was in a huge, drafty but elegant old stone manor house on the Île de la Cité in the middle of the Seine near the Notre Dame Cathedral. The front of our building faced the Quai aux Fleurs, the famous old Paris flower market. We entered through a tiny unmarked door in back. The French judges and prosecutors who taught us were an energetic group, well experienced in both the theoretical and the practical sides of the complicated French legal system. Although veterans, they were gung-ho. Apparently our group were the only Americans who'd ever been admitted to their special school, and they were eager to interact with us, which they did for ten hours every day—and every evening as well. I still have several thick books of notes I took during those intense weeks the twenty French lawyer/teachers gave us. Most of them spoke some English, just as most of us Americans spoke some French, so the cultural divide was not as great as it might have been. Although the lecture portions of their classes were always in formal French, they were delivered slowly and distinctly for our benefit. The Q&As which followed were usually an interesting blend of French, English, and *franglais*, the bastard form used by those who know just a little of both.

The subject matter was both broad and deep, but before getting into too much law, the teachers recommended for us in true French style all the best French bistros, brasseries, and wine bars within walking distance. A couple even gave us the names of particular waiters to ask for. Also very French were their recommendations for Paris movie houses that ran classic French films, stressing a good way to learn real French law was by watching French crime films. They all loved the slang of the French underworld, constantly tossing in and explaining words like *indique* for "informer" or *caïd* for a gang leader. The classes were anything but dull and formal.

The biggest shock to us Americans was how frank and critical our French teachers were about the flaws in their system. A typical lament was that "the French people do not understand their system, and to the extent they understand it, they don't like it," a surprising statement from natives of the country that invented and gave its name to "chauvinism." On the other hand, they did not exactly flatter what they always called the "Anglo-Saxon" court system. Although they rarely mentioned our US legal customs explicitly, professing to know little or nothing about them, they reveled in mocking the British system, which they called "antique and Germanic" rather than "Roman and classical" like their French system.

We were especially puzzled when the lawyers stressed, almost universally, how utterly different and incompatible the vocabularies of our two systems were. More than one of them used the same phrase: "It takes a whole paragraph of French to explain one word from English law, and an entire paragraph of English to explain one word from French law." When we first heard that statement we doubted it, but as we became more familiar with the French system, we came to agree, and I still feel the same way.

We grateful Americans had to admit that the French had gone all out to provide us with the best and most experienced of their law teachers. Most spoke in slow, clear French, which was very helpful. The only hard times we had were when a couple of them tried to teach entirely in English. Their accents were painfully hard to follow, and their attempts to use English words to explain French legal practices helped to prove even more persuasively how difficult it is to translate from one system to the other.

Over the course of the weeks, more than twenty French lawyers and judges taught us everything from courtroom manners to their idea of a "jury" system, which could not have been further from ours. To take an easy example, in a French criminal jury trial, the verdict need not be unanimous, as in US federal courts and most state courts. In France just eight votes out of twelve are needed to convict, and the quality of proof needed to establish guilt is not the strict "beyond a reasonable doubt" standard required in all US courts, but simply to the juror's "satisfaction on oath and conscience," a truly vague and arbitrary standard it seemed to us.

Our lawyer/teachers began with an interesting discussion of their juvenile justice system, then moved on through money laundering and protection of victims to the management of prisons and their attempts at rehabilitation. The most frequent theme, repeated by almost every presenter, was "the French legal system is only good *in principle*," not in practice. A couple said that to understand the French system it was necessary to understand the national character: "We are a nation of rebels. We need strict rules to keep order and avoid chaos, our national malady." At the same time, as one said, "The French people have two great loves: strict rules and breaking those rules as often as possible without getting caught."

It was a constant theme that the French man in the street did not trust the judicial system and would do anything to avoid becoming entangled with it. That same idea had been repeated to me many times by my good friend Leo Kelberg, an American expatriate who'd lived in Paris for twenty years and never tired of analyzing the French. Leo had great insight into Parisian life. He lived frugally at the Pension Orfila where I first lived, taking all his meals there. Every day consisted of getting up late, sitting in his favorite cafés for hours nursing cups of espresso while reading the French papers, then spending his evenings at one of the unending free art exhibitions and free concerts in churches and parks.

Leo Kelberg was one of the happiest people I'd ever met. Once I asked him how a native New Yorker could leave home at age thirty-eight and never return, and if he ever got homesick. "Well, maybe a little sometimes. But Paris is my life. The way I live, if I went home and sat around like this without a job, they'd call me a *bum*," he said forcefully. "Here in Paris they see my lifestyle differently: Here I'm not a bum; here I'm a *philosopher*." Only in Paris.

Our French teachers explained to us, with considerable understanding, how the basis of much of their crime lay in a sort of permanent underclass of North African immigrants, all Muslims, especially those from Algeria, who either could not or did not want to really integrate into French society or accept its values and mores. They explained how, after many attempts at reform, most people in the system, from police and prosecutors to judges and probation officers, eventually just gave up on ever changing things for the better. What we used to call ghettoes they called "zones of non-law," where the police never ventured and seldom interfered with local, informal Koranic justice unless a really serious crime was reported to them, especially if a "real" French person was a victim.

We had learned early on that the French prosecuted very few fraud cases unless a really big fraud was perpetrated against some rich or powerful person with influence. Otherwise, they all stressed that their system was based on self-reliance. It was the citizen's duty to be wary against being cheated, and if they were cheated, it was probably their own fault for not being more responsible. The old Latin cliché *caveat emptor*, "Let the buyer beware," came up frequently.

Violent crime in Paris, and the rest of France for that matter, was much less of a problem than in America, they thought. The French expressed amazement at why we Americans allowed so many guns, which to them, if not the root cause of all violence, at least made our violence infinitely worse. Most of us agreed with them and were basically at a loss to explain Americans' insane love for guns, except to stress how close we still were, in spirit at least, to the Wild West and cowboys and the American spirit of self-reliance, and how we did not look to the government to protect us. We explained, and the French agreed (somewhat) that the government that protects you today will take away your rights tomorrow.

One surprisingly positive note came from their comments on their prison system. One day an American mentioned the problems we have with constant lawsuits by prisoners. We told them how many of our federal judges have special, full-time law clerks who do nothing but handle prisoner complaints. The French said they had a solution for that problem. Every French judge must spend some time, usually six months or a year, serving as a "Judge of the Application of Penalties." In that role, a judge is required to review, in person, with each inmate assigned to him, the inmate's current situation and attitude. A penalty judge apparently has fairly plenary powers to either reduce or extend the inmate's time to serve based on the judge's assessment as to whether the inmate needs more punishment or will no longer be a danger to society if released early. As far as we could understand it, the French system also had much more strict, and more helpful, probation and parole supervision, although we did not have enough time to go into the subject long enough to feel we really understood it.

After two intense and interesting weeks in Paris, our group moved on to Lyon, where we were official guests of Interpol, a rare honor. Once again, on the first day we were given extensive lists of the best restaurants serving the best wine at the best prices, especially the unique Lyon institutions known as *bouchons*, or corks, so named because of their deep, narrow, hole-in-the-wall shapes, like long, narrow wine corks. Also explained to us was the beauty of the ancient *traboules*, little covered tunnels between buildings which pedestrians used to go from place to place in Lyon without getting wet, a tradition which is apparently unknown in rainy Paris, where I often wished later it would be adopted. My most unpleasant memories of Paris are of having wet, cold feet from the daily showers, a feature of romantic Paris that you never hear about until it is too late.

From Lyon our host, chief guide, and teacher was a young but experienced prosecutor, a native of Lyon named Bernard Rabatel. While he was still new in his position, his obvious talent caused him to be named one of the lead prosecutors of the infamous Nazi Klaus Barbie, the "Butcher of Lyon," whose specialty was catching and torturing to death members of the French Resistance. Shortly after our visit, Bernard became a *magistrat de liaison*, the French version of our resident legal advisors under OPDAT. We became, and remain to this day, close friends, writing often and visiting in each other's homes in France and in the US. When Bernard was later assigned to Washington, he often invited me to lunch at the French ambassador's tiny, private dining room deep in the elegant French embassy, where his special personal chef provided for privileged diners at five small tables some of the finest French meals I've ever enjoyed. With his excellent English, Bernard later served in the same role for several years in London, then in Kosovo, and for four years on the French island of Martinique. If I have achieved any depth of understanding of the French legal system and how it compares to our American system, it is thanks mainly to my friend Bernard.

In Lyon we did not stay in a hotel. Interpol gave us much more interesting housing: elegant private rooms in a big, beautiful old converted convent. As the French became less Catholic and more agnostic, there was no longer a need for convents, there being few nuns left in Lyon to house. As renovated, it was a uniquely comfortable place to live. Our classes in Lyon, as opposed to those in Paris, were more advanced and focused much less on the French system and much more on its differences with ours. They especially wanted to discuss our plea bargaining, which they thought at first was terrible, and our undercover operations, which they thought were totally immoral. "Assuming a false identity is not consistent with the ethical requirements of a true legal system," they would say. A different issue altogether was our frequent use of wiretaps, which they also said publicly were improper. Later, as we got to know them better and after a long night of wine drinking, my favorite *juge d'instruction*, or investigating magistrate, a Monsieur Taillebot, finally explained to me how their system really worked, not *en principe* (in principal), but in reality: "We use wiretaps all the time; we just claim we don't. In the file, we report what we get from wiretaps as coming from informants." When I stopped laughing, Judge Taillebot went on: "It is ironic to think we French accuse *les Anglo-Saxons* of hypocrisy, when hypocrisy is actually a French *specialite*."

One subject of debate at Lyon among the French themselves was Judge Taillebot's long-term assignment as a *juge d'instruction*, a position which at that time was under attack by some of France's leading prosecutors. One of them had even written a long diatribe of a book arguing that the investigating magistrates, who function as a sort of one-man grand jury, should be abolished outright. The prosecutor's book had the self-flattering title *Long Live the State Prosecutors*. It quoted Napoleon, who once famously called investigating magistrates "the most powerful men in France" because of their independence and broad power to bring, entirely independently and on their own, serious criminal charges and to order the accused taken into custody. Personally, it did not take me long from personal contact with both the prosecutors and the investigating magistrates, to favor the latter totally. To me, and I haven't changed my mind since, without those magistrates, the entire French criminal justice system would collapse.

Top Ten Differences between US and French Trials

At the conclusion of our sessions in Lyon, we Americans and the French came up with a rough agreement on the top ten differences between our system and theirs.

First: The roles of the players. In an American trial, lawyers call all the witnesses and ask all the questions. The judge acts as a silent, impartial referee. In France the presiding judge decides what the evidence will be, and to the extent there are any live witnesses at all, the judge calls them all and questions them himself, while the attorneys watch. The judge also keeps the file himself; it is not even available to counsel in a clerk's office. Asked which system they would enjoy working in, the French lawyers all favored the American system, saying, "Although you do all the work, you have much greater satisfaction—and much more fun."

Second: The American system is mainly oral. The witnesses must be there in person. In France the system is almost entirely written. Witnesses appear only through their prior written statements, usually mere summaries of testimony like what the FBI calls 302 reports. The French worship the written word.

Third: The French have *no hearsay rule*. Their written reports often rely on secondhand information we would never allow. To them, hearsay is "secondary" evidence, and often most of the evidence in a French case is in fact nothing but pure hearsay, a remarkable difference.

Fourth: In the US the jury is made up entirely of lay persons, or peers, of the accused. In France judges, even court of appeals judges, *sit in* with the jurors. There is thus no need for jury instructions. The French asked, "How can you expect someone off the street to understand the law?" The Americans responded, "How can you expect jurors to be independent when pompous judges sit in with them and dictate to them how to decide?" The French judges voted unanimously for the French system, saying it was "more professional." The Americans disagreed 100 percent.

Fifth: In France civil cases and criminal cases arising out of a single incident are tried *together*, which means our idea of differences in the *quality* of evidence go out the window. Proof in our civil cases is by a "preponderance" of evidence, i.e., only 51 percent. A criminal case in the US must be proven by much stronger evidence "beyond a reasonable doubt," a vastly different standard and a bulwark of all American criminal defense cases. Even more important, in France a twelve-person jury verdict need not be unanimous. A mere 8–4 majority for guilt suffices. Prosecutor heaven.

Sixth: In France there is no Fifth Amendment. A defendant has *no* right to remain silent, and one who does is basically presumed guilty. French judges can force defendants to testify and then subject them to blistering cross-examinations. Prosecutor heaven, once again.

Seventh: In France the main issue at trial is not whether the defendant "did it." That issue is basically the judge's decision and usually decided before trial based entirely on written witness statements. The main issue at trial is the defendant's character, an issue US prosecutors are strictly forbidden in most cases even to mention. In the US defendants are tried for *what they did*. In France, they are tried for *who they are*. In France the first witness (and often the only) called by the judge is a psychologist, psychiatrist, or social worker who gives an opinion on whether the defendant probably did what he or she is charged with based on what sort of life he or she has led. You could not invent two systems more opposite if you tried.

Eighth: We often debated which of our systems is most just and finally took a poll. The majority view of the French was as follows: "If I were guilty, I'd rather be tried in America, where justice is just a game filled with constant tricks and traps and ways for defendants to escape justice. If, on the other hand, I were really innocent, I'd much rather be tried by trained professionals as in France, where the goal is to arrive at the truth, not to play games." *No American wanted the French system.*

Ninth: Americans are much harder on fraud than the French, who claim their tendency to blame victims encourages self-reliance. We disagreed so strongly on this point that we could hardly discuss it calmly and certainly never reached any sort of agreement on it.

Tenth: We did, on one issue, reach a surprising agreement: The examining magistrate, a one-person investigating grand jury, which is now under serious threat of being abolished in France, is a great institution and should definitely be kept. Napoleon himself once called the examining magistrate, who can investigate and indict the politically and economically powerful, "the most powerful public official in France."

In the end, we all concluded that it is impossible to harmonize our two systems. Emerging democracies should adopt either the French/Roman written system or the oral Anglo-Saxon system. No country should ever try to combine them as Russia has tried to do. Marriages of the French and US systems are destined to be unhappy ones. To make peace at the end, we agreed that both systems have both good and bad points and both at least try to achieve justice.

IN THE REPUBLIC OF MOLDOVA:
LEGAL CULTURE IN THE BALKANS—
WITH WINE (1995)

I had thought Algeria and Tunisia were exotic destinations, but in 1995 I was to find a beautiful, totally unknown country, formed when the Soviet Union broke up in 1991: The Republic of Moldova. Called Moldavia by the Russians, it was originally the easternmost province of Romania in the heart of the volatile Balkans region. In the 1830s, Russia assumed control of Moldova to "protect" it from conquest by the Ottoman Turks. Its capital, Chişinău [KEE-SHEE-now] was called Kishinev [KISH-ee-noff] by the Russians and was a fairly typical Balkan capital: conquered, burned and reconquered and reburned many times during the wars of the sixteenth through the twentieth centuries. For a time during World War I the region was renamed "Bessarabia" after a noble family, the Bessarabs, causing many people to think, wrongly, that it was somehow an Arab country in the middle of the Balkans.

The Russians did effectively keep the Turks out of Moldova, calling themselves the Moldovans' "Big Brother," but they also tried violently but unsuccessfully to turn the defenseless little country into a Russian-speaking vassal state. The Moldovans strongly resisted, keeping their Romanian language and even declaring independence, briefly, following the Russian Revolution in 1917. The Russians soon reinvaded and once again ruled the country with an iron hand. Bordered on the west by the lovely little Prut [proot] River, in which I loved to swim, and on the east by the Dniester River, both of which eventually flow into the Black Sea, Moldova is nevertheless landlocked due to its eastern neighbor, Ukraine, which controls its southern border, a land of mostly coastal swamps, thus depriving Moldova of its most promising avenue for foreign trade.

Moldova is mostly a farming country, like a large truck farm really, with beautiful tomatoes and other vegetables and fruits. But its primary crops are its fine wines and its abundant fruit and nut trees. Without its years of stifling Soviet bureaucracy, Moldova could have become a little France. Today, however, it looks more like France might look if it had suffered two centuries of Communist mismanagement. The most striking thing to me upon my arrival in Moldova was its women: petite, dark, and beautiful. By nature many Moldovan women are reserved, not looking one readily in the eye as Russian, French, or Georgian women do. So sought-after were they as beautiful, obedient wives by Russian military officers that I was told by both Moldovan and Russian guides that Russian officials often paid bribes of half a year's pay to be stationed there long enough to obtain a Moldovan wife. There is also a Moldovan story about how life there was so pleasant that even the children of *two* Russian parents never wanted to leave, wishing to continue to live the warm, relaxed Moldovan lifestyle. The rhymed little saying about it needs no translation other than noting that "Ivan" stands for a little Russian boy:

> Mama Rus [rooss]
> Papa Rus
> Dar (but) Ivan [ee-VAHN]:
> Moldovan [mohl-doh-VAHN].

The dark side of the story of the beautiful, submissive Moldovan women came when the Soviet Union collapsed and Moldova, with no industry or foreign trade with other former Soviet Republics, became the poorest country in Europe. As result Moldovan women became by far the most exploited in the world in the sex-trafficking trade.

Historians say that Romania, and by extension its former eastern province of Moldova, was once a regime with rich land but too few people. The Roman Emperor Hadrian (he of the famous local wall) deported thousands of the poorest Roman citizens, both slave and free, to the region, thus resulting in the name "Rome-ania." The story is highly plausible.

One historic character of whom the Moldovans are particularly proud is their fifteenth-century king, Stefan cel Mare [chell-MAH-ray], or Stefan the Great, who defeated the Turks in a famous battle. He then negotiated a most unusual peace treaty under which Moldova agreed to be a vassal state of Turkey, paying heavy annual taxes in its main crop, wheat, but only through Greek Christian intermediaries. No Turk was to set foot on Moldavan soil and no mosque was ever to be built there. Under the peace treaty, the Islamic religion was forever banned, a ban which still stands. One result was that Moldovans stopped eating wheat products altogether, relying entirely on corn, a new import from the Americas, which went untaxed. To this day the main staple of their diet is mamaliga [ma-ma-LEE-gah], a sort of corn meal mush, and beans. Knowing only that brief background, I landed at the rundown airport in Chişinău.

In the Republic of Moldova

A Trial in Chişinău

Thursday, August 10, 1995

An early introduction to Moldovan legal culture was attending in Chişinău a real Moldovan criminal trial, one of the first held under the new "adversarial" system which only went into effect on July 1, 1995. Judge Vieru [vee-AIR-oo], a former police officer, received us into her chambers and outlined what the case was about and how the proceedings would be different from a traditional Soviet trial. My interpreter was Christina Sturza, the daughter of the minister of justice, who was fluent in Russian from living for several years in Transnistria and also fluent in English from spending her senior year in high school in a small suburb of Cleveland, Ohio.

The defendant was a police officer accused of two crimes: beating his wife and son and falsifying official reports about a large theft. Strangely to an American lawyer, the totally unrelated cases were tried together. The trial began with the judge on the bench and her male secretary beside her. No verbatim transcript is made as in our system. The secretary handwrites a summary of each witness's testimony, which the witness signs immediately after testifying, as in the French system. Their statements are further verified by putting their inked thumbprint at the bottom. The courtroom was similar to ours, minus the jury box and witness chair. The prosecutor and defense attorney sat at separate tables as in our system. Most striking was that the defendant was made to stand alone throughout beside the seated victims rather than beside his attorney. It was like an English dock, but even more disadvantageous for the accused.

The rule excluding witnesses from hearing each other's testimony was invoked, just as in our cases, but was not followed. The Moldovans have "civil parties," basically victims, as in other continental systems. The judge advised all parties of their rights, learning in the process that the wife's attorney, whom she had already paid in full, had failed to appear due to a conflict with another trial. Apparently there was no rule requiring him to contact the court. He simply did not show up. Nevertheless, with a promise from the judge that she and the prosecutor would assist in representing the wife's interests, the victim wife agreed to proceed without her attorney.

The judge had independently contacted the ten-year-old victim son's teacher and also had her there in court as his representative. At that point a further victim appeared. The judge explained how she had joined for trial yet a third separate charge against the same defendant: failing to file a report on an incident in which supposedly he had returned, seeking a finder's fee, several thousand dollars in found currency to its owner, whose name was not disclosed, and who turned out to be either a total imposter or, more likely, an accomplice of the police officer who had helped him steal the money. The victim of that third offense, who had lost his money under very unusual circumstances, also waived his right to have counsel. The judge then obtained, under the new legal code, everyone's consent to conduct the trial in Russian rather than in Romanian/Moldovan, as required by the new legal system.

After the judge had advised all parties of their various rights, she handed the file to the prosecutor, who read what was translated as the "arraignment," a lengthy handwritten statement more like a summary of evidence than an indictment. The defendant denied failing to file a report on the seized money, blaming a subordinate. He admitted beating his wife and son during alcoholic binges but denied doing it quite so many times. The judge commented to the parties that she hoped the new legal reforms would soon permit guilty pleas and plea agreements as under the American system, having already introduced us to the parties in flattering terms as being there to help reform the Moldovan system. In the meantime, the courts would be required to go through the useless motions of trying the whole case, regardless of a defendant's in-court confession, just as in the famous trial in Dostoevsky's *Crime and Punishment* in tsarist times.

The judge told the prosecutor to call her first witness, to which defense counsel objected, saying that the defendant had a right to testify first. The judge disagreed, saying she had total discretion to control the trial and the order of witnesses. The judge called, sensibly, the male victim of the lost property, as the first witness. The prosecutor being a last minute replacement who knew virtually nothing about the case, the judge chose to question the victim herself, since she was the only one there at all familiar with the file, much as in the old Soviet system. The supposed victim, a fat, sleazy-looking guy who called himself a "capitalist," not a compliment in post-Soviet countries, claimed he had "accidentally left" a bag with over five thousand dollars in cash in several different currencies on the stairway of a friend's apartment building during a "diabetic seizure incident." The judge noted that it was more likely the "capitalist" was drunk but ruled he still had a right to his money, however he had obtained it.

The victim explained why he failed to report his loss for over three weeks, saying it was such a large sum of cash by Moldovan standards and everyone was so poor that he just assumed no one would ever turn it in. The male victim made a very poor witness, but did sort of establish the loss. A friend of his, equally bogus-looking, was the next witness. Strangely to me, the judge first asked the defendant personally if *he* wanted to question the witness himself, but the defendant deferred to his attorney. The defense attorney asked two or three poorly planned questions that did his client no good. The forlorn-looking defendant was still standing alone out among the audience.

The judge directed the prosecutor to call the defendant police officer's assistant as the next witness, learning in the process that he had sat in the courtroom during the entire proceeding in violation of the rule on witnesses. The judge had questioned the defendant fairly extensively about his defense during the "arraignment," so the witness knew pretty well by then what he needed to say to keep their stories consistent. The prosecutor took the assistant on cross-examination as a hostile witness, badgering him with the help of the judge, both of them informing the witness and the defendant that they were themselves former police officers and already knew that neither officer had followed proper procedure, berating them for being dishonest and implying they basically stole the money together. The judge said flatly she might well ask that the assistant be joined as an additional defendant in the case at a later time.

A sworn statement from the neighbors who found the bag of money on the stairs of their apartment was summarized for the record, but the judge said she wanted to recess the trial on that issue until the witnesses could appear live, since they seemed to be the only independent and possibly credible witnesses. They did not appear, probably from fear of the police.

The judge finally let the defense attorney call the defendant himself to explain his failure to make a report. Both the prosecutor and the judge cross-examined him at length on his misfeasance, with the defendant blaming everything on his subordinate, whom the judge then recalled for further cross-examination by the court, most of it not really questioning, but more of a US Senate–style monologue giving her opinions on the witness's shortcomings, without waiting for any answers from him.

The judge then announced that she would hear the victim wife and her son's testimony on the beatings. The little boy had repeatedly run out of the courtroom crying and seemed really shaken by the whole proceeding and very much afraid of his father, who stood not far from him throughout. We had to leave at that time for me to address a group of judges and prosecutors from the Ministry of Justice. We spoke briefly with the judge in her chambers before leaving. She stressed how totally new and utterly different this type of trial was for them, clearly hoping we would be impressed. She said her son would be studying in the US next year. I withheld any criticisms, mentioning only that in our courts the defendant sat by his attorney and the investigating officer sat by the prosecutor for better communication. She immediately agreed to start doing that. I also asked how subpoenas were served and if trials ever had marshals or bailiffs to keep order and enforce the rule. She said such officials were used only in really critical cases, due to a severe shortage of funds to pay their salaries.

A further trial problem arose when nearly all the witnesses strongly disagreed with the secretary's summaries of their testimony, partly because he was so far away from them that he couldn't hear very well. He had to amend each statement before they would sign it. The judge said that was just how it had always been done, but she could possibly arrange things differently so the secretary could better hear the witnesses. She seemed more eager for praise of the progress made than for tips on how to do better, so we did not openly criticize what one of our television judges would no doubt have thought a wildly disorderly proceeding even if presented by non-lawyers.

If this was meant to be a model trial, it certainly was not. On the other hand, the judge was bright, keen, fair, and very impressive, and I suspect it was a fairly typical trial. The defense attorney put his head down on his table and appeared to sleep several times. The judge did not seem at all surprised or try to wake him or correct him. I mentioned to later groups in our conferences that attorneys, in order to be more alert and forceful, should always stand when questioning witnesses and addressing the court, but I did not want to critique this able and helpful judge any more by noting that both attorneys did all their work seated. The whole thing was utterly disorganized but was certainly "transparent," and a spirit of fairness seemed to pervade the proceeding, thanks entirely to the judge. She may well have been selected by the authorities for us to observe because she was one of their most able.

All in all, the trial showed sincere effort to implement a new system. Perhaps in the absence of juries, Moldovan judges will be successful in claiming, as have their American counterparts, that they act better as factfinders than lay jurors. And perhaps in time they would never, in a single trial, try a defendant accused of failure to keep proper records and of being a thief and an admitted wife beater and child abuser. But I doubt it.

The trial was, as we say, somewhat down and dirty, but no worse than one of our old justice of the peace trials with a good judge seeking against the odds to obtain a just result. On balance, I was somewhat hopeful for the future of the Moldovan legal system and believe we could be of practical help to the Moldovans later by attending more actual trials and advising them on their trial procedures from personal experience, not based on theories and promises. Nuts and bolts are what they need now. We also badly need a good English translation of both their procedural and substantive legal codes to advise them more helpfully. All I had was their constitution, which they seemed intent on obeying both in its letter and its spirit. Future visiting Americans will certainly need at least some familiarity with both the wildly different Soviet system and the equally different continental or "civil" law systems before trying to advise the Moldovans.

In the Republic of Moldova

The Maximum Security Prison at Cricova

Friday, August 11, 1995

On Friday we visited Cricova [KREE-koh-vah], the maximum security prison for all of Moldova. Located just thirty miles from Chişinău, Cricova now holds all prisoners repatriated from Siberia upon the breakup of the Soviet Union, many of them formerly under death sentences that were commuted to thirty years under the new post-Soviet code. We were guided by Miron Timofti, supervisor of prisons for the prosecutor's office. The warden, Col. Alexei Rusu [ROO-soo], greeted us. Mr. Rusu explained he had thirty-nine guards for 510 prisoners. One-third were kept in solitary confinement, customary upon incarceration for violent crimes. All guards were army officers. Four doctors and three nurses were on call.

The mess hall looked like one on a rural military base in the US, but no worse. Pictures of macho American stars like Rambo covered the walls. The kitchen was grim, smelling heavily of cabbage. A one-eyed inmate cook reminded me of someone from Parchman penitentiary, our own huge prison in the Mississippi Delta, often fictionalized by world famous Oxford novelist John Grisham. The whole scene was right out of *Cool Hand Luke*, but with economic conditions as bad as they were on the outside, the prison was comparatively better on the inside than some of our jails in Mississippi.

I asked Col. Rusu about gangs in prison. He said that Cricova had them and that just as in the US "they who control information control the prison. If they learn something before we do, we lose." He said there were no real ethnic tensions or gangs based on language but much more informal, classic bands of thugs. The Moldovans had a special swat unit like we do to handle violence. The inmates looked typical, no worse than in the US and not nearly as muscled up or tattooed. Several were mixing mortar and putting mosaic tiles on a large central wall facing a large, attractive fountain—which was actually working. The courtyard itself was also surprisingly attractive. On one side an all-denominational church was being constructed. The warden said most inmates claimed to be Baptists based on recent visits from foreign missionaries, but few showed any credible religious beliefs after seventy years of official atheism under the Communists.

The buildings were well painted, the tables made of strong steel. The bathrooms were not much worse than those elsewhere in Moldova, which were almost universally deplorable. If anything, the prison bathrooms were cleaner. We used a couple of them. Of course they knew we were coming.

The warden mingled easily with inmates, probably better than most American wardens. He said that under the Soviets all prisons for felons were in the Ukraine and Russia and none in Moldova at all. Apparently Moldova used army officers as prison guards partly to keep them employed and because the country has no trained civilian guards and no money to train them. In theory using military personnel as guards might seem questionable, but based on what we saw, and the economic picture, it probably made a lot of sense at that time.

Col. Rusu asked if we wanted to question some prisoners, so we did. I picked out the most vicious-looking one, a Turkic guy with a mean stare and lots of facial scars. I asked what "they said" he had done. "More murders than you could know." What about robberies? "More than I myself could know." A real humorist, he was much enjoyed by the other inmates. I looked for an educated, political-looking type and asked a slimmer, younger inmate with thick glasses what he was in for. "Attempted murder, but I didn't do it. The prosecutor was mistaken." My instincts about his background were not so good. He said he was a maintenance man with little education. I asked if this was his first offense. With a classic inmate sneer he said, "The first time they got me I really killed the guy, but I did my time and never told on the guy who paid me to do it." So much for political prisoners. If there were any, they had to be on the third floor, in isolation cells, whose tiny windows we could see from the courtyard. No one seemed defensive or fearful among the guards, however, and to my experienced eye the inmates did not seem as servile or brutalized as I have so often witnessed in the US, but more like above-average American inmates. They wore civilian clothes, not uniforms. I saw no shaved heads and few tattoos.

I asked the warden if the inmates worked, and he said only about 20 percent of them. They simply had nothing for most of them to do except fix up the prison. They were too dangerous to let out for roadwork, even supervised. He showed us a woodworking shop and later presented us with the gift of some elegant little wood carvings, which I photographed for the illustrations after staining them myself and hanging them in my library. One object was a club, representing the guards. A shovel represented the inmates. Above them was a vampire bat, to remind everyone how close Moldova is to Transylvania. Several Moldovans had Dracula-like accents. Inmates are allowed to make and sell wooden wine bottles and boxes to foreign visitors for a surprising fifty dollars each. At that price I did not buy one.

The ten-bed prison hospital was smelly, grim, and crammed with some really sick-looking people. We were supposed to visit it, but just as we reached the door, the warden mentioned in passing that several had tuberculosis. I was glad I had already declined to go inside or shake hands. We didn't stick around.

A few prisoners were used in the huge Cricova winery, which has over forty miles of underground roads through limestone tunnels. We passed huge pits and visited these tunnels, where the wines are fermented and aged.

Local prisoners were used by the Soviets in the 1950s and 1960s to dig the limestone, which was used for construction of public buildings and roads all over Chişinău and which I had seen stacked in blocks and piles along the roads everywhere across the country.

The visit concluded with a lunch of fresh vegetables, fruits, cheese, bread, and very good champagne labeled "Cricova," served in the warden's office. They called it in true Russian style "Champanski." The warden's huge assistant, Melnik, who did not drink, pointed out that Lenin's picture, which once hung over the warden's desk, had recently been replaced by symbolic portraits of a large and a small German shepherd, representing the warden and his assistant.

After a few glasses of champagne, the warden began telling jokes about what would happen if Presidents Clinton and Yeltsin began swapping secretaries, the punchline being that Mr. Yeltsin's secretary would not object to Mr. Clinton's sexual advances and his insisting on her shortening her miniskirt, except that she worried he would find her KGB pistol in her underwear. Despite his name, Mr. Rusu was not pro-Russian but outspokenly very pro-Moldovan, extolling the beauty and charm of the Moldovan women, who look rather Italian. He said that "even if your wife is Russian, if your father is Moldovan, your children will still be beautiful." He also stressed how easily Russians "became" Moldovan, giving again that Romanian proverb: "Mama Rus, Papa Rus, Dar Ivan Moldovan; i.e., "Mother Russian, Father Russian but Little Ivan (born here) is Moldovan." He also repeated a saying I heard several times: "The Russians say they are our friends, but behind our backs they call us 'gypsies.'" He wanted to make it clear how friendly Moldovans were toward America. Of the Russians he said, "A wolf changes its coat, but not its heart."

I asked about conjugal visits. He said that a facility was currently being built for them. I told him Mississippi had pioneered the idea, but while it relieved some tensions, it often led to corruption, rivalry, and the use of prostitutes instead of wives. He said the prison was guarding against those dangers and that because his prisoners were long-term, the guards knew their real wives and children from dinner visits which were already being allowed. Freed prisoners had a duty to stay in contact with their guards, but our system of parole was just an idea at that time because the Moldavan system lacks money to have supervisors trained to help released prisoners find work. Personally I've always doubted whether our system really works much better, considering our high recidivism rate, due likewise to lack of funds and motivation.

The Moldovans would have liked to provide education and job training in prison but had no funds. Their problems sounded remarkably like ours, although they have less crime and our prisoners appear to me considerably more violent and hostile. All in all, given economic conditions, this one prison offered nothing, from what we saw, to shock the conscience, although the practice of "orienting" all new prisoners with a period of six months' solitary confinement on short rations was something I had not encountered before. It probably makes them pretty pliable.

Law and Order in the Breakaway Republic of Gagauzia

Tuesday, August 15, 1995

Going south from Chișinău the countryside was lovely, all rolling hills with vineyards, somewhat reminiscent of Champagne fifty years earlier. The highway was three-lane without a sufficient underbed, but not bad. The drivers were much less wild than the Tunisians, whom I had just left. On one hill we passed some huge trucks going up with them coming down way too fast. Our driver Alexei referred to the road as "the mother-in-law's dream."

We visited Hincesti [hin-CHEST] where Australians from the famed Penfold winery were helping the Moldovans modernize. I later tasted a Hincesti sauvignon blanc and a cabernet-merlot blend in a restaurant. They were both smooth and tasty and just three dollars in the restaurant. There is definitely a market in the US for Hincesti's more modern table wines and the excellent sparkling wines from Cricova. The ones I tasted there would appeal to the American palate.

The land going south was so rich and black and closely planted that the only pasture was along the road, where skinny-looking cows were tethered. I saw almost no good beef in any restaurant in most of Moldova and little meat of any kind in Chișinău except for excellent pork shashliks at the open air market, or *tolchuk*, but there was plenty of both pork and beef on the collective farms in Gagauzia [gah-gah-OO-zee-ah]. Fields of sunflowers were everywhere, as were the small dark sunflower seeds everyone breaks between their teeth as snacks. The wheat had just been harvested, and there was healthy-looking corn everywhere.

The most striking features along the roads were the little bus shelters covered with colorful mosaic tiles. Beautiful little shelters were also built over the many water wells. The telephone poles were extended by being strapped together inside short concrete poles placed in the ground, a system I had never seen before. Everywhere were big stacks of limestone blocks. There were very few elderly babushkas or real signs of poverty along the roads. Most people looked healthy if not exactly jolly. Of course the weather was perfect, sunny and 75°F. There were no soldiers anywhere but lots of traffic police. Surprisingly Moldova had a freer feel than Tunisia, which was more of a police state. Everything here was fenced. An odd and frequent sight was big motorcycles with people riding in sidecars as in old World War II movies.

Fields of potatoes, cabbages, tomatoes, corn, and flowers went on forever in all directions. It would take really bad planning for this country not to be prosperous. Our interpreter, Ilian, would confidently describe various villages as clearly either Moldovan or Gagauzian as we passed by, although I could not have told the difference. It was an unpleasant reminder of Bosnia in the ways people perceive each other as so ethnically distinct.

As we went farther south, the country got drier and gradually poorer, much like crossing from California into Mexico. Our destination, the Gagauz capital of Comrat [kohm-RAHT], could be seen for a long distance. For the first time in Moldova, all the writing was in Russian Cyrillic letters, with no Latin signs in sight anywhere. The drought here was evident: dusty fields, empty reservoirs, all of which intensified the pollution left by the Soviets. There were lots of what look like abandoned small factories. Near Comrat there was a huge area of well-irrigated greenhouses, big as I ever saw.

A big sign announced "Gagauz Republik." Our guide, Misha, said they had just arrested the local militia leader last week. The language here in court and otherwise is not Romanian but sometimes Russian or often Turkish. At the city hall, or *bash khanat*, we were to meet the mayor, or khan, whose title reminded me we were definitely not in Kansas. Everywhere on doors and gates were vivid red Communist stars. A few had been painted over in black but not removed. Lenin's statue was still prominently in place on the squares. The people looked very different, non-Romanian. A few were blond and fair skinned like Russians, but most were darker and Turkish-looking with good features. We walked the narrow, dusty streets from office to office, getting a feel of the place, which was very different from Chișinău, like a totally different country.

We met first with Mr. Stefan Gradinar, chief prosecutor at Comrat. He explained his salary was comparatively good vs. other Moldovans at fifty dollars a month, except that his rent was thirty dollars a month and conditions were getting worse. He said prosecutors used to get unofficial supplements, but that now all the best people were quitting, especially all legal experts. Mr. Gradinar, who had not been to the US, seemed well respected by his colleagues and appreciative of our visit. He introduced us first to Peter Pashali [pah-SHAH-lee], new president of the National Assembly of Gagauzia, who was also bright and positive. He chatted about his family history in the Balkans and how "pasha" meant not ruler but "leader," while "gagauz" was Turkish for "traitor," referring to his people's early adoption of Christianity.

Several people in Chișinău had told me, somewhat ominously and apparently erroneously, that the Gagauzians were really "muslims at heart," just waiting to rejoin the Turks. I certainly did not get that impression at all. Mr. Pashali noted that since Gagauzia's, "autonomy" in 1994, things had gotten no better, but at least they'd gotten out from under the problem of being required to speak Romanian, which no one knew. He said he knew that sometimes "dual power means no power" and that their future definitely lay with Moldova, not in being some tiny independent breakaway state, although many Gagauz favor that approach. "We just need a viable status *within* Moldova," he said.

Mr. Pashali professed himself pleased with America's efforts to help former Soviet countries. Recently departed US Ambassador Mary Pendleton had personally visited his home district and helped the Gagauzians with their economic problems, and he welcomed as many US visits as possible in all fields. He showed me on his desk copies of the US and Moldovan constitutions in Russian, saying he liked the simplicity of our constitution and the way people actually lived by it, unlike the Soviets. He noted that only on the past Saturday did his government actually appoint a real Moldovan prosecutor for Gagauzia, who was going to move his office from Chișinău to his ancestral home in Comrat. It was obvious that relations between the national government and the Gagauz were in transition and little actual legal work was being done on a daily basis.

Mr. Pashali said the biggest current legal problem was that there were too few lawyers of any kind and no law school to train new ones. Only three of the fifteen members of the Gagauz parliament were lawyers; "How can you write laws without lawyers?" He was optimistic about how his region would somehow operate within Moldova while maintaining its own language and institutions, suggesting it would be like Hawaii within the United States, like a state with a different original culture.

After the legal seminar, which was lively, we were taken to lunch at the nearby collective farm at Bugeac [boo-ZHAHK], which my hosts readily admitted was a model, far above average or typical. Inside a cellar decorated as a dining room we had my finest meal in Moldova, a monster groaning board of meats and fresh vegetables like an old Midwestern thrasher's dinner. Huge pieces of pork, first lightly boiled to tenderize them, then grilled over an open fire, and finally simmered in their own stock, were truly delicious, as were the little tomatoes and new potatoes, good as I ever ate.

The boss of the collective farm, where nothing had changed since the Soviets, undertook to debate with me the glories of Communism versus our decadent capitalist exploitation of workers. Mr. Gradinar tried to stop the boss but was overridden. The boss asked me to drink a toast to Stalin. In reply I gave a toast to Stalin *only* as a military leader who joined us in defeating the Nazis. When I asked him to join a toast to President Reagan, he made a similar sidestep and offered his toast to the actor Ronald Reagan, who, despite other shortcomings, was "an excellent cowboy."

Professing total ignorance of economics, I reminded the boss that I was a prosecutor who specialized in eradicating public corruption and violent crime and in protecting minorities from exploitation. I told him how my father had founded and managed a "people's" REA government-sponsored cooperative, which brought electricity to US farmers in the 1940s and 1950s and that I personally saw it happen. I also told him of my "capitalist" experiences in high school in leasing a hay baler and baling hay by myself for local farmers, even though my father was technically a government member of the *nomenclatura* and a protected *apparatchik*. Somehow, over a two-hour period of eating, toasting, mutual challenges, and cajolery, the whole dispute became defused and the boss began praising Americans as honest and straightforward people. We parted on excellent terms.

While he went off to arrange a swap of farm produce (wine for fish) with a group of Latvians, the rest of our group, including the mayor of the village and the judges and prosecutors, seemed relieved at the outcome of the great luncheon debate. They appeared reassured that we Americans were not as arrogant as they had expected but also were not going to be run over by old-school Communist hardliners. In some ways, though not involving legal issues, this encounter was perhaps my favorite moment of the Moldovan trip.

Our wine, a cabernet sauvignon served in unlabeled bottles, was the best I tasted in Moldova. We drank multiple pitchers to make sure. It was light and fresh, more in the style of a Beaujolais, tasting as if it were made by the carbonic maceration method. The wines of Comrat were generally not yet as highly rated abroad as they should have been, mainly due to bad storage and shipping practices under the Soviets and more recently poor handling *after* they were made, but this wine was a hint of what Moldova *could* do in the wine business if its excellent products were properly stored and well marketed. Wine could be a key to developing closer US-Moldova commercial and other relations.

"The Eyes of the Tsar"

Wednesday, August 16, 1995

The road north from Chişinău to Bălţi [belts (The final *i* in Romanian is pronounced *s*.)] was wide and bouncy but adequate. The houses and farms became steadily more affluent as we traveled north until the area looked more like Austria than Mexico. There were still plenty of two-wheeled horse carts and field huts built of corn stalks, but overall the area looked like it could have been a rich farming country if well managed. It looked like France might have looked if the Soviets had managed it for fifty years. As always, our driver's papers were checked several times by the traffic police, who seemed to outnumber real police by at least a thousand to one in the country. They wore funny Tyrolean-looking hats, which people said were donated to them for some reason by the state of Florida along with their uniforms. I didn't know whether to believe it or not, or whether they even believed it.

In Bălți we met with an assortment of prosecutors, judges, and defense attorneys, who were alert and ready with practical questions. By far the most interesting were the comments of Chief Prosecutor Ion Morei [ee-OWN moh-Ray], on which I took several pages of notes. He visited the US April 3–14, 1995, and was obviously impressed and eager to proceed with real legal reforms, although not agreeing with every one of our ideas. He described the northern part of the country, Bălți in particular, as the most reformed, anti-Communist, and anti-Russian of all Moldova. He said Moldovans worked harder and cheated less than the Russians. My own impression was that the Russians are more aggressive and the Moldovans more laid back and passive, probably from centuries of foreign occupation.

At lunch, in the lovely sixteenth-century dining room in the cellar of the Casa Mare on the city square, I noticed a picture of Jesus on the wall. "He replaced Lenin," my companions said, laughing. Mr. Morei said that until 1989 he had spoken only Russian, but now used more Romanian. He transferred his son to the Romanian-language school but had so far kept his daughter in the Russian one. He had his children baptized in the Moldovan Orthodox Church, and he and his wife were recently remarried in the church, something which was "too dangerous for my job" under the Soviets. His wife is of Ukrainian origin. His parents, as large landholding boyars, were sent to Siberia after World War II. He was himself born in Siberia, where the family lived for nine years until Khrushchev ordered them repatriated. They got some of their property back but no reparations until Gorbachev in 1989, thirty years after they were "rehabilitated." Unfortunately their restitution money, which would have bought seventy cows when awarded, was worth only seventeen lei when they finally got it, or about four dollars.

Mr. Morei volunteered many interesting opinions on Moldovan and other legal systems, old and new. As we strolled around the city, he stressed how prosecutors still supervised factory bosses, mayors, prisons, and other institutions, and exercised far too many functions unrelated to prosecuting cases, many of them "unnecessary." As for the famed prosecutorial control of judges, he said that it still existed, but mostly at the Supreme Court level, not at trial; however, since trial judges knew the prosecutor could always reverse their decisions on appeal and embarrass them, they usually knuckled under to politically influential prosecutors.

He said that under the new system the judges had to approve arrest warrants and most did not want that responsibility. Many of them, more out of fear or laziness than corruption, would dismiss arrest warrants without even telling the prosecutor. Under the old Soviet system only the prosecutor general could cancel an arrest warrant. Mr. Morei said that under the Soviets the judges denied having any jurisdiction of organized crime and gangs and wanted it to stay that way, fearing violent retribution. He felt that Moldova had the worst of both worlds, with the judges having enough power to be corrupt but not enough power to act against organized crime. I suggested both "judge shopping" and going to the media, time-honored prosecutorial techniques we used when faced with the same problems in the US. He laughed and said he'd tried both, with the media avenue being more successful because "the people are more reform-minded than the judges."

One of Mr. Morei's more interesting comments was that people in general had little faith in the judiciary because judges were so often corrupt, but they trusted the prosecutor's office *too much* because of its broad powers as the "Eyes of the Tsar" (a phrase I heard a lot) since the time of Tsar Peter the Great. Mr. Morei's candor was striking, and he seemed to want to impart to us as much information as possible in the few hours we had to share, carrying us into a number of offices, businesses, and shops to show us the pros and cons of the changes in the economy and laws. He certainly could not have been more open or frank in giving us his views and accurate facts on the current situation so that we could offer appropriate help. He was the only one to tell me that Moldovan wines had been infested by the radioactive fallout from the Chernobyl nuclear plant disaster in nearby Ukraine.

Mr. Morei's most original remark to the seminar group was that he had come away with one powerful impression of the US justice system: it functions on common sense and practicality, not empty formalities. Everywhere he went in the US he saw people wanting results, not theories, which was the greatest need of Moldova. Along this line, before I arrived, Bălți and Chișinău had already done one of the things I suggested: establish a special unit of experienced organized crime prosecutors and judges to handle cases of violence and intimidation. Attending our lunch was just such a prosecutor, Anatoli Dolgi, a muscular, formidable-looking little man dressed all in black who was in Bălți to try an organized crime case later that week. It illustrated what is to me our biggest shortcoming in helping the Moldovans: we know so little about what really happens in their legal system that we can't advise them as helpfully as we would like. I guess that's why they sent us here.

The only statistics on crime I received while in Moldova came from Mr. Morei. He said there were 4,200 criminal cases filed in Moldova the previous year and that his office had 437 of them. If Bălți has 160,000 people and Moldova 4.5 million, it either had a lot more crime or a lot more prosecutions there. In comparative terms, the atmosphere and spirit of Bălți compared to Chișinău reminded me of Milan compared to Naples: one vigorous and energetic, the other laid back and decadent. He noted as we walked that the people had recently lost their traditional joking, friendly Mediterranean manner and become glum and grouchy due to economic hardship and uncertainty. He said the atmosphere in the streets was much less happy than a few years ago despite their new freedoms. Many missed the security and predictability of the Soviet system.

Most state factories were closed, but many small private enterprises in clothing, fur hats, and cognac were growing, and factory outlet stores were becoming popular. Education in Moldova generally lagged behind Romania, but the university at Bălți, built by the Turks, was much more attractive than the rundown Soviet pile I visited in Chișinău. The square had a lovely fountain which the city couldn't afford the power to operate. Sidewalk moneychangers, which I didn't see in Chișinău, were common in Bălți. In a large department store only Russian was spoken. Bălți still had special relations with the Baltic states and a lot of tax-free bartering apparently went on.

Mr. Morei said that formerly Bălți was home to many Jewish citizens of high standing, most of whom had long since left for Israel. Anti-Semitism remained a touchy subject, long after the Russian pogroms ended, but he said that some Jews were coming back to Bălți because of ethnic violence with Muslims and other hardships and strict rules in Israel and because of new economic opportunities in Moldova. He felt the Jews could be a key to economic recovery, but said that very day a bank teller had been killed in a daylight robbery at the only Jewish bank in Chișinău, illustrating their dilemma.

Prosecutor Morei said one of his office's best anti-gangster moves in Bălți had been to close off the main downtown squares to automobiles. Since most citizens had no cars, the thugs constantly drove through in their black Mercedes, intimidating everyone. In the months since the closing, street life had livened up considerably. Four more theaters opened downtown, and many citizens had begun to engage in old-style strolling about. Mr. Morei also tried closing the town's only sex toy shop, but had to let it reopen by popular demand. Apparently the prosecutor could exercise a sort of injunctive power to abate nuisances without going to a judge. Again, it is hard to transpose values from one system to another. As a French judge once told me, "Each of our systems is internally consistent and complete, but if you change one part, you change the relationships of all the others." Moldova was trying to do just that in a time of political uncertainty and economic hardship. On our part, patience, persistence, and plenty of candor about the shortcomings of our own society and legal system were useful in our relations with Moldovan legal authorities. They wanted our help, but we needed to be thoughtful about not humiliating them.

I had one vivid personal experience with crime in Moldova. One pleasant evening, standing alone in front of the parliament building on my way to dinner with my interpreters, I felt a sharp blow to the back of my head and fell on my face. I'd been carrying my suit jacket slung over my shoulder, John Kennedy–style, and as I lay on the ground I felt someone strongly tugging on it, eventually pulling it away. Two muscular teenagers went running away with it, laughing. An adrenalin rush made me run after them, loudly yelling, "Police, Police," which I assumed sounded the same in Romanian. Of course no police came. To my surprise, I was gaining on them, but then I began to be out of breath. I realized that my passport and wallet were both stashed deep in my pants pocket, not in my jacket. Just then the young thugs, one dark and one blond, probably Russian, vaulted over a tall hedge. It suddenly occurred to me to ask myself what I would do if I caught them. Probably get the stew beaten out of me. So I stopped and let them get away with my favorite suit jacket. Oh well, the suit pants would become slacks, and I would have a nice dinner with plenty of fine Moldovan wine, which I proceeded to do. I reported it to the Moldovan police, but never heard back from them.

A Little Bit of North Korea in the Heart of Europe: Transnistria

Thursday, August 17, 1995

My last visit in Moldova was certainly the most eventful and unusual. Justice Minister Sturza and Prosecutor General Postoban both politely but firmly refused to help us with introductions and documents to visit Transnistria, the breakaway neo-Soviet "republic" on the eastern side of Moldova. The local deputy prosecutor, however, Mrs. Raisa Batsura [baht-SOO-rah], agreed to guide us through the tanks and military checkpoints with her boss, Prosecutor Ivan Glavchev [GLAHV-choff]. It is interesting to note that evaluators of Mrs. Batsura's April visit to the US found her "quiet, with little to say." On home ground she was quite the contrary, bold and forthright, and was an excellent choice for a US visit. She was an outstanding discussion leader and obviously learned a lot while being quiet but attentive in the US.

Transnistria was under a ceasefire maintained by elements of the Russian 14th Army, a handful of Moldovan police, and a Transnistria militia. The

Russians were identifiable by light blue circles on their helmets, looking ironically like small halos. The prosecutors gave us a tour of the scene of the biggest battles of the 1992 civil war, in which over a thousand were killed and many others just "disappeared" and were still unaccounted for. It was, at that time, easily the worst violence in the former Soviet Union outside Chechnya. Along the entrance road are rows of concrete crosses to mark where particular deaths occurred. All along the Dniester Bridge are similar crosses of iron. Bendery [ben-DARE, without the "y"], like the regional capital Tiraspol, is an old Russian fortress built to hold back the Turks and Tatars, but more recently, before the Soviet Union collapsed, it had been a vacation spot with hot spring baths for Russian tourists. The region looked much more industrialized than most of Moldova.

For centuries Transnistria has been an especially Russified enclave, even though 70 percent of its residents are ethnically Moldovan. Everyone now speaks almost exclusively Russian. An international outcast, Transnistria is now recognized by no nation, but protected by Russia. The old flag of Soviet Moldavia flies over public buildings along with red flags and banners. The fighting on the Transnistrian side was allegedly done mainly by unemployed mercenaries recently mustered out of the Soviet army, but most Moldovans believe the Russians would like to keep it as their westernmost military outpost, beyond Ukraine, and their closest base to Serbia and the rest of the Balkans as it was before World War II. It was here that I felt most strongly how Moldova was still a part of the volatile Balkan region.

Mrs. Batsura showed us several destroyed buildings and lots of others heavily pockmarked by bullets. Sniper fire here was said to be every bit as bad as at Sarajevo. The "rogue" commander of Russia's 14th Army, General Lebed, had been forced out only two months earlier by Mr. Yeltsin, and had stated he would run for president of Russia. He was described as a "Zhirinovsky-type strongman," but better educated and fairly popular. At the time of my visit Transnistria had 440,000 people and distinctively Moldovan, Ukrainian, and Russian villages and neighborhoods were pointed out to us. Our interpreter Ilian characterized the area as "a little North Korea in the heart of Europe," complete with its own currency called "ruble coupons," so worthless that a thousand-coupon note won't buy a box of matches. Mrs. Batsura gave me some as souvenirs.

According to our hosts, the whole Transnistria idea was economically ready to collapse, being held together by Communist officials only so they would still have their jobs, cars, and apartments. It had thirty government ministries, far more than all of Moldova itself. Gagauzia in contrast had just five. Fear of the West remained strong here. Several of the plotters of the failed coup to overthrow Mikhail Gorbachev were either from here or fled here after its failure. The prosecutors were heavily and repeatedly intimidated. Under a dual system the Transnistria prosecutors occupied all the buildings and the Moldovans had just one small office, but all the experienced ones stuck with Moldova.

It would seem difficult to discuss legal reform and the rule of law under such circumstances, but our small meetings actually went quite well. Under the watchful eyes of a Russian captain, Alexei, who declined to give his last name, Mrs. Batsura explained her visit to the US, saying that our system was as "near perfect" as could be fashioned and that we had many aspects which could be immediately applied in Moldova. I gave a typical speech, stressing my long experience as prosecutor, professor of trial practice, former defense attorney, assistant to a judge, and legal counsel to a US senator who was chairman of Armed Services. The questions were enthusiastic and surprisingly hopeful about the future considering the gravity of the situation. The Russian captain was friendly and even agreed to swap his cloth Russian POCCIA arm patch with me for my FBI and Marine Corps badges. The more sensitive political topics we reserved to talk about privately in the car or at dinner. I now wear his badge sewn to my jean jacket.

Our most interesting visit was an unauthorized one with a Transnistrian prosecutor, Mr. "X," which was held with a Moldovan prosecutor in his former office. Mr. X was very courteous and his assistant spoke good English. Beneath a picture of Lenin and a map of the old Soviet Union, the two old prosecutor friends discussed how their personal cooperation had kept the justice system functional by informal means throughout the civil war. Most Transnistrian defendants wanted their cases tried by the Moldovans, mistrusting the "rigged" Soviet justice system. The two prosecutors still somehow worked closely together, dividing up the cases, trying to do rough justice as best they could. The Transnistria prosecutor said he understood even Russia was changing its legal procedures to be more western, that they wanted to protect human rights and wanted an adversary system, but that it would take much time. The Transnistrian government, on the other hand, rather than decreasing "investigative" detention without a warrant as was done in Moldova from three days to twelve hours, had increased it to thirty days, unheard of even under the Soviets. "You are not the same person after thirty days in detention," he commented.

Detainees could also be held without the knowledge of the prosecutor, an even more ominous new development. The Transnistrian prosecutor was firm on one point: Yeltsin's decree to fight organized crime was not working. "Stronger measures are needed. We need more and better investigators, prosecutors, and judges. The gangsters are out of control and getting worse." On the other hand, the prosecutors want to cooperate with the US, which no one during my trip ever seemed to blame for the problems either of Moldova or of the Soviet Union generally. Perhaps the Moldovans were just being hospitable, but I don't think so. Even those who were in open ideological disagreement with us never blamed us for their plight. Gorbachev was unpopular everywhere, but his former populist protégé Luchinski, originally from Moldova, was often named as a likely new president over Mr. Snegur [SNAY-goer]. In Bendery, as everywhere in Moldova, the mention of the former Soviet "jury" system, two lay judges voting with the real judge, provoked laughter or a heated debate, sometimes both. Some said the lay judges were just rubber stamps called "nodders," who had no input. Others complained that ignorant co-op farm workers, characterized as "Martha Milkmaid" and "Tommy Tractor Driver," were moved to tears by emotional defendants and often outvoted the professional judge to acquit obviously guilty defendants. That seemed unlikely, but was repeated to me by several persons on several occasions.

The biggest supporter of juries was Mrs. Batsura, who said she had seen them work well in the US, especially because people have faith in the judges. The impression of venality and corruption of Moldovan judges was widespread. I had once assumed that the prosecutors were the KGB types and the judges the helpless pawns, but that is not the way the Moldovans perceive it. The judges themselves seemed demoralized and dispirited and for the most part lacked confidence in their own roles. One told me in a typical comment, "Lay judges didn't work, but without them the real judges are even worse."

Across the street from our meeting were the burned-out police department and passport office where the civil war began with the killing of a police officer, the son of one of the judges. September 3 would be the third anniversary of the civil war and was to be "celebrated" by Transnistria. The Moldovan prosecutors feared real trouble then but said they were the frontline and could not let their country be divided up. The Russian military "authorities" came to me and said there was a case of cholera in the military barracks where the peacekeepers stayed, and they demanded we leave Transnistria immediately. Our hosts said it was just a typical Soviet pretext to clear everyone out for September 3. The chief of police moved out of town with some of the soldiers, but most police officers stayed because it was the only place they had to sleep. Increased pressure against them is expected and violence is not unlikely.

All restaurants being closed, at least to us, Mr. Glavchev invited us to lunch at his home, recently purchased with special loans from three credit unions. It was a beehive of construction in the rear courtyard where a cellar, gardens, and outbuildings were being constructed. At the door we all had to remove our shoes because there were fine Caucasian carpets on the floors as well as the walls. He explained that he was ethnically Bulgarian and his wife Russian.

She had killed two of their best rabbits to make our lunch on short notice, all other meat being unavailable. The food was excellent, but no doubt a huge expenditure for them.

Mrs. Glavchev had spoken just that week on television against the breakaway republic, saying that though an ethnic Russian herself, she was as Moldovan as anyone and wanted to stay that way. She supervised fifty-six train repair stations and was an impressive and forceful woman of considerable charm. As we proceeded through several courses and innumerable toasts in champagne and later cognac, she told some really funny and mildly raunchy ethnic stories with Ukrainians the butt of most of the jokes, apparently the Moldovan tradition. Moldovans readily admit they are often the butt of jokes by Romanians, being portrayed as bumpkins and country cousins. The Tunisians, whom I had just visited, treat the Libyans the same way, as the Algerians do the Tunisians. Having myself grown up near Chicago, once home of ubiquitous anti-Polish jokes, I saw that human nature doesn't change much regardless of geography.

The two prosecutors said how much they like our system with the judge as referee versus the old system where the judge gathered the evidence and the prosecutor dictated the outcome but often did not even bother to attend the trial, leaving all that up to the judge. Mrs. Batsura lamented the habit of being so unprepared that neither prosecutor nor defense attorney knew enough about the case to question the witnesses. Our spirited cross-examinations were a marvel to them. Even as a prosecutor, she liked the judge being "at the top of the pyramid."

She also liked our federal system of having the lead investigator sit beside the prosecutor and the defendant sit beside his attorney so that maximum knowledge of the true facts of the case is available to both sides, live, in court. Under the old system technicalities reigned. The slightest procedural error caused not only a whole new trial but an entire reinvestigation, with every witness re-interviewed, sometimes several times. It sounded like our old English "forms of action" in civil cases and our old antique indictments with their flowery, hypertechnical allegations, such as "against the peace and dignity of the State."

I did warn Mrs. Batsura, however, as I did all prosecutors, to beware "the rule of judges." If the balance went too far, with no lay jury as a check as in our federal equity cases, judicial tyranny was a real possibility, especially with lifetime judicial appointments. We talked again, as with each group, about elected vs. appointed judges. We liked their new method of selecting judges by panels of experienced magistrates, or by the parliament on their recommendation, first for a five-year appointment, followed by a ten-year reappointment upon good performance, then a possible lifetime reappointment, which seemed to be a good balance given all their circumstances, somewhat like what is called in the US the "Missouri Plan."

A really surprising report they'd heard from the prosecutors in Bendery was that their new adversary system was *already* working better, despite the unsettled social and economic situations. They reportedly had held several trials, and the attorneys were better prepared, the trials went faster, the victims and witnesses could understand what was happening, and most of the rote reading and empty formalities of Soviet courts were easier to drop than they had supposed.

As we drank a last glass of cognac before crossing the checkpoint back into Moldova, the prosecutors gave us a toast to *druzhba*, or "friendship," noting we had to have the *botul calului* [cah-LOO-loo-ee] or "mouth of the horse." The origin of the old Moldovan phrase, meaning "one for the road," came from the practice on cold nights of allegedly sticking your glass under your horse's warm breath to thaw it out so you can drink it. We were thus toasted safely out of Transnistria and my Moldovan legal odyssey was over. I would readily do it again.

Throughout my two-week stay in Moldova I had remained sober and in control by drinking only wine, always declining brandy and vodka. But under the warm hospitality of the photogenic Mrs. Glavchev, however, I relented and toasted repeatedly in Moldovan brandy. The next morning my interpreter Ilian informed me of my final toast at the border, of which I had no recollection. According to Ilian, when Mrs. Glavchev removed her gloves for the final toast, I replied, "If the rest of your body is as beautiful as your hands, it must be a pleasure to behold." Ilian said she and her husband both seemed pleased, not offended. So much for prosecutors as diplomats.

A Contrary View of Moldova

Soon after editing this chapter on Moldova, I came across a book written in 2008 by NPR and *New York Times* foreign correspondent Eric Weiner. Entitled *The Geography of Bliss*, it details Weiner's travels in ten countries, from the Netherlands and Thailand to India and "America" (i.e., the USA) trying to learn which countries are happiest and why. Oversimplifying his conclusions, as Weiner himself does, he finds most countries a mixed bag. Switzerland is comfortable but boring, Qatar rich but soulless, America too complicated, Bhutan way too exotic and complex to classify as a true Shangri-La, but then he decided that dark, frozen, tiny Iceland is probably the happiest country. Weiner stresses that money is not enough alone to guarantee happiness, although it softens troubles.

In a thirty-four-page rant, Weiner unfairly judges poor, impoverished Moldova as the unhappiest country on earth. His basis for this slander is, to me, a brief shallow trip, during which he totally missed the point of Moldovan culture, ignoring its poetic and artistic side, denouncing its women as painted tarts in short skirts, and concluding that its only virtue lies in its excellent fruits and vegetables, which are indeed superb. Weiner saves his bitterest venom for Moldovan wines and foods, obviously having visited neither Cricova nor Comrat nor Hincesti. While it is true that Moldova is the poorest country *financially* in Europe, partly due to its citizens' foolish atavistic habit of electing Communists as their presidents, behind the outward poverty lies a vibrant, interesting culture waiting to bloom into a healthy, modern country. My last word on the subject.

Return from Moldova: Ilian and Azret— the Balkans Meet the Caucasus

As I was leaving Moldova, my trusted guide and interpreter, Ilian Cashu, without question the best guide I ever had in any of the countries the DOJ sent me to, asked me for a "little favor." Though raised under a Communist regime, Ilian had somehow survived with a strong personal moral system. He never hit me up for money or any other favor, so when Ilian finally did ask, I was eager to hear what it was. "I want to study in America so I can return to Moldova with some education and skills and help my people."

For a minute I was disappointed. It seemed like every person I met in every former Soviet Republic, not excluding Russia, wanted to escape to the West, anywhere in the West, but America most of all. Now Ilian sounded like all the rest. Former Soviets would declare that they wanted to help their country, when all they really wanted was to get the hell out of where they were, which they universally felt had no future, at least not for their generation, and probably not for their children's. But for Ilian I felt differently. He had worked so hard, he *deserved* to get out. Without ever being allowed to leave the Soviet Union, he spoke at least six languages fluently, all learned in public school and from talking constantly with foreign visitors. Thanks to being a Lenin scholar, a high academic honor, he had visited *every* Soviet republic, but had never been able to leave the Soviet Union. His English, although it had some occasional gaps, was fluent. His French was even better. In Moldova we often spoke French together so the Moldovans around us could not understand our observations about them. Ilian was a very subtle character. In some ways he became like a son to me. Of course I would try to get him a scholarship to the US, but I also told him honestly I knew nothing about how to do it. I would try, but it was a real "long shot," a phrase that he, as a lifelong deer hunter in the forests of rural Moldova, always liked.

The day after I arrived back in the US, I called Susan Oliphant, director of the Ole Miss Study Abroad Program, who had helped my daughter Lydia get a full year on scholarship in southern France and another year teaching English at a high school in Le Mans in western France, known mainly for its twenty-four-hour road race. Susan's first reaction was to say, "Oh no, not another eastern European. Once they're here, they'll do anything not to go back. They'd rather be in prison in the US than back in their own countries." I asked her as a personal favor to please try anyway. That very afternoon she called me back: "John. Can you believe this? We've just been offered two George Soros scholarships, good for two years of study at Ole Miss with not only all tuition and travel paid, but room and board as well. And so far we have zero applicants."

I soon had in hand Ilian's academic records, certified in Russian, Romanian, and English. His Soviet high school picture was startling. I had known him only as a clean-shaven, short-haired young college student. His high school graduation picture showed a heavily bearded, wild-eyed mountain man right out of the old *Duck Dynasty* television series. Later I asked him about it. "Winters were very cold in the mountains when I was growing up. Our house was not heated. Hair is like clothing, Mr. Hailman." Nearly as surprising was his academic record. Written in the stilted language of the Soviets, it showed clearly how Ilian became a Lenin scholar, a rare and highly privileged position, due to his gift for languages. Although never trusted to visit any western country, he had been from Moscow to Vladivostok, from Yerevan, Armenia, to Bishkek, Kyrgyzstan. "It was easier than it sounds," he said modestly. "Everyone everywhere is required to study and speak Russian." He had been to so many places I'd always dreamed of: Samarkand, Tashkent, Ashkhabad. "But it is not all gravy, as you say. Everywhere you go everyone tries to exploit you. Everyone must be paid off. As a Lenin scholar, they even give you special cash money just for bahksheesh (small bribes)."

Ilian's adaptation to American life was amusing to watch. We went to lunch together often. His introduction to our wildly different American culture left him shocked but always positive. "Mr. Hailman, tonight I must drive a car for some foreign students. They all want to get drunk and I am the only one with a driving license. They never drove before. Tell me, please, what is the appropriate bribe to give a US policeman when he stops me and asks for money? I do not wish to be cheated."

When I stopped laughing, I told Ilian that police were different in America. They are paid well enough that they do not have to make a living by shaking down people affluent enough to drive a car. "Never, ever offer them money. Not only will they arrest you, they will be so offended they may even bust your head," I told him. Ilian said, "What a great country, where the police are honest. Amazing."

Although he could have lived cheaper on campus, Ilian chose to live unsupervised by authorities in a ratty little hellhole of an apartment right off campus that catered entirely to foreign students. The place was cold, dirty, and depressing. All sorts of exotic but tempting smells came from the cooking in the rooms. He once counted students from eighteen countries in his apartment complex. Out of ten thousand Ole Miss students, he was one of a handful who rode a bike to class. He was *really* foreign to the affluent Delta frat boys and gorgeous coeds from Dallas in their BMW convertibles. One of the first questions he asked me was how to meet girls. Once they heard his foreign accent, they brushed him off, politely and not so politely. "They have zero interest in me or my country. They are the most provincial people I ever met." I told him to forget sorority girls. They just want rich husbands, not adventure. Look for female graduate or law students, especially from cities in the north.

One Monday, a saddened Ilian told me about his weekend, sounding like one of those old *Saturday Night Live* skits with Chevy Chase and Dan Akroyd talking about American girls "with big American breasts." He also once volunteered that American food must be "incredibly nutritious" because "look at how fat that lady is." Fortunately, the lady did not hear him. One night Ilian met a dark-haired graduate student in psychology from Boston at a bar called "The Library," noting, "I like your American humor. Giving the name 'Library' to a bar so you can tell your parents you are at the 'library.' What a great country." The girl had agreed to let him buy her a drink, and they had danced together several times. She even told him he was cute. "I remembered what you said about American women being different, idealistic, so I did not just ask her if she want to have sex, as with Soviet woman. I wait for her to act." The woman invited Ilian to her apartment for a drink. "She let me touch her breasts. When I try to go further, she ask me a very American question: Did I think I was falling in love with her or did I just want sex. I try to understand your culture, so I say I think what it supposed to be: love. This girl, she say in very northern, nasal manner: 'Wrong answer. I just wanted to see what sex with you would be like. You are too serious.' She then asked me to leave. I feel very bad. I lose my big chance."

Later Ilian had better luck, sticking to foreign women students. I felt bad that he didn't know more American Ole Miss students, but they simply had their own narrow lives to lead and were totally uncurious about whether Moldova even existed. Then one day Ilian showed up unannounced at my office. With some difficulty I convinced the federal court security guards to let him in. "John, you really know some strange people," they said. Ilian had a problem. He had ordered an expensive computer via the internet and it had not arrived. Or rather it had arrived, but had been stolen before he ever saw it.

"Do you know a guy, Mr. Hailman, named Azret?" I had never heard the name. "He is a really big deal with foreign students. A real Soviet gangster." I asked Ilian to explain. It seems Azret was the main assistant to a faculty chairman and carried a big stick among foreign students. He was also a real Russian-style gangster wannabe who exploited the more naïve foreign students. He had an illegal "black box" phone he used to make illegal international calls for free, then made the foreign students pay him huge fees for using it. He had also assembled a pretty good arsenal of illegal weapons and shook down students from former Soviet states, who understood and accepted that way of doing business. If they didn't pay him, bad things would happen to them or their belongings or their student status.

Azret exploited the Chinese, Indians, and others, but his favorite victims were the lonely Muslim males. Using trashy white girls he picked up in local bars, he would pay the girls a little to ride around with the lonely Muslim boys, who then paid Azret handsomely for the privilege of just sitting beside the girls with their short skirts and their bare legs touching the boys'. For a really good payment, the girls might even let themselves be kissed. Azret had the makings of a pimp, but just hadn't gotten there yet. Always an operator, Ilian had secretly gotten a key to Azret's apartment from the manager. The inside, he said, was amazing. Every inch of every wall, even the ceiling, was covered by huge pictures of American gangsters from the movies. Ilian went into the apartment because he had been told by the postman that the guy in that apartment, the big one with the heavy beard, was the one who had signed for his computer.

What did Ilian want to do? I offered to take the case and get Azret indicted in federal court for fraud on the telephone company and extortion of foreign students. That scared Ilian to death. "You do not know the Soviet system, Mr. Hailman. Azret is from Caucasus. Everyone there is gangsters. Foreign students know all about him. He has power. He would get me and the others sent home." Ilian told me he had checked Azret's story of his background. He came from the tiny north Caucasian republic, still part of Russia today, called Kabardino-Balkaria. The whole place has fewer than a million people and is best known for breeding fine thoroughbred horses. Ilian had verified that Azret's father had been a high-ranking officer of the KGB who had been killed under suspicious circumstances. Azret apparently had earned his fearsome reputation. I asked Ilian how badly he wanted his computer back. He said not enough to confront Azret or even enough to have him know he knew about it.

I called a detective at the Oxford PD and put together a search warrant for Azret's apartment for the black box phone and some other items, but not the computer. When the detective searched the apartment, Azret was scared to death. He still had a Soviet idea of what the police would do. He confessed right away and admitted to things we hadn't even heard of. He gave back Ilian's computer without even being asked. The Oxford officer loved the caper. As he was leaving, evidence in hand, he told Azret, "You need to get rid of that gangster stuff, man. That shit could get you deported." Ilian loved it when I told him about it. Azret never even suspected Ilian was behind it all.

As I pondered whether to go full bore and do a federal indictment of Azret, weighing the potential damage to Ilian and other foreign students, I got a call from a professor. He was upset. "John, I've got my best graduate assistant, Azret, here with me. Ilian Cashu tells me you may know something about it." I explained to him that rumors had led to the Azret arrest, leaving out all mention of Ilian's role. He said Azret wanted to transfer somewhere far away in the US to another university. The professor wanted him back at Ole Miss, but Azret was too scared. We never heard from him again.

Ilian was another story. He accelerated his program at Ole Miss, receiving not only a master's degree but a full scholarship to Syracuse University in its prestigious doctoral program in international studies and had completed all but his dissertation. He called me again later from Harvard, where he was being paid to lecture on reforms to the pension systems in former Soviet states. He had married a beautiful Moldovan woman, and while she was stationed in Berlin as a Moldovan diplomat, he was doing broadcasts in Romanian for the Voice of America. They are now back in Moldova, contrary to Susan Oliphant's fears and Eric Weiner's slanders. Ilian regularly emails me pictures of his beautiful wife and two fine children. It was a most happy ending to a most unusual story.

IN MOSCOW, IN SEARCH
OF THE NEW RUSSIA (1998)

This chapter on Moscow was supposed to be easy and fun to write. I had deliberately saved it for last, as a sort of dessert. Then I tried to write it. It was unusual for me to find it so hard to get started. I found the "new" Russia so complicated it was hard to find a place to begin or a point-of-view to write from. When I was living it, my time in Moscow was both exciting and encouraging. My love of Russian literature, which has lasted all my life, always gave it a sort of romantic glow, but as I fumbled with my pen for an opening sentence, nothing came. Finally I decided to call my old friend, former federal prosecutor Mark Bonner, now a law professor in Florida, to refresh my memories of our times together in Moscow and to add a few details. Mark and I first knew each other, as detailed in *From Midnight to Guntown*, under interesting circumstances: We investigated together and helped convict Arab terrorist Abdel Ashqar, the treasurer of Hamas, who was once a graduate student at Ole Miss, right under our noses. Ashqar later ran for president of Gaza from prison, but lost.

I called Mark and reminded him of his promise to help me one day in return for enlisting him in the Ashqar case. I told him I badly needed him to refresh my memories of our times together in Moscow in 1997. For some reason, the Moscow "mission," as I had called that naïve, youthful junket, was the only such foreign DOJ trip for which I wrote no official mission report like the ones I relied on in writing my other travel missions described here. Also, my parents having died in 1992, there were none of the long, detailed letters about events during my travels which I had always written to them and which my mother had always dutifully saved for me. Mark Bonner was, unfortunately, of the opposite school. When I asked him what reports or photos or other documents he'd saved from his three years as RLA (resident legal advisor) to our ambassador in Moscow, he said proudly, "None. When I retired, I shredded every last document from my entire career. Didn't you know you were supposed to do that?" Whether I was supposed to or not, I definitely would never consider bringing myself to do such a thing.

Happily for me, Mark does have an excellent memory for what we did in Moscow and faithfully answered the multiple pages of questions I'd written up to ask him based on my own vivid memories and especially the thick reporter-style notebooks I'd kept during the mission. Mark also had the new telephone number of his brilliant Russian assistant, Irina Dline [ee-REE-nuh duh-LEE-nay], whom he had helped come back with him to the US and gain US citizenship and a good job with the US Treasury. Mark also had the telephone numbers of the most fascinating woman I met on the trip, former Chicago federal judge Suzanne Conlon, who had earlier prosecuted with Rudy Giuliani in New York the famous "French Connection" drug case. I had also known Suzanne after the Russia trip through the large coincidence of her meeting at a judicial seminar one of my best friends, US district judge Neal Biggers of Oxford, with whom she formed a long-term relationship extending beyond her chambers in Chicago to her large ranch in Montana and on to her mother's home in beautiful LaJolla, California, and finally to our own home in Oxford. Having gathered all the facts I could from those highly reliable sources, here are my recollections of Moscow.

One reason it is hard to re-create now what Moscow was like in 1997 is the vast changes in both America and Russia in the past twenty years. In those days, America was riding high as the world's sole "superpower" after the breakup of the Soviet Union. Harebrained professors were confidently predicting the "end of history," that the whole world would soon be made up of liberal democracies, and that there would never be another war. Russia would be America's new best friend. Now, Russia is *ruled* by a lifelong KGB agent, Vladimir Putin, a brilliant, sophisticated, well-educated but ruthless lawyer-autocrat and assassin many now call the "The New Tsar." He seems to be giving Russians what they want, restoring their confidence and desire to be a great world power again. We in the United States are now a deeply divided country having, with some clandestine Russian help, foolishly chosen as president the most unprepared, emotionally unstable, all-around incompetent US "leader" in our nation's long history. As aptly stated by former New York mayor Michael Bloomberg, we now have our first "con man" president.

How times change. Russia's president now openly laughs at us and mocks us while "we" threaten to abandon NATO to the Russians, insult our neighbors and allies, and cut taxes for the rich while blithely throwing away vital, carefully negotiated trade treaties around the world. Russia has meanwhile boldly invaded, conquered, and occupied the vital Crimean peninsula on the strategic Black Sea and then occupied, almost without firing a shot, key portions of Ukraine, Georgia, and Moldova, and is now threatening the Baltic states. Mr. Putin has now built an eighteen-mile, multilane car, truck, and railroad bridge directly from Russia to Crimea. And we've not even mentioned our negligence in allowing a vital new Russian naval base on the eastern Mediterranean on the coast of Syria. Considering all of the above, it is easier and more pleasant to return to a happier past, which had such promise in 1997.

On a warm, sunny day in March 1997 my secretary Brenda Gill buzzed me and said, "Mr. Hailman, another of your foreign friends is calling you. He says he's Russian, but he sounds like an American to me. Here he is." A familiar voice boomed out, in mock Russian: "Golitsin Hailman. Golitsin Bonner here." At the time I had no idea that "golitsin" [goh-LEET-sun] meant "mister" in Russia's post-Communist vocabulary, so I answered him with "Tavarish [tah-VAH-rish] Hailman here," using the old Soviet word for "comrade." Mark couldn't resist: "Well, my old friend, I was going to invite you for an all-expense paid junket to Moscow, but if you insist on talking like a Commie, I may have to rethink it." After a little good-natured sparring, I agreed to the trip. Mark, who was then the energetic, newly appointed legal advisor to the US ambassador to Russia, had managed to wangle out of the Russians an invitation for three veteran US prosecutors to attend, for the first time ever, the annual conference of senior Russian prosecutors from all eleven oblasts, or regions, of the new Russian republic. It was exciting and quite an honor.

"There is one downside," Mark added. "In true Soviet style, the Rooskees insist that each of us present not one but two long, boring scholarly papers on some aspect of prosecuting organized crime and violence. Based on some of the war stories you've told me, I propose you do Murders for Hire and Civil Rights Murders. People in even the most remote parts of Russia have heard of Mississippi, you know." Ouch. That hurt, but it sounded easy. The papers were duly written and translated into Russian and presented to us on arrival in handsome, bound volumes. It was a promising beginning.

Mark said DOJ would pay our travel and the Russians had agreed to put us up in their finest hotels and feed us in their best restaurants. "You'll be in the newly renovated Hotel Nacional, where Lenin once lived, right across from the Kremlin. The food may be a little pricier, but if you like vodka and caviar, you should survive."

The trip sounded wonderful. The first warning sign was the airline routing, which took me through JFK in New York, which I've always avoided after I once watched a woman have a shrieking, screaming nervous breakdown there while waiting in a typical JFK mob scene for a multi-delayed flight. My worst fears were soon realized. After a pleasant, uneventful business class flight from Memphis, with first-class wines, I stood in line waiting for a connecting flight via the Russian carrier Aeroflot, which I'd heard called "still afloat" by some detractors. All was well until a cold, heavy rain started falling on New York. "It can't last," the gate agent assured us. So there I was, having left warm, sunny

Memphis with my only worry being the weather in Moscow, which Mark had already said was unusually cold for April. The flight was to leave at around 7:00 p.m. It was delayed first for an hour, then two, then three. Finally, around midnight, they announced they would be taking us by bus to a motel in "nearby" New Jersey. As I started to step up onto the bus, with icy rain soaking me under an airport-furnished umbrella, the bus suddenly jerked forward, causing me to slip and stick both feet into a concrete ditch of knee-deep, ice-cold water. We got to the motel around 2:00 a.m. I tried to dry my socks and pants on the heater in my room and fell asleep pretty quickly. At 3:00 a.m. the phone rang with orders to come to the lobby immediately, our bus was leaving. I got my slightly less wet socks on under my soaked shoes, donned my soaked pants, and headed out. All our dry clothes were of course already locked up with checked baggage in the hold on board the plane.

The passengers were a surprising group. About half were Americans traveling to Russia to adopt children from orphanages, which was all the rage back then but is now banned by Mr. Putin. Once on board, the good-looking Russian stewardesses plied us with large amounts of every kind of adult beverage. Before leaving, being strictly a wine drinker, I'd promised myself not to touch any vodka, no matter how tempting, based on a bad experience in Moldova on an earlier trip. I kept my vow all the way to the new Sheremetyevo Airport in Moscow, named for the tsarist-era estate the Soviets seized to use in building the airport, which turned out to be clean, modern, cheerful, and efficient. I thought I'd be tired after the fourteen-hour flight, but the idea of being in Russia shocked me into a wide-awake state.

The countryside from the airport to the city fulfilled all my most positive stereotypes of Mother Russia from Tolstoy. Beautiful birch trees with white bark stood out under green canopies of freshly sprouted leaves. In the background was pure-white snow with huge snowflakes like white cotton candy. Maybe those stories about Russians always creating Hollywood-like *Potemkin* scenes for tourist eyes were true. We passed only a few exceptions, but they were memorable: dirty little hovels made of packing crates and tree branches with smoke coming from inside indicating someone, certainly someone very poor, was actually living inside. Except for that one sad note, everything looked beautiful along the road.

I have no recollection of who from the embassy met me at the airport, but I was whisked through the diplomatic line, avoiding customs entirely, and into a big, black ZiL limo, all by myself. Mark was obviously looking out for me. Before the trip I had tried to re-immerse myself in Russian history, ancient and modern. I had learned that 1997 was the 850th anniversary of the official founding of Moscow. I reread a little Tolstoy, not only from his weighty masterpieces *War and Peace* and *Anna Karenina*, but also from my own personal, much shorter favorite, his first novel, *The Cossacks*. I also reread some of the difficult, pessimistic, apocalyptic writings of Solzhenitsyn, who knew both Russia's frozen gulag prison camps and the pampered life of a famous writer in the US.

I always especially liked the travel account of Mother Russia by the nineteenth-century Frenchman, the Marquis de Custine, who is still to Russia what his countryman Alexis de Tocqueville is for America through his perceptive work *Democracy in America*. Finally, overwhelmed by too much complex and conflicting history, I turned for some clarity to a brand-new American book on Russia, *Resurrection*, by a *New Yorker* staff writer I'd always enjoyed and admired, David Remnick, who is now the editor of the *New Yorker*. *Resurrection*, which was named as a reference to Tolstoy's novel of the same name, finally gave me the orientation I felt I needed. Remnick had just returned from several years as foreign correspondent in Moscow for my old paper, the *Washington Post*, while his wife held the same post for the *New York Times*. His four hundred insightful pages resulted in my own making of over fifty pages of notes and highlighted quotes. With Remnick in my head, I felt ready for Moscow and the "New Russia," which quickly exceeded my expectations.

The timing was good. Much of historic Moscow had just been restored to its former bright-colored glory: The Bolshoi Theatre was magnificent; classical, old, Italian-style yellow buildings with white trim and bright-orange buildings with green roofs stood out all over the city, including the Tchaikovsky Concert Hall, which I could see from the window of my glorious hotel, the Nacional. The red-brick Kremlin, which I knew from my readings was a huge fortress (all Russian cities have kremlins), was filled with tall, wildly decorated cathedral roofs but was not as beautiful as it had been in the eighteenth century, which I knew from old paintings, when its walls were cream-colored limestone. The Kremlin museums turned out to be the biggest revelations. Moscow, under the yoke of the authoritarian tsars, had missed both Europe's sixteenth-century Renaissance and eighteen-century Enlightenment. The city was burned in the nineteenth century by Napoleon, then had survived in the twentieth both the spectacular financial mismanagement of the Communists and the massive Nazi invasion and massacres of World War II. Despite all its suffering, Moscow had somehow been resurrected. It looked clean, bright, even fresh.

Mark Bonner had warned me that the weather was very cold for April and I was partly glad: a warm Russia didn't sound right. My first surprise about the weather came from the roofs of Moscow, which were covered with inches of fast-melting ice. City workmen with long poles were punching on the bottom edges of the roofs, causing huge sheets of ice to fall onto the sidewalks with loud crashes. Because of the thick, every-year ice, Moscow roofs have no gutters, only thin, flat, downward-facing sheets of metal from which the big thawing sheets of ice can slide off without tearing down the gutters or the roofs. It was a dramatic introduction to Russian weather. One familiar sight was the broad streets, the surfaces of which had been plowed up and placed in the median to be reworked and covered with new hot tar, exactly as we sometimes do to our roads in Mississippi after really bad winters.

The Nacional was beautifully restored to a state resembling something under the tsars. My high-ceilinged room had deep-red velvet curtains. Out the window I could see the Kremlin and several other beautifully restored buildings. At a little shop nearby I found several bottles of exotic dessert wines from the Crimea, which I never dreamed made wine. They resembled Spanish Pedro Jimenez or a sweet old red port gone brown, and were a welcome substitute to replace the vodka I'd sworn to myself not to drink.

On the ground floor of the Nacional was a ridiculously overpriced outpost of Paris's famed Maxim's restaurant where it was obvious the nouveaux rich "New Russians" were showing off their wealth. Mark called it "a tacky, little island of western luxury." It reminded me of a joke from Remnick about two new Russians who were trying to outdo each other: "I bought this tie for $300 during my trip to Paris," said one, to which his proud friend boasted "I paid $400 in Paris for the very same one."

But cost was not all pretension. The Nacional breakfast, which cost at least five times what it would have in New York, featured an "all you can eat" buffet of excellent smoked salmon, by wading through which I proved on the first morning that it is impossible to make yourself sick from eating too much smoked salmon. The helpings of all three types of caviar were ladled out carefully by the servers but were still wonderful. The beverage of choice, which I declined, was a big glass of ruby port from Portugal, a breakfast drink I'd never seen before. Until then my biggest breakfast walk on the wild side had been my mornings at the old Santa Maria Inn in California where in 1967 I somehow formed the happy if unhealthy habit of drinking an ice-cold bottle of Budweiser with a big bowl of hot, deep-dish cherry cobbler, something I'd nearly forgotten till I saw the Nacional breakfast menu. Instead of ruby red port for breakfast, I opted to try Kvas [kuh-VAHS] in special blue and white porcelain cups. It was surprisingly delicious. I wish we had it in America. Kvas, they told me, is made from leftover brown bread marinated in lemonade with raisins. It tastes much better than it sounds and is also low in alcohol.

My first morning around 10:00 a.m., after an ample breakfast, Mark Bonner sent a driver to take me to the embassy, which was another revelation. "Of course they say the Cold War is over," Mark noted as we walked across a broad, grassy "soccer field" in the middle of the embassy compound. "Some of the younger guys actually *play* a little soccer here sometimes, but in reality they keep this space open to land helicopters to evacuate us just in case the current tensions get worse." Of course that would have only saved a select few, since the embassy had over two thousand employees at the time. Apparently the rosy news stories about our new Russian "friendship" were a tad overly optimistic.

Inside the embassy I saw an even more ominous warning. "Why is that big swimming pool so green? Don't they have enough chlorine?" I asked. Mark's response was blunt. "I would never swim in that thing, but it's not here totally for swimming. Just in case they decide to lock us in here without food or water, just to get our attention, that pool is our reserve drinking water." For emphasis, as if it were needed, Mark added that the embassy, not trusting the Russians to give it clean gas for the large fleet of embassy vehicles, had decided to truck in its entire supply all the way from Finland. He hardly needed to add that no Russian workmen were allowed to do any repairs or other upkeep in the embassy. "The trust factor right now is rather low," he said in an understatement, reminding me of another time, when Russians planted listening devices throughout an entire American embassy building, causing a massively expensive rebuild.

Despite these dark early warnings, the entire visit went well. The Russians, ignoring their economic problems caused by the painful transition from a Communist to a capitalist economy, treated us royally, and with obvious good will. On the person-to-person and prosecutor-to-prosecutor level the whole visit was friendly and open. As a veteran of many foreign missions, Mark knew the importance of a rested and well-briefed team, so he had set aside four whole days for us to recover from jet lag and to meet our Russian counterparts socially, in relaxed settings, before we started serious seminaring.

The first night Mark and Irina took us to a Georgian restaurant named *Pirosmani* after their beloved primitive artist. His picture was on the cover of all the menus, one of which I brought home with me and still have framed on the wall of my study. Just before leaving home I'd read a fascinating, in-depth nine-page article in *Esquire* magazine by a veteran American chef. It had aptly predicted precisely the dining experience we had. Irina explained the dishes as they arrived. First we were served delicious *pelmeni*, which someone called Siberian ravioli. Others dissented, saying they were cheese turnovers, more like dim sum from China. Dolmas, which I called *Greek* stuffed grape leaves, were actually from Soviet Armenia. Especially delicious were the *blini*, or buckwheat pancakes; *borscht*, a soup made from beets and red cabbage with sour cream and served just warm with a cup of Kvas; a cold sturgeon and cucumber salad; and several slices of various jellied meats. I could not keep up with the order of delicious, fast-arriving Russian and Georgian dishes, which culminated with a platter of *shashlik*, delicious skewered pork shoulder from Georgia, accompanied by an array of Georgian wines. It was quite a feast.

During the dinner other Russian hosts, whose names I failed to note, recommended their favorite "New Russian" restaurants in the capitol, which they said were recently privatized and excellent, replacing the horrific, evil-smelling handful of former Soviet establishments. I managed to visit, but could not afford to eat in, the lavish Boyarsky restaurant in the newly restored Metropol Hotel, which also had a great bookstore and was modeled on an aristocratic boyar mansion, and the Tsar's Hunt, which had real wolf skins on all the chairs. The waiters wore traditional belted tunics with rows of shirt pockets to hold rifle shells, just as I saw later in Georgia. Most expensive of all was the Up & Down Club, which was guarded by thugs with Kalashnikovs and featured topless waitresses and several tables of beautiful blond Slavic prostitutes. For better or worse, Moscow was living up to all of its reputations.

During our own much more decorous and peaceful dinners, we were still pretty excited. As always when in a new country, I tried to acquire some useful new vocabulary, featuring first the essentials like "Thank you" (*spasiba* [spah-SEE-bah]); "please" (*pashalsta* [pah-ZHAHL-stah]; "how much" (*skolka* [SKOHL-kah]); and, to my surprise, the odd-sounding word for "happy to meet you" (*rat* [raht]). Of course I already knew the famed Russian *nyet* [nee-YET], the strongest word for "no" on earth. Several volunteered the real Russian meanings of words we were familiar with from the space race missile and rocket competitions, including *mir* (peace), *soyuz* (union), and the supremely ironic name of the main Soviet propaganda newspaper *Pravda* ("truth").

Someone handed me a sheet of translated words Americans usually found amusing: *zup* [zoop] for teeth; *dzhinzi* for jeans; *tufli* for shoes from the French *pantoufles*, or house slippers; *pilyuli* for pills; and *petroushka*, which I associated mainly with the classic Greta Garbo movie, though it means nothing more exotic than "parsley." *Limichiks* referred to country people in Moscow who were "limited," i.e., had no papers. The best word, we were told, was *krasnoya* (red), which was always popular, indicating "good luck" long before the Communists co-opted "red" as their flag and symbol.

Other important words were *medved* or *piva* for beer and others which I already knew: *ikra* [ee-KRAH] for caviar; *isba* [EEZ-bah] for old, traditional, cozy log houses, several of which I later visited and enjoyed; and *kashmer* (not cashmere like a sweater, but "awful") from the French word *cauchemar*, or "nightmare," a word I didn't need nearly as much as I'd feared. The Russian use of so many French-derived words is not surprising when you consider that under the tsars the people at court always spoke French when in company, using Russian, which they considered primitive until it was popularized by great writers like Tolstoy, only at home.

The Russians asked if there were any unique American words I'd like translated. I explained, somewhat boastfully, that in the US I was reputed to be good at getting freebies, whether wines or dinners, by writing newspaper columns on them, as well as free foreign trips from DOJ for teaching the US legal system abroad. The Russians fell out laughing. "You must have Russian blood somewhere. Such people are well known here as *khalyavchiks* [kahl-YAHV-chiks], sometimes admiringly, as 'clever ones' who outwit tyrannical Soviet restrictions on freedoms, at other times disdainfully, especially among official bureaucrats, as 'freeloaders.'" The Russians said they had especially admired *khalyavchiks* under the old system because, as the popular saying goes, "Whatever is not forbidden is required." There was no space for personal freedom of movement or even thoughts under those rules, which led either to illegal acts or extreme frustration.

The next morning, after another ample and expensive breakfast far exceeding my government per diem, but worth it one more time, I met again with the energetic federal judge Suzanne Conlon and famed Notre Dame law professor Jimmy Gurule. We were shown around the city, including Pushkin Square, which had Moscow's first McDonald's, there called "MacDo." The old Moscow University, in yellow trimmed in white, looked surprisingly like the 1830s University of South Carolina Law School where I taught for years when DOJ had its courses for new federal prosecutors there. Ugliest of all buildings in Moscow were the towering gray Soviet skyscrapers known as the Seven Sisters, constructed mainly by German prisoners of war under Stalin after World War II. One held the Foreign Ministry, another the Hotel Ukraine, another the hideous "new" Moscow State University, which was as ugly as the three-million-book Lenin Library, which is utterly uninviting to readers.

Surprisingly to me, the old KGB headquarters on Dzerzhinsky Square were much more attractive—until you thought about what had gone on in the torture chambers of its Lubianka prison, right in the middle of the city. The statue of Dzerzhinsky, founder of the secret police, had been discreetly removed to a museum in the Kremlin, like most Soviet statues, but the big one of Yuri, supposed founder of Moscow, still stands, its rider on horseback holding out his right hand at shoulder level, palm down. Our guide said Muscovites now mock it because of the corruption, quoting Yuri as saying, "The shit is piled up to here."

Mark Bonner gave us the option of a night-train trip to St. Petersburg. Most took him up on it, but it would have taken at least three days away from the capitol, so I stayed in Moscow. Our Russian guides, some of whom were *from* St. Petersburg, said so much of Moscow had been refurbished that it looked like St. Petersburg anyway. One guide said 80 percent of Russian money and culture was now in Moscow, which was the "Number One" city of Russia, so far ahead that "There is no Number Two." I later "got some back" from my intrepid traveler daughter Allison, who spent ten days in St. Petersburg but missed Moscow altogether. We now share memories and dispute who made the better choice.

Suzanne Conlon persuaded me that we should see Tolstoy's winter home near Moscow, which we visited by private bus. It really struck me for the first time just how rich and powerful Count Tolstoy had been and that he was not only a world-class novelist but an immensely rich humanitarian, who in his old age freed his serfs and became religious to the point of zealotry. But considering his long life, eleven children, blissful marriage, and those freezing winters, he no doubt needed some solace in his old age. The estate, which is now a museum, made us wear strange little rattan booties upon entering, which I thought scratched the ancient wooden floors worse than our socks would have done, but the guides said the floors were way too wet and cold to enjoy sock-footed.

Suzanne had also convinced me we could not afford to miss the great *tolchuk*, or open-air market, at beautiful Ismailovsky Park in the outskirts of Moscow near the old city wall and the modern Ring Road. It was fantastic. At the entrance, ageing babushkas sang old Russian songs while central Asian dancers did those leaping, squatting, athletic dances I'd seen earlier in the US during a Moiseyev Ballet visit. The market had *everything* for sale from sad little black bears to harried chimpanzees dancing by hurly-gurly accordions. That part, but only that part, was the cruel side of Russia. My big regret was that I was unable to buy a beautiful brass samovar which was fitted out to make Russian tsai tea from an electric burner rather than using the usual inner cylinder of burning charcoal. Just as I asked the price, an American woman elbowed past me and, speaking fluent Russian, stole it for a song. All my life I had admired the beautiful samovar in the old Peabody Hotel lobby in Memphis but could never find one for less than a thousand dollars. The pushy lady got it for a hundred. Unlike the Peabody samovar, which has its brass namesake duck on top, this one had a beautiful Russian eagle, not a bear, on top. I still regret losing out on it.

I was really lucky, however to let a Russian lady persuade me to buy, for just seven dollars, a light gray *shapska*, a fur cap with those big ear flaps tied up on top. It was hard to the touch and still damp, but made of beautiful Siberian hare with a sheen like mink. "Keep it out in the open, never close it up or it will rot and spoil and stink. Let it dry, and in two or three months it will be soft and comfortable and, believe me, waterproof." I followed her advice and she was right to the letter. I still wear it every winter in Mississippi, but when I tell people how I got it, they tend not to believe me. But the hat's softness and ability to shed cold rain without the inside getting wet, now convinces even the worst unbelievers.

Several years later, my good friend retired US customs agent Doug Evans, one of the Hailman Hall of Fame great investigators and a fearless international undercover agent, brought me a beautiful, genuine, deep-brown mink cap; it glistens with or without snow on it, and I now wear it on more formal winter occasions, when I want to look presentable. Doug's mink cap is a traditional Russian military one, soft inside but so tough on the outside I suspect it has a bulletproof Kevlar lining. It's another precious possession.

Looking for presents for Regan and my daughters, I loaded up on little carved wooden boxes, intricately hand-painted and signed by the women who made them during the long, dark Russian winters. Beside me as I write is a red one with black and gold designs which holds my paper clips and a black one with a lovely blue and white painting of an onion domed church from the "Golden Ring" of monasteries at Vladimir north of Moscow. The array of items available was astonishing, no doubt brought in by the long row of eighteen-wheelers that bordered the park, several bearing plates from Kazakhstan and Tajikistan. I bought several of those lovely, colorful central-Asian round caps which Russians like to wear to parties. The ones my daughters didn't get now hang on hooks in my library. I haven't had the nerve to wear one to a US party yet.

With the expensive array of goods on display, I was surprised there were no police. Women even had big display cases of cut but unmounted semiprecious jewels. As I was examining one, I learned why they needed no police. A pair of cracks, like rifle shots, suddenly rang out from near the entrance. A slim man with a very white face and coal-black hair, dressed all in black with red piping and tall felt boots was walking my way. Fortunately he walked on, coiling back up as he passed me the long, woven, light-brown rawhide whip that he'd used to make the menacing sounds. He had no gun or other weapon. I whispered to the saleslady, "Who is that?" She replied with respect, "One of our Cossack guards. We only need two for this whole place. They are ferocious. If someone was stealing something, his family will probably never see him again."

I was disappointed by my ignorance. I not only had read Tolstoy's great book about his five years in the tsar's army living with the Terek band of Cossacks on Russia's southern border along the Caucasus, but had even read a whole separate history of the Cossacks, which pictured them as big, beefy soldiers, rough with heavy beards and colorful if dirty clothes. The lady told me, "Some old Cossacks are like that, but ours are special. They have to be slim to ride horses the way they do."

Claiming my bad back, I begged off from riding with them, but Suzanne Conlon, who had and still has a big horse ranch in Montana, went riding with them and held her own quite well. She even rode bareback, but wisely declined to ride standing up on the back of a galloping Cossack pony. I hoped to buy a pair of the thin, light, waterproof, knee-high felt Cossack boots, but could not find any my size. As a really poor consolation prize I have a small black-leather Cossack boot which I use as a pencil holder.

The dramatic history of the Cossacks, whose name is said to derive from the Turkish word "Kazakh" (as in Kazakhstan), meaning "freeman," is too long to recount here, but I've listed books about them in the Further Readings section at the end of the book. The short version is that the Cossacks are a mix of escaped serfs and/or convicts from the gulags who live as peasant farmer/warriors along the Russian frontiers and protect citizens from marauding Mongols and Islamic fighters, who for centuries have raided Mother Russia. At times Russian governments have tried to tame them by offering them commissions in the regular army, but the Cossacks have generally refused, preferring their traditional life of freedom. Attempts to compare them to anyone in America, like the earliest Texas Rangers, totally fail to capture their unique character, including their strong religious preference for what they call the "Old Religion" and their surprisingly puritanical family lives. They have always been to me my favorite part of the rich culture and history of Russia and are a good lesson in not trying to oversimplify Russia and its people.

The next morning after the open-air *tolchuk* at the park, Mark sent us with guides to the Kremlin, which was across the street from my room at the Hotel Nacional. I had intended to walk around the whole triangular complex, said to be nearly two miles, but never had the time. One of our guides apologized for there not being even more of the massive Orthodox cathedrals, many of which were torn down during and after the 1917 revolution, but said at least most of the best stones from there were used to build the interior pillars, walls, and benches of the magnificent Moscow subway, to me perhaps the single most unusual place in Moscow. It is an artistic gem and calling it a mere "subway," as if comparing it to the efficient but smelly metro of Paris, the plain vanilla but nice metro of Washington, or the filthy crime-ridden real *sub*way of New York, or even to the better versions I'd enjoyed in London and Montreal, is totally misleading.

The most surprising thing about the Moscow Kremlin, in fact much more surprising than its great size, was the number and impressive quality of its museums, the best known being the Tretyakov, which features paintings, sculpture, and wonderful rooms full of costumes from tsarist times. Russian paintings are rarely seen outside Russia. Having myself studied for a year at the Louvre in Paris during my junior year, I understood the critical attitude of some of my companions, who said the nineteenth-century paintings were "too derivative" of the French artists of the same periods. I totally disagree with them. Although clearly following the trends of those periods, the paintings did remind me of Manet, Cezanne, Degas, and others; however, they were not mere stylistic copies but individual works of high art all to themselves. I respectfully didn't mention that to my companions. Since I can't paint a lick or even draw a straight line or a round circle myself, I kept my mouth shut rather than be a phony. My personal favorites of the Tretyakov, which is named for the family of a great collector, were the paintings on purely classical Russian themes such as arctic wolves, birch forests, and cozy log houses with fireplaces deep in the Urals, or of Cossack villages along valleys of the Don and the Volga. Mark promised me a return trip one day for a boat trip down the Volga to visit the court systems of "deep Russia" cities like Samara and Saratov, but after relations with Russia cooled, and Mark came back to the US, we could never pull it off.

My personal and surprising favorite of the Kremlin museums was the Museum of Military History, which was rich in weapons, uniforms, and battle-plan maps. Elaborate panels visualizing campaigns against the Mongols, the Tatars, Napoleon, and Hitler were illustrated with vivid mementos and letters about the sieges of Leningrad and Moscow and the incredible courage and suffering of the Russian people and their soldiers through the ages ever since Moscow was officially founded 850 years earlier.

After the Kremlin we went for an early dinner at a most unusual, informal restaurant, the Patio Pizza, part of a recently established joint venture between Russian and Italian "beez-nessmeni," as they were called. The restaurant was located on an enclosed terrace in front of a handsome building, which was formerly, with supreme irony, Communist Party headquarters. My companions at table, also a surprise, were an Italian anti-mafia investigating magistrate from Milan named Dottore Vigna and his bodyguard, who looked nothing like one our Secret Service agents: Armani suit over his .38 Beretta, slim, big smile, relaxed manner. The judge noticed how I was looking at his bodyguard and remarked, "Don't be fooled by his cool demeanor. He knows that when several of my fellow judges were assassinated in the past few years, their bodyguards died with them." The judge, called "Doctor" for his Italian PhD, said, "Milan is a city of bribes," so pervasive, especially in the construction industry, it has led to massive inflation from the flow of money for bribes. He said the mafia always tries bribery first but turns to murder when necessary, which is often. I kept a copy of the Patio Pizza bill, which was in Russian and shows I paid 15.00 in some currency, perhaps dollars, noting at the bottom 87,000 in another currency, perhaps rubles, but at that time *USA Today* listed a dollar as worth 5,000 rubles, so it didn't compute. The date was April 26, 1997, and the time was 10:26 p.m. The food was excellent, especially the imported green olives from Italy, some of the best I ever ate.

My judge and I had spoken entirely in French, since I knew no Italian and he knew no English and neither of us knew any Russian to speak of. But we had a great discussion of our trial experiences. Mine fascinated him because the US system seemed to him so "remarkably complicated" to be so clean. Our talks led to a lucky break for me: later that week the Italian ambassador to Russia was hosting a big dinner for law enforcement leaders from Russia and Italy. The judge was to be a guest of honor, and he asked if I would be "willing" to attend and act, if needed, as an interpreter. I agreed almost before he completed stating the invitation. I enjoyed the dinner company in the beautiful old mansion, but like all interpreters I had no time to eat. I sat between and interpreted for the head of the Russian "tax police," or IRS, and an Italian prosecutor. I had a late dinner at the hotel by room service, which was excellent, maybe better.

Returning to the hotel full of enthusiasm, I began mounting the four or five steps to the handsome entrance when the doorman opened it and two tall, uniformed Russian officers stepped out, followed by a burly general. I immediately recognized him as the famed General Aleksandr Lebed [LEH-bud], who had commanded the Russian paratroopers who captured and occupied Transnistria when I was in Moldova. Forgetting for a moment how insignificant I was, I stepped up and offered to shake hands with the general, who was famous as a heroic "fighting" general who always parachuted in with his troops, especially during their unfortunate adventures in Afghanistan. Fortunately for me, rather than busting my head, his officers let me pass, and we shook hands warmly. He spoke a little English and was very gracious, saying he was pleased to see such "kindness" from one of our "friends," the Americans. I wasn't too sure exactly what his position was at that time in the military but thought he was somehow involved high up in Russian politics. He politely moved on, and I went and sat in the lobby.

In a major coincidence, there was a front-page story in the hotel's copy of the *Moscow Times*, a surprisingly free and open, German-owned newspaper which people at the embassy had told me was fairly truthful, surmising the Russians wanted to appear that way to Americans and other English-speaking foreigners, and surmising further that few if any ordinary Russians would ever read it anyway. The story said that General Lebed, who had just been named head of the State Security Council the previous year, was under consideration to run as Boris Yeltsin's vice president, possibly even to become his successor. The article told a number of things for which General Lebed was then being criticized: that he'd taken to using a silver cigarette holder when speaking "like an English Lord"; that he had disobeyed orders in Afghanistan by flamboyantly parachuting into the middle of a firefight, receiving serious wounds for which later he received several medals; that he had made anti-Semitic remarks; and that he had recently indiscreetly opined that US Secretary of State Madeleine Albright "needed a big kick in the ass" for her negative remarks about the "new Russia."

The article concluded by saying that due to his recent indiscretions, President Yeltsin was rethinking his idea of Lebed as vice president and would probably drop him from the ticket shortly and cool their relations. Although he had officially retired from the army in 1995 and run for and won a seat in the duma, or legislature, he continued to wear on occasions, like that evening, his general's uniform, claiming it was proper in keeping with his role as head of Yeltsin's Security Council. The article ended with quotes from Lebed's autobiography *I Pity Our Great Power*, where he said that despite his love for democracy, his hero and role model was Charles De Gaulle, a broad hint that a fighting general might one day *rule* Russia just as De Gaulle as "president" had ruled France.

After the article on Lebed, I glanced through the rest of the paper. On a back page was a small, unusual announcement about an event that very night: "Planet Hollywood/Kodak Cinema will present a one-time-only screening in English, with Russian subtitles, of the Academy Award–winning movie *The English Patient*, best film of 1997." The showing was to begin at 1:00 a.m. Blown away to think I could see, in English, in Moscow surrounded by Russians, the famous movie I'd never yet seen of one of my favorite books, turned my head totally away from common sense. The ad gave the nearest subway stations to the theater. Although I'd visited several of them including Tverskaya and Pushkinskaya, the ones nearest the cinema, I knew I could never navigate them knowing no Russian.

So I foolishly stuffed most of my cash into a thin pocket I'd had sewn inside my shoe sole and asked the concierge to call me a taxi. I also asked her how to pronounce the name of the cinema and the address and how much the fare and tip should be. Five minutes later I was in a Russian cab headed for the theater. The driver let me out, smiled, and seemed pleased with his tip. Alone on the well-lit street, I noticed that although there were business-looking buildings there, I saw no sign of a theater or anything else still open. I walked down the street, unable to read the Cyrillic characters on the street signs, but I could tell they were not the same ones listed in the ad. After two or three tries at different corners, I was about to panic. It had turned much colder and windier and felt like rain. How stupid I had been to do this. Excited by meeting General Lebed and the mafia judge and my other noteworthy adventures that day, I'd totally lost what I thought was my common sense.

Just then a tall, lovely Russian woman turned the corner facing me. She must have seen the fear on my face, for she walked up and said something in Russian that sounded friendly. I blurted out stupidly, "Do you speak English?" She smiled and shook her head, then said, "Mais peut-être vous parlez français?" Sweetest words I ever heard. Recovering my confidence, I noticed her floor-length black wool coat and stunning dark mink hat against her shining blond hair. She had that blond Viking look I'd begun to notice on several Russian women, and then there was her height: at least six feet two in her high heels. The woman walked me about three blocks and around a couple of corners when suddenly there was Planet Hollywood. She apologized for rushing off but said she was late getting home to relieve her babysitter. In my haste—and hers—I failed to get her name or address to send her a thank-you present from the US. She seemed pleased to have met an American.

When I approached the cinema, it was a startling contrast with the lovely blond. The men nearly all were carrying short-barreled automatic rifles, probably some version of AK-47s, easier to carry in a crowd. Their women—they all had one—wore a variety of shining expensive mink coats of various colors, some shaved, most not, all stunning, all floor length. I nervously approached a sort of cashier to ask about the movie, being almost late and fearing I might not get in. He pointed upstairs and said something I didn't understand in Russian. The downstairs had dining and dancing on one side. The other side appeared to be some sort of casino with slot machines and roulette, card, and dice tables. It looked and felt like a good place to get killed; not robbed, killed. One Russian prosecutor who owned a health and exercise club on the side had told me earlier he had been making lots of money from the new rich but had problems keeping clients. They kept getting rubbed out in "business disputes." This place looked like their home base.

I quickly climbed the richly carpeted stairs. There being no one either selling or taking tickets, I quietly slipped in an open side door. On stage, in front of a blank white movie screen, two tough-looking guys were having a violent argument with the audience cheering and jeering them. I tried English on a guy next to me. He replied, in good English, "Just a little political discussion. Quite amusing really. You American?" When I said, "Yes," he shook my hand vigorously and smiled broadly. There was too much yelling for us to have a conversation and the movie soon started. I enjoyed it a lot, but toward the end, around 4:00 a.m., I got really sleepy. My neighbor helped me get a cab and even paid the driver in advance for my trip. Later I somehow lost his number and regret that I could not thank him properly.

Back in my room, after a couple of glasses of sweet, brown Crimean wine and many long looks out my window at Moscow by night, I fell happily asleep. In my dreams, scenes from the movies of Pasternak's *Doctor Zhivago* and John Le Carré's *Russia House* with Sean Connery and Michelle Pfeiffer competed with my own incredibly vivid memories of that extraordinary day as I slept well past noon.

On our last night before beginning our lectures and meetings, the embassy took us to the Bolshoi Ballet, which had just been magnificently restored, its twenty columns glistening in the Moscow night. Although I've long been an opera and classical theater buff, I'd never really been to a serious ballet performance. The women always looked beautiful to me on their toes, but the guys flitting around always gave me negative vibes. Frankly, the Bolshoi was no different in that respect. They still pranced around in tight jock straps, but the sets and music were transformative for me. Sitting by Irina Dline was a big help. She explained background points I'd never considered, since the ballet we saw, *Swan Lake* of all things, was well known even to me—but I left the theater all aglow with at least some of the emotions ballet is supposed to evoke. The Russians had once again altered my preconceptions.

The next morning they roused us before dawn, which in the far north was *really* early, since it stayed light nearly all night. We got in a ragged, muddy little bus and headed for the Procuracy School, which was about forty minutes away outside the Ring Road. I'd planned to sleep during the ride, but seeing new parts of Moscow was impossible to resist. At first we drove past beautiful yellow, white, and burnt orange Italianate tsarist buildings. Then, as the road got bumpier, a darker, grayer, lower set of buildings began to appear. The vestiges of Communist realism and decadence surrounded us. Our Russian comrades apparently were willing for us to see some of Moscow's warts, not just its glories. We saw poorly dressed people shuffling along the grim streets between dismal Soviet-style apartment complexes.

The Procuracy School was quite a contrast. A converted old-style movie house, like some of those in America that have survived from the 1930s, it looked welcoming. Even more welcoming was its director, General *Smirnov*. We had a hard time keeping a straight face when we heard his name. Somehow, I can't recall if he was wearing a military uniform with medals, at least for the first day; perhaps that is just a fixed image in my mind, but I think he did. I have no mental ambiguities about our reception, however. After shaking our hands vigorously, he stepped through a hidden little door I didn't notice at first, leaving us standing there. His office was handsomely appointed with fine leather chairs and leather on the tables and even on the main door, like in Persia. A row of finely bound books covered the wall behind his desk.

Just as I was telling the others how impressive his office was, General Smirnov reappeared on the opposite side of the room through another well-hidden door, enjoying having deceived us with his hidden doors. "How Russian was that?" I wondered. He immediately reached into a tall cabinet and pulled out a handful of fairly tall, expensive silver cups, which he placed on a highly polished table. Including Mark, Suzanne, Jimmy Gurule and me, there were six of us, including DOJ Violent Crime Chief Dana Biehl, who had just arrived.

Smirnov reached into another hidden cabinet, which hid a refrigerator, and pulled out a large, heavy bottle, probably a gallon, not of his namesake Smirnov, but of finest Stolichnaya, and began filling our silver cups. I estimated mine held well over two large shots. The general then showed us the proper procedure for drinking it: Elbow out, head up, then head back, swallowing it all in a single long gulp. It occurred to me that it was probably not yet 8:00 a.m., but I did my duty. We could handle it, although I remembered our numerous Washington briefings about never getting into drinking matches with Russians. To my surprise, unaccustomed as I was to ever drinking any alcohol before lunch, even wine, I did not seem to feel the vodka. If anything, it cleared my head from the early awakening and long, bumpy ride.

Then, as we looked on in shock, the general began *refilling* our big silver cups with a second round of double shots of vodka, giving some sort of welcoming toast. To our relief, he quickly led us straight into a sort of amphitheater much like the Sorbonne. He had told us that the amphitheater held about five hundred prosecutors. Present were the top one hundred prosecutors from all eleven Russian provinces, or oblasts as they called them, plus all their principal assistants.

In my notebook are summaries of the long, rambling lectures given by the panel of experts (Russian lawyers are really big on the use of experts), but the notes are as tedious as the lectures were. I barely recall giving my own talk, which was about murders-for-hire in Mississippi, which are much more common than most honest, trusting citizens realize. I do recall one question I was asked about jurisdictional problems. Our long panel, consisting of three or four Americans and three or four Russians, looked formidably boring and intimidating, and probably was as we tried to explain our "federal" system of dual, overlapping federal and state systems.

A Russian prosecutor, a rough-looking guy from deepest Siberia with a mighty beard of Biblical proportions, directed a question to me: "Under Soviet Union we had unitary system. Now, eleven independent oblasts. We have problem, happens often. If gangster from mafiya kills a guy, he just cuts off his head and carries it to the next oblast where crooked prosecutor says he won't give it to us. Under new Russian law, we cannot prosecute murder because new law says we must have *whole body*. What would you, as American federal prosecutor, do?"

Repressing my initial instinct to tell him to revert to Soviet methods and steal the head or hire a hit on the hitman, I flailed around looking for an answer, finally settling on inviting the prosecutor from the neighboring oblast to a fine dinner and bribing him with plenty of vodka and caviar. I foolishly promised to talk with him further at dinner that evening—my biggest mistake of the conference. After that otherwise fine dinner, a sort of drinking party, the guy came quickly over to see me. Until then, one of the most pleasant parts of our stay had been socializing with our interpreters, who were mainly beautiful women in their twenties and thirties, most of whom told us they had been with the KGB before 1991. Most openly told us they were married to Russian military officers with military intelligence. That particular evening, my assigned interpreter was a particularly gorgeous woman with a powerful resemblance to Julia Roberts, right down to a mole on her cheek. She spoke perfect English. The only problem was that all the grosser Russian prosecutors, especially those from the Far East, were constantly hitting on her, to the point of repeatedly patting her bottom.

I am no hero, but her beauty and seeming fragility (even though she probably had a pistol hidden somewhere) led me to try to become her protector. It was not easy. She was a heavy smoker, so I agreed several times to go outside with her in the cold while she smoked. Using my presence as an excuse, my drunken questioner tried repeatedly to join us so he could "share prosecutor ideas with me." I asked the woman, who was really deft and obviously experienced, to tell him something, anything, in Russian. Whatever she told him sent him quickly scurrying back inside.

Before he went, however, he gave me a back-breaking bear hug around a ruptured disk I had back then, and with his nauseating breath and scratchy beard, he tried to give me a hearty Russian kiss directly on the mouth. After that day, I participated in the lectures but always ducked out immediately after the dinner before the drinking began.

By far the best part of the legal mission was meeting alone with individual judges and attending real Russian jury trials, the first ever in Russian history. Under both the tsars and the Soviets, attempts were made to involve the "people" in the justice system by having two lay assessors, ordinary citizens, flank the judge on the bench and participate in the verdicts and sentences. All our Russian counterparts agreed the assessors were a miserable failure. The Russian people despised them. For the most part, uneducated and scared to death, the assessors just did what the judges told them, to the extent that their nickname all over Russia was "the nodders." Some called them, even in the classless Soviet years, "Tommy Tractordriver and Martha Milkmaid."

Then came the new American-inspired system of twelve fairly selected jurors, chosen from among educated, registered voters from the region of the trial. For the Russians this system was truly revolutionary, and the prosecutors seemed to be heavily in favor of trying it. Before I watched my new first Russian trial, however, I recalled the words of David Remnick, whose every prediction had proven true: "By far the weakest institution in the new Russia is the new legal system." One of the Russian prosecutors had also told me, along the same line, "In the new Russia anything is possible—except reform."

From interacting with Americans eager to understand Russia, our guides, Tatiana and Anatoly, loved making instant proverbs in English. On the new status of Ukraine, Tatiana said one day, "It is so odd under the new system.

When I go to Kiev, the original *Rus*, I must now go as a foreigner." Anatoly said to me, somewhat strangely I thought then, "We Russians badly want to be Europeans, but our fate is to be Americans." Tatiana had similar feelings but was glad to the point of gleefulness to be free of the Soviets and their authoritarian ways. Our Russian guides rarely ever said they wanted to join a religion but still respected the Orthodox Church as an institution and a pillar of their ancient civilization. Tatiana volunteered one day, in that regard, "In Soviet days they always used to play on television and in movie houses the best new movies only on Sunday mornings, to discourage people, especially young people, from going to church, as if tearing down the cathedrals was not enough."

My first one-on-one meeting with a Russian judge came on a cold morning late in the month. The beautiful yellow building was unheated and had no working elevators. Aleksandr Baitsurov [BITE-soor-off] was deputy chief judge of the vast Moscow Oblast, which had 7.5 million people and 153 trial courts. His office held major trials and was also the court of appeals for all lesser courts of the oblast. As we began to talk, a judge came in to report. She was holding an apparently typical joint jury trial of several defendants accused of hijacking eighteen different trucks and killing all their drivers and any girlfriends riding with them. Judge Baitsurov advised her to deny all defense counsels' motions for continuance of the trial. Even though two had doctors' letters saying their hearts needed rest, the judge said, "They're always faking. It's too easy to forge—or buy—such letters. This trial has already been going on for six months."

The judge explained that Russia's rules were tougher on defendants than ours: just eight guilty votes out of twelve were enough to convict. Nevertheless, 80 percent of all defendants in jury cases still went to trial since guilty pleas were "too Communistic" to be allowed. "We constantly fear a return to the old days." So far, jury trials were required mostly for cases where the maximum sentence was fifteen years or more. All lesser cases still went to single judges with two assessors, exactly as in the old days. Judge Baitsurov said eight other oblasts also had "some" jury trials. The Moscow Oblast had already had them for four years. Results were mixed. Although *no* defendants had been acquitted yet, there were way too many problems. There was no money to pay jurors, whose bosses often fired them for missing work; judges often paid jurors out of their own pockets from money they still made from unnamed "private" businesses on the side. Russian jury trials were an honest effort, but again right out of the old days.

The judge sent me with one of our best interpreters, Anatoly, to my first in-person Russian jury trial. As in all European courts, including France and Italy, there was a cage-like cell at the back of the courtroom for defendants who had not made bond, which was basically all of them. In the first courtroom the judge was an intelligent, stern-faced woman with a good haircut and neat black robe. The jury was the surprise: only twelve of them, with no alternates. One man was wearing a white shirt and tie with a business suit and took notes during the testimony. From appearances, we could have been in the US..

The only light came from a high row of double-paned windows. "We cannot afford electricity, so all trials are strictly by daylight," Anatoly noted. When the judge asked a defense attorney a question, he said, without standing, rather disrespectfully, "Ask my client what he wants." A marshal rapped on the bars of the defendants' cage, pointed to a ratty-looking young man and said, "Stand up and answer the judge." The defendant stood and said, sneering, "Why ask me? How would I know? That's why I have a lawyer." The jurors looked at him with disdain if not total hostility. It was clear verdicts of guilty were guaranteed. The trial was mostly for show, to follow the new laws. Anatoly remarked on the absence of the victims' families, who had a right to attend and receive damages. "They are fed up and no longer care. They need to be at work, and they know neither the defendants nor the government itself has any money to pay any damages that might be awarded."

We went to a second courtroom, which again was presided over by a very polished, professional woman judge. An elderly, white-haired defense attorney was examining his defendant, who was trying to explain why he'd taken a machine gun to what turned out to be the murder scene. The prosecutor was a very young man, badly dressed. He laid his head on the table part of the time and appeared to nap. He always addressed the judge seated and with little respect. Again, a guilty verdict seemed a foregone conclusion. We left quickly to a third courtroom. The judge again was a woman. Again one juror was wearing a tie. It was a group of twelve solid-looking people who I'd have been happy to have for one of my own more important jury trials in Mississippi. One defendant was a woman, much the least menacing of all the many defendants I saw that day.

The prosecutor, wearing a badly patched black leather jacket, called a male defendant to the stand. "You recall your prior statements?" Defendant replied, "Not exactly." The judge, who was not wearing a robe but was well dressed, told the prosecutor he could read the defendant's prior, signed statement, which bore his inked thumbprint. The other defendants, the victims, and the attorneys agreed to that. The judge then asked for the statement and read it herself, with feeling and a sense of drama. The jurors listened with great attention.

The statement began, as did many I heard that day, "We first drank way too much vodka. I just remembered he had offended me deeply. I saw a knife in my hand covered in blood. I remember hitting him with it three times. The floor was slippery with his blood." In this case all three defense attorneys were women.

The prosecutor explained that his next witness, in rebuttal, was a nurse who could not be found, believed to be in hiding out of fear. The judge then gave the jurors a cautionary "unavailable witness" instruction almost identical to one of ours. The statement was interesting. The nurse was from Bokhara in central Asia and did not speak Russian well. A translator had prepared her statement. In it she stated that two strange-looking young men with the female defendant entered the victims' kitchen, all drunk, all three holding knives. The jurors were riveted and leaned forward to hear the judge read the statement, which was full of hearsay about all the nurse had *heard* about prior, similar violent, knife-wielding crimes by these same defendants, apparently admissible because they were thought to be related to the *motive* for the current crimes.

The judge announced, when there was no cross-examination—you can't cross someone who's not there—that the next witness would be the eleven-year-old son of the female victim, who was killed during the crimes. The boy was accompanied by a teacher from his school and looked terrified. Incredibly, he had been seated near the defendants' cage where they repeatedly cursed and spit at him during the trial. Several times, the boy had rushed out of the courtroom in tears, only to be dragged back by the marshals. "One guy hurt my mother and said he'd kill her and looked at me and said he'd kill me too. His girlfriend sort of warned me he was capable of murder and told me I should leave." The boy continued, shaking, "Mother said Uncle Vitaly is okay, he's just drunk, but I knew he had just stabbed her last August. At that point Uncle Yuri ran out, but Aunt Angelica told me to stay, to go back in my room. I didn't see it but about then someone stabbed my older brother."

At the end of that sad chapter of a trial, the prosecutor called the female defendant as what we would call an "adverse" witness. The judge gave her what was, to me, a bizarre instruction. Even though she could be compelled to testify, the judge told her, and the jury, "You are not required to incriminate yourself or *any close relative*," a strangely humane idea we've never considered in the US to my knowledge. When asked why the terrified boy would lie, the female defendant, who up to that point had looked decent, completely convicted herself by giving an ugly, criminal sneer and saying, "How should I know? He's just a nasty, lying little devil." The jurors visibly shook their heads, looking like they'd like to slap her and go ahead and vote guilty. She had removed all doubt.

After that trial, Anatoly took us back to Judge Baitsurov's chambers. After asking what we thought, he said that even though Moscow had already used juries for four years, people in most oblasts had no idea how juries worked or that they even existed, although television and newspapers said they did. Judge Baitsurov volunteered several colorful observations on how the new Russian jury system was actually working. "Since the members of the duma are mostly uneducated crooks—they run for office mainly to get immunity from prosecution—the laws they pass are done largely without thought or purpose. Their left and right feet rarely walk together. They keep trying to reinvent the bicycle. Hardly ever have any of them seen any kind of trial. Their goals are to *avoid* the courts. If they want justice, they turn to a mafiya; they believe in guns, not laws." He added, "There are virtually no lawyers in the duma. How can you make laws without lawyers?" which reminded me of how sadly things have changed in our own Congress since the founding fathers, who were mostly lawyers. The judge went on, "Our jurors are honest, but they are like baby birds, helpless. Anyone with good sense tries to stay off juries. They fear what will happen to them. Only 20 percent ever show up and there is not even a punishment for not showing up. The jury lists are often rigged by bribery. There are many dead people on the rolls. It is sadly amusing that one group of people always shows up when summoned: convicts. It gives them immunity while the trial lasts."

On that grim note, the judge launched into statistics, a sacred subject to Russians, especially Russian lawyers. Just as we refer with a straight face to political "science" (at least the University of Virginia has now changed the name of its course on the subject to just Politics), the Russians always refer not to law schools but to judicial "science" schools. The judge's big book of Moscow Oblast convictions showed 27,000 cases for 1995 and 33,000 for 1996. For 1996 only 200 were by jury verdict; there were 150 for 1995, which shows the true lack of importance of jury trials in the new Russia.

The judge laid out further some of its worst problems. Prosecutors, although still powerful and still called "The Eyes of the Tsar," are still grossly underpaid and must somehow supplement their meager salaries, even though they are paid more than judges, who must do more of the same. Prosecutors generally have so many cases they have no time to prepare for trial, nor do the judges. The defense attorneys are even worse off, although little is expected of them. "Who wants the guilty assisted anyway?" the judge said. Trying to be positive, Judge Baitsurov added, "Corruption used to be universal; now it's down to about 80 percent." He said with some wonderment, "You should appreciate what you have in America. There you actually *expect* honesty and *expect* things will be done *by the book*. You are exceptional but hardly know it."

Tired but grateful, and with a notebook brimming with quotes, I thanked the judge for his time and candor and his wise insights into Russia—and the US as well. Walking away from his handsome building, it struck me how so many Moscow walls were plastered with huge signs for the Marlboro man, for many Russians the primary image of an American. Not exactly healthy, but at least we don't look weak. Anatoly told me as we walked, to my slight surprise, that he had been trained as a lawyer but quit because he was sickened by all the corruption, saying he made a good enough salary as a tour guide and interpreter for English speakers, especially Americans, who tipped really well. I made a mental note of his gentle suggestion, and we both enjoyed quite an experience together. "Americans are so open and honest," he said. "It continues to astonish me, the contrast with my people. We have a desire to be honest, but the system is aligned against us, always has been, and probably always will be."

Our last night in Moscow, Mark and Irina took us back to the Pirosmani Georgian restaurant where it all began. The two weeks had been like two years or perhaps two decades, everything being so wildly different. I wished once more that I could speak Russian, recalling the old French saying, "Who speaks a second language has a second soul." I wondered to myself what it would feel like to have a second, Russian soul. I knew well from experience that I am a pretty different person when speaking French: older in attitude, much more aggressive and cynical than when I'm speaking in English.

Now I had had a peek inside the Russian soul and hoped to get more. I never did, but recalling all I witnessed so many years ago in Moscow was the next best thing. No books, no movies, no amount of money could buy or replace that experience.

Looking back today on our Russian mission, I realize we were naïve in our hopes that we could begin to make any difference in Moscow or Russia generally. From the perspective of our current more cynical and pessimistic time, our former hopes to help Russia with reform now seem like a tiny rowboat on a vast ocean. Obviously, what we tried to do has failed, but I still believe, perhaps even more strongly now, that our efforts were worth it. It sounds like a cliché, but in a vast, popular democracy, every person must do his part or the whole enterprise fails. Hundreds of thousands of individual Americans are needed if our endeavors are to succeed. I know nation-building does not work, but I'd like to think that even today in Russia there are people, now probably elderly, or their children whom they've told about it, that there were once good Americans who came to help them try to improve their country and their personal lives, making both more free and fair, and that there must still be many Americans of the same kind, still ready to befriend and help their country. Even age and experience have not altogether dimmed my hopes.

MISSIONS TO THE SULTANATE OF OMAN, PEARL OF THE PERSIAN GULF (1999, 2002)

In early March 2002 I flew back to Oman from Memphis via KLM to Amsterdam and on to the capital, Muscat, stopping briefly in Dubai, which was like a more lavish version of Las Vegas. We arrived just before dawn. Richard Wilbur from the embassy and Michael Hager of Harvard, head of an important NGO, met me at the airport with a hired driver. We sped along a smooth, four-lane divided highway lined with elegant royal palms. It looked nothing like any other country in the Arab world. I had thought I would be too sleepy from the long flights to notice the scenery, but it was so spectacular it woke me up totally. Dick, a graduate of the University of Virginia and the Kennedy School of Government, whom I had known earlier in Tunisia, began showing me the local sights. The first was a large, colorful ticket stuck on the windshield of a car in the airport parking lot. "That is not a parking ticket," he noted with a chuckle. "It's a fine for having a dirty car." The car, an expensive one, looked fine to me, just dusty. "The Sultan is very proud of his capital city's ranking as the second-cleanest capital in the world, second only to Singapore."

Dick next said, "The medical care here is excellent. No worries in that quarter in case you're wondering. They have American doctors and American nurses right in the embassy." That statement and others told me Oman was not going to be any ordinary visit to a dusty Middle Eastern capital. As we whizzed toward town, Dick and Michael began regaling me with stories of Oman and its ruler, Sultan Qaboos [like a train's "caboose"]. His father, uneducated and a severely religious man, decided years ago to send Qaboos to England to study, not to Oxford or Cambridge but to the Royal Military Academy at Sandhurst. There Qaboos not only learned perfect English but decided his country needed to modernize. At the time, his father the king always locked all the old gates to the city and had his police keep everyone off the streets after dark. Many Omanis left their country, which was said to be one of the grimmest places on earth, less violent than Yemen next door but deeply depressing.

In the countryside it was even worse, if that was possible. The king did not control anything in the back country desert and mountains beyond Muscat

City. In fact, under international law, the place was treated as two countries, one called "Muscat," the other "Oman." The rugged interior, which borders both Saudi Arabia and Yemen, where the frontiers are neither guarded nor even marked, was ruled by fanatical, fundamentalist imams, each with his own little autocratic fiefdom, which were constantly at war with each other in petty, longstanding local vendettas.

Qaboos returned to Muscat in 1970 with a classmate and close friend named Tim Landon, a keen military strategist. With Landon's help, Qaboos carefully staged a quick, bloodless coup d'état, exiling his father to a quiet retirement inland. With Landon as his chief of security, Qaboos used his new army to reunite the country, relegating the local imams to subservient status as mere local notables. When they asked that he call himself imam, he rejected that idea as well and chose for himself the traditional title of sultan. For those interested in Omani history, I strongly recommend by far the best books I've read on the subject: *Oman: A Comprehensive Guide* by Hatim al-Taie and Joan Pickersgill and *In the Service of the Sultan*, by Ian Gardiner, an outstanding study of how a British coalition helped Qaboos suppress a violent Communist insurgency in Dhofar, along the border with Yemen.

Qaboos began modernizing the country, carefully investing its considerable oil reserves, ordering two houses be built for every family, one of stone in the oasis towns for winter and another, simpler one of palm leaves and other inexpensive natural native materials in the hills to occupy and stay cool in the long, dry, hot summers. Modern education and healthcare were suddenly free for all, paid for by the country's then-ample oil reserves. The education had to be mainly in Egypt, Jordan, or Morocco due to lack of local schools. As in neighboring Saudi Arabia, foreign workers, mainly from Pakistan and the southern Philippines, were brought in to do the hard labor. Eighty percent of the Army of Oman comes from the Baluchistan region of Pakistan, as I learned from several later meetings with Omani officers.

At first, all went perfectly. The violent vendettas were suppressed. As one of his ministers told me, tribal peace was restored with surprising deftness. Speaking of another minister in Qaboos's cabinet, the minister told me, "Not so many years ago, his grandfather killed my grandfather in an old tribal feud. Now we serve the sultan together as friends."

As Dick Wilbur was discussing Tim Landon, I was surprised to learn that the military strategist had a brother in the US, a history professor schooled at Oxford, England, but who was then teaching in Oxford, Mississippi. "I know him," I said. "He's a good friend, *Michael* Landon. He teaches English Constitutional History at Ole Miss, where I teach law. He never mentioned he had a famous brother." Dick explained, "They are very discreet here about matters regarding Mr. Landon."

Sadly, Tim Landon was out of the country that month, traveling somewhere with the sultan, so I never got to meet either of them, but I got a real earful about him from the Omani officials I met. Said to be a billionaire several times over, Tim Landon was called all over the Middle East "The White Sultan." It was said, and never denied, that with Qaboos's approval Tim Landon made most of his considerable fortune as an arms dealer. When he died young of cancer in 2007, his renown was such that Queen Elizabeth herself attended his funeral. His brother Michael and his wife Carol, who are now retired but still live in Oxford, had also attended and later told me all about it after I got back to Oxford.

The rosy picture of life in Oman seemed too good to be true, and I suppose in a few respects it was, although not many compared to every other country in the region. The first problem the Sultan encountered was similar to what almost every rich parent faces with his children as they grow up: they are so used to having everything given to them that they have no ambition to work or "make anything" of their lives. Dick told me I would see as I interviewed lawyers and other public officials during my stay in Oman that they were all foreign; Omanis do not work, much the same problem that Saudi Arabia's rulers have encountered over the years. I was personally somewhat familiar with that situation from my own experience.

When my daughter Allison, now a successful family doctor, was a rebellious fifteen-year-old, she asked if she could live for a while with the family of her best friend Naj [NAZH], a Saudi girl, also fifteen, whose father taught political science at Ole Miss. The Saudi father, Salem, had just divorced his Saudi wife, Zina [ZEE-nuh], and gone back to Saudi, leaving her unemployed and temporarily virtually penniless in Oxford. Zina did not want to go back to Saudi because, as a woman, she would have had few rights and might never have been allowed to return to the US, which she and her four children had grown to love for its many freedoms.

After surprisingly few negotiations, my wife Regan and I agreed to let Allison live with Zina and her children on a trial basis. In return I would pay for their rent, electric bill, and food until her family in Saudi could decide how to support her financially. We had our doubts, but I felt fairly confident because of my own upbringing. My grandmother's best friend was a Syrian lady who ran a Middle Eastern deli two blocks from her house. I thus grew up with a lunchbox full of kibbe and baclava instead of Twinkies and corndogs. Although Louise, my grandmother's friend, was Christian, not Muslim, I felt comfortable with Arab culture and with at least giving the project a try.

Without going into a long story, the arrangement worked beautifully. Allison was soon spouting Arabic proverbs (*In Shah ALLAH; Al HAMda-Leelah*) and doing really well in school under the stern but loving tutelage of

Zina. The experience altered my thinking about our modern cultural clashes and later eased my adjustment to my own extensive travels that are the main subject of this memoir. After a happy, productive year, Allison returned home and the Baeshens got a quieter household.

Back in Oman, Dick Wilbur was explaining to me the other problems in Oman. First, the sultan's oil reserves were much more modest than thought earlier and would run out entirely in ten years or so at the rate they were being used up. There were still vast reserves of natural gas, but no pipelines to export them, or even to use them locally, so Sultan Qaboos began building, with US help, a vast bottling factory and port on the Indian Ocean on the southern coast at Salalah to liquefy reserves of natural gas into propane for export, a project still struggling to succeed on the competitive world market.

The third problem facing Oman was of a totally different order: the succession to the throne. There being no legislature (except an informal but effective traditional *majlis*, or consultative assembly of wise men) and no elections of any kind to be held, when Qaboos died, who would succeed him? Always a man ahead of his time, Qaboos was also way ahead of his time in another social way, especially for his region: He was and is what we would now call a confirmed bachelor, who would be having no children and had no eligible nephews. It was such a sensitive topic that I feared to broach it with most Omanis, and the several Western expatriates I asked about it said that no one seemed to know anything about it and most feared even to speculate about it.

The most common rumor was that the sultan had written the name of his successor on an official royal decree and sealed it in a safety deposit box to be opened only upon his death. No one seemed to have any idea who had the key or what name might be on the document. The question became more acute after the death of the sultan's most trusted confidante, Tim Landon. As he neared the age when most men die, people around the region, and in the US, which counts on him as a crucial Middle Eastern ally (he helped broker the Iran nuclear deal among others), no one seems to have any idea what will happen when the inevitable occurs. It is so unsettling, both there and here, that most people don't want to talk, or even think, about it.

With Dick Wilbur's excellent summary of the history and current Omani situation still ringing in my ears, we arrived at my hotel, the Hyatt Regency. Dick sort of apologized for not putting me up at the Al Bustan Palace down the beach, where every emir of the United Arab Emirates plus most other Middle Eastern leaders keep permanent suites, in some cases entire floors. Dick said he thought I would prefer the atmosphere of the Regency better, and I certainly did. Although we later dined several times at the Al Bustan, which had lavish buffets with the cuisine of at least a dozen countries, the Regency is incomparable. You enter into a vast palace out of *The Arabian Nights* with beautifully carved balconies facing a six-story atrium. In the center is a large bronze statue of a man resembling the sultan, hunting on horseback with a falcon on his arm. The statue very slowly revolves, almost imperceptibly, just once every twenty-four hours. In the four corners of the lobby are four large, exquisite silk tents designed so that the sides may be let down, enclosing the diners and the large, low central table and cushions so that conservative sheikhs from the desert can dine with their wives, unveiled, in privacy.

On the wall by the entrance is a huge, beautifully carved and stained wooden marquetry map of Oman with all important cities, oases, markets, and other landmarks handsomely and colorfully portrayed. On a mezzanine just above the lobby are shops with exquisite silk rugs from around the region, especially Kashmir, and one of the finest English language bookstores I've seen anywhere with titles of books on the region I'd never seen or heard of anywhere else before or since. My credit card was groaning when I left, but my library is rich and happy.

The best way to portray the splendors of the hotel and the views of the city on one side and the Indian Ocean on the other side, not to mention the beauties of the Omani countryside, are through the many rolls of film I took during my stay. As shown in those photos, all of which I took personally, the interior country of Oman looks like the better parts of Afghanistan: steep, stark, rocky mountains with patches of beautiful green valleys. The bus stops and signs for villages are magnificently carved from beautiful local stone.

The sign to Nizwa [NEEZ-wah], the capital of the interior, is typical. There I almost lost my life when some local boys dared me to walk the hundred-yard length of an uneven path around the inside wall of the sixty-foot-high old central fort, an ancient baked-mud structure whose narrow inside path has no handrail. I foolishly did it, not looking down, and lived to tell about it. The fear of such a height did not hit me till I was back on the ground and my knees started shaking so violently that I had to sit down. The boys seemed much more impressed by my overcoming my fear than by my dangerous walk itself. Being locals, they had probably done it, after daring each other to do it many times. Or maybe not. Maybe they had more sense than that. Somehow it's always been easier for me to take risks in foreign places than it is at home.

Most of Oman's impressive sights I saw with one of my favorite people I've ever met, who would no doubt have been a friend for life if circumstances had been different. When we arrived at the embassy, Dick Wilbur said, "I want you to meet one of my assistants, Said al-Harthy. Said [sah-EED] is from the richest, most powerful tribe in this part of Arabia and has seen and done everything. His family owns half of Muscat and his uncles are all cabinet members." A tall, lean young man of about thirty came in wearing the most unusual, expensive-looking, floor-length, dish-dash robe I'd seen, a dark shade of gray I never saw anywhere else. "I'm Said," he said. "John." From that moment, we were friends. "Said has a wonderful camp deep in the 'real' desert, the Wahiba Sands, similar to the desert on the border with Saudi Arabia," Dick said. When Said asked how soon I'd like to visit, I said, "I'm ready now."

We left that night. Said had a big Range Rover with stacks of large water tanks on the roof. As we drove he explained many things. "What you in the West call 'deserts' we Arabs call 'sands,' only if they have drifts. Otherwise, to us with our land and our climate, *everything* is a desert, except it's mostly rock not sand." He explained that much of Oman had almost no roads except between cities because nearly every inch of the country which was not impassible sand dunes (vehicles detour around those areas) is made of naturally crushed rock just like a road for the four-wheel drives used by every Omani. I hardly ever saw a regular sedan except on the few main roads to and from the airport on the road to Nizwa. "Also, we never ride camels as transport. They are far too valuable as racing stock. My son is a jockey. I will show you tomorrow."

We stopped at a small concrete building in a little oasis of palm trees where a butcher cut up a small goat at Said's direction. "My wife made an excellent local rice dish with shrimp from the ocean, but I thought after your long voyage you might need some red meat. He had also brought along, amazingly, two bottles of generic French Burgundy from the Marquisat firm, which must have cost him a bundle. I had paid him a fixed price for the whole trip, all included.

That night, at his camp, as a black sky filled with thousands of stars, we ate the goat and the rice, which was like a paella, beside a toasty fire as the temperature fell quickly. After the wine, he asked if there was anyone I'd like to call. I thought immediately of my well-traveled daughter Lydia, who'd been with me to Tunisia and had spent her junior year in France in Montpellier on the Mediterranean. Said pulled a cell phone from the pocket of his robe and asked for the number. It rang and rang and then a sorority girl voice came on and asked us to leave message. Full of good wine, I said, "This is for Lydia from her father. I'm in the middle of the desert with a sheikh of Araby as in those old Hollywood movies." Said confirmed that he was indeed entitled to call himself a sheikh [shake] but never did. "There are too many people calling themselves that nowadays who are not entitled." I soon learned he was right.

The next morning we headed for the large oasis at Sinaw [SEE-now] where there was a large, open-sided, multi-roomed desert souk that sold everything from farm animals to gold bars and jewelry to long Bedouin swords and intricately carved khanjars [CON-jars], once used for disemboweling enemies in tribal wars but now supposedly largely ceremonial. I bought several of each and took some perfect photographs of the whole scene. One currency used there really surprised me: large Maria Theresa silver dollars. I brought several of those home too for framing as cameos on necklaces for Regan and my daughters.

Beside the souk were several pickup loads of leafy green substance, too green to be marijuana. Said said it was alfalfa, much prized as food for camels to supplement and balance their diet for racing, which otherwise consisted mostly of large burlap sacks of cheap dates from the oases. They also sold little sacks of dried and crushed shark meat, which was supposed to be an aphrodisiac and which they called "the Viagra of the desert." What a world. My favorite pictures are of a beautiful young Bedouin girl, young enough to be unveiled, saying goodbye to her pet sheep, which was being sold, and a greedy, ugly gaggle of Bedouin women with shiny black masks with those hook noses that the desert women wore instead of veils. They were shouting and arguing over the price for the young girl's sheep while she looked on and cried.

Another favorite picture is of a tall, scrawny, hook-nosed Bedouin man holding up first a dagger, then a long, narrow sword. When Said asked him the price, he gave us a little sales pitch. "Sir, with this sword an eight-year-old boy can cut off a man's arm." He then paused and added dramatically, "But it takes a *man* to cut off a head." I bought the sword, which looks just like one of those from the movie *Lawrence of Arabia*, and it now hangs on the wall of my library, right above a khanjar dagger given to me by the attorney general of Oman. As he promised, in the fifteen years I've had it, the silver khanjar has somehow never tarnished. A good khanjar in Oman is handed down from father to son through generations. It is also a vital part of an Omani gentleman's wardrobe, hung from a silver-colored belt around the waist. To go to a formal occasion without one's khanjar is to Omanis like going to a formal dinner without a tie would be to us.

That afternoon Said took me to see his son's camel race. It was a startling scene. Deep in the middle of the Wahiba Sands was a large flat space the size of three or four football fields. Underneath the sand was solid rock. The footing was excellent. The twelve or fifteen jockeys were all the same age, about six, and the same size, very small but wiry and energetic. I'd always held the opinion, or prejudice really, that one problem Gulf Arabs have is that their oil wealth imprisoned them in a soft, easy, sedentary lifestyle, where women and foreign servants do all the heavy domestic chores, depriving young men of exercise and too often leaving them listless and overweight. Said's appearance and lifestyle certainly exploded that idea, let alone his son's lifestyle as a jockey.

For that reason, I was all the more incredulous when I got a stern lecture from a state department bureaucrat after I returned home about how negligent I was for not objecting to Said's allowing his son to risk his life racing a camel, not to mention how dangerous it was for the poor camels, whose fragile legs were allegedly often broken (like those of our American thoroughbred Arabian race horses) in such "foolish" sports. I laughed in her face and gave her a tongue-lashing of my own that kind of surprised even me. I quickly regretted it, fearing they would put a big black mark on my file and never send me abroad again. Luckily, I never heard any more about it.

The racing camels were nearly all of a beautiful golden shade, sort of a palomino color. They did not even have to walk to the racetrack. Each one had its own special trailer or big four-wheel drive. The race course itself was laid out naturally. There were two long, parallel piles of sand about six feet high, two hundred yards long, and twenty yards apart. The riders milled around at one end waiting for the start while scores of male spectators sat on their heels on top of the berms of sand. Numerous other spectators, apparently fathers of jockeys and those who owned the camels, were aligned outside the berms in their trucks. The boys all wore bright little colored crash helmets like small motorcycle helmets, all with chin straps. They were grinning furiously and turning their nervous mounts around and around. Suddenly they all took off running. The men in the pickups drove madly along outside the berms on both sides, honking wildly. Not a single rider or camel fell, although there was so much dust and sand from the camels and the trucks you could hardly see.

Said had wisely positioned us near the start and got us quickly into his truck. We beat the riders to the finish line just in time for Said to congratulate his son. There was no real winner proclaimed, the camels all riding so wildly it was hard in the dust to see much, but Said's son was clearly one of the leaders. As the boys dismounted and did high fives (they knew all about American ways and copy us a lot), I noticed for the first time a big round hill not far from the finish line on one side. On top was what first appeared to be a series of black tents. Then I saw movement. Finally, one of the little jockeys, without his father, approached the "tents." Said said, "They are not really supposed to be here. They get much too excited." The "tents" were the black burkas of the boys' mothers who had violated the rules and come to watch the boys ride. I *really* did not mention that one to the state department lady, although I would have had to agree with her totally about the disrespectful, segregated treatment of women on such occasions.

Throughout the rest of my stay in Oman, Said continued to entertain and instruct me. He taught me a lot about life in general and not just about his own country. He told me once of his life as a boy. His grandfather had owned a large, seagoing dhow, those tall ships the Arabs once used to trade to the west with Africa and to the east with India. Said had shipped out several times, from the age of about ten upward, as a crewman with his grandfather. The dhows had motors but they were not powerful enough to use on the rough open seas. Nor were their sails. The ocean currents in the region were powerful and seasonal and they could sail only when the annual, alternating ocean currents and monsoon winds were in the right direction. In one season they would sail west to the island of Zanzibar or the port of Mombasa on the coast of Kenya to pick up a load of products (I've since forgotten which) to bring home. In the other season, they would sail east with a load of Omani products such as cloves and frankincense for the southwestern Indian port of Callicut (not the northeastern city of Calcutta in Bengal) to trade for Indian products. The sea voyages were tremendous adventures for the young Said, who wished that the trade had continued. Now it has been mostly replaced by huge oil tankers and massive ocean liners.

One important social impact of the trade occurred during a period when Oman had bad rulers like the father of Qaboos. In those periods many Omanis stayed on in Mombasa or Dar es Salaam and Zanzibar. There they married African women, later bringing back their biracial children to Oman, which explains why there are so many mulatto Omanis, including members of the royal Yahyah family tribe, as depicted in one of my photos.

After our dessert, Said introduced me to the second Omani who became a close personal friend. Colonel Ali, formally known as Col. Ali Nasser al-Bualy [BOO-ah-lee], is from a small but highly influential tribe well known across southern Arabia, which was known to the Romans as "Arabia Felix," or "happy Arabia," because of its mild maritime climate and its strips of green land, both along the coast and in inland villages that grow wheat and even cattle, not just dates and figs at the oases. Col. Ali, as I always called him, was a short (five feet four), stocky, athletic man of forty-some. He was Oman's attorney general, grandson of a former Omani ambassador to England and nephew to Oman's ambassador to Yemen. Educated in Cairo, he spoke perfect British English and had a keen interest in, and knowledge of, world history, including American history. He had visited the US several times and hoped to continue his education to a PhD in international relations at Georgetown, where I had once pursued a master's degree in law as an E. Barrett Prettyman Fellow.

We hit it off immediately, one of those relationships which, as the Arabs say, *mektoub*, (was written). Oman left me with a much stronger natural belief in Fate, a belief that our destinies are written before we are born, although it is also part of our destiny to struggle to succeed and to help Fate out a little bit. That faith goes way beyond mere Presbyterianism, although there are some shallow similarities.

Col. Ali entertained me constantly during my stay in Oman, opening for me doors to all sorts of experiences and people I'd otherwise never have seen or known. Most important was his invitation to his home for dinner, an unusual honor. When I arrived at around dusk, he ushered me into his salon, which was furnished not with the customary elegant silk cushions around the walls, but with western-style sofas, which he said he'd learned about in the US and thought were much more comfortable for backs and knees than his own country's traditional seats. My first surprise upon entering was that the entire living room was filled with the smoky, powerful aroma of incense, so dense you could hardly see. He said, "I wanted you to have the whole Arabian experience. This is frankincense, which is common here and is featured so prominently in your Bible's teachings about our region."

Col. Ali later showed me how frankincense bushes grow and helped me buy several small sacks, which I brought home along with little cans of Biblical myrrh. I was amazed at how closely frankincense crystals resembled crack cocaine and how brown myrrh looks like hashish. The boys at US Customs in Atlanta, where I reentered the US, required a lot explaining about those items. Only when their drug-sniffing dogs approved them did they allow them. I personally felt a special kinship with those dogs, Belgian shepherds like my own dog Max, the greatest dog of my life. Belgians make wonderful drug dogs as well as pets. They are calm and never bark (although I always had to keep Max in at night because he could not stop howling at the moon). When I gave samples of frankincense and myrrh to my pastor, Alan Cochet, along with little traditional clay pots in which to burn them, he asked me, "Where is the gold?" Preacher humor.

After the surprise of the incense, the biggest revelation of my visit to Col. Ali's home was his children, a girl and a boy of preschool age. They were happy, laughing, and completely out of control, although not mean or spoiled in the slightest. Both hopped up on my lap, messed up my hair, and laughed hysterically when they tickled me. They were utterly charming, unspoiled, and truly childlike in the best sense. With puberty, all that would change and the boy and girl would follow radically different paths. Meanwhile they chattered away in Arabic spiced with little bits of English phases. "I'm teaching them English slowly so they will love it and not consider learning it a chore," Col. Ali explained.

When servants brought in the dinner, the children hugged us and left. Col. Ali and I moved off the couches to sit on cushions at a low table totally covered with an elaborate *mechoui* [may-shwee] feast, the first of many, featuring skewered lamb and goat with lovely little pots and bowls of every kind of tasty dishes. "You can carry Western customs too far, you know. I still prefer our food and style of dining." In keeping with Omani custom, Col. Ali's wife never appeared, and during my entire stay I never met her, nor was she ever mentioned.

This memoir would be way too long if I described all the wonderful days and evenings I shared with Col. Ali, but one more cannot be omitted. One afternoon, after a series of business meetings, he said he knew I missed my

Part of the author's ticket to a *Swan Lake* performance at the Bolshoi Ballet in Moscow.

A band of Cossack soldiers in winter camp in the early twentieth century. The photo was given to the author by a granddaughter of one of the Cossacks.

PRODUCE OF THE REPUBLIC OF GEORGIA

GWS
GEORGIA 3000 YEARS OF WINE CULTURE

KHVANCHKARA

ხვანჩკარა ХВАНЧКАРА

12% vol

SEMI SWEET WINE

e 75cl

ГРУЗИНСКОЕ ВИНО
G.W.S. COMP. LTD. GEORGIAN SPIRITS AND WINES COMPANY LIMITED, TBILISI, REPUBLIC OF GEORGIA
BOTTLED BY NL-HPA 100, 5000 AP TILBURG-NL

A label from the favorite red wine of Josef Stalin, the former Soviet Russian dictator born in Georgia. Some Georgians, ashamed of his crimes, claim his biological father was actually Persian, not Georgian.

Extinct ancient volcanoes called *puys* in the remote Auvergne region of central France.

Sailing in an illuminated grotto on the Mediterranean coast of Mallorca, the beautiful island east of Spain where the author lived in the summer of 1964. The author once had a vision he would die there. Fortunately, it never happened—yet.

Parsee children from India with their unique Persian caps. The author once lived for some months with a beautiful Parsee woman in London and agrees with the statement by Mark Twain that "the Parsees are the most handsome race of all Hindustan."

The author's name in Arabic script.

حثد* ؛تجج جت دت حثدح

Traditional hand-woven Berber carpet from Tunisia now on the floor of the author's library. The gazelles are for good luck and are also the symbol for beautiful young girls. Under stricter forms of Islam, representing animals is forbidden, but the Berbers, a fiercely independent people, take a more relaxed view of such religious rules.

CHIŞINĂU

Statue of the heroic Moldovan warrior-king Stefan the Great, who defeated invading Muslim Turks in a historic fifteenth-century battle. Moldova has remained Christian ever since.

Unique marquetry picture of a Moldovan farm girl, intricately carved from thin slices of wood from five different Moldovan fruit trees. She is holding a strip of linen used to wrap the trunks of fruit trees in winter to protect their bark from wild deer. The author acquired the piece in Chişinău from the woman whose husband made it.

Unusual wood carving, made entirely by prisoner artisans, given to the author by the warden of the maximum security prison at Cricova, Moldova. At the top is a vampire bat from nearby Transylvania, offset by a "lucky" hexagonal pineapple in the center. The shovel on the left represents the prisoners; the club on the right represents the prison guards.

In the lobby of the Hyatt Regency Hotel in Muscat, Oman, a slowly revolving statue of Sultan Qaboos hunting with a falcon on his arm. The tent in the background has flaps that fold down so desert sheikhs who dine there can entertain the women of their harems unveiled.

View from the author's window in the Hyatt Regency Hotel over the beautiful, blindingly white houses of downtown Muscat.

Traditional Omani entrance gate to a horse-breeding town in central Oman.

A beautiful Omani bus stop of carved stone on the route to the inland capital of Nizwa, which allows in breezes while sheltering travelers from the 120 degree heat.

A colorfully dressed Bedouin mountain woman known as a *shawawi* tries to catch her goat, who does not want a bath. The author had earlier drunk downstream, without incident, from the same stream after she had washed her herd of silky-haired goats.

Trusted Omani guide and friend Sheikh Saïd al-Harthy with his son, an enthusiastic camel racer, awaiting the start of a race.

An intricately handmade *khanjar* dagger presented to the author by the prosecutor general of Oman, Ali Nasser al-Bualy, as "a parting friendship gift." Just as Ali promised, the silver dagger was so made that after ten years of exposure to the air, it has never tarnished.

Colorful Omani key ring festooned with bright red wool, especially practical in a desert country where keys dropped in the loose, deep sand are often never otherwise found.

The author's beautiful, open-sided bungalow on Bali in the beautiful Ubud region of the island, home to most of its unique artists.

A colorfully decorated "good luck" shrine dedicated to the goddess said to protect the author's temporary home.

The shrine beside the author's bungalow in Bali, one part of a time-lapse series of photos taken by the author tracking a spectacular sunrise.

A typical Balinese rainstick made of a hollow length of bamboo beautifully stained and hand-carved and filled loosely with seeds. When shaken, it sounds like rain falling on a traditional roof of woven palm fronds. On top is a carved turtle, the Balinese symbol for the earth, which they noted long ago is curved and often moves like a turtle.

The Author with Y Made Yasa, attorney general of Bali, whose handsome features reflect the Polynesian origins of many Balinese. He personally prosecuted the infamous "Bali Bomber" who killed dozens in a terror attack on Australian surfers on a Bali beach right after the author left the island.

Summer day in a remote alpine village in the Caucasus on a plateau high on the slope of
Mt. Kazbegi, tallest mountain in Europe.

A Georgian *tamada*, or toastmaster, leading toasts from a typical drinking horn. His classic
Georgian shirt has rows of pockets made to hold rifle shells, often replaced in civil society
by silver cylinders, which are handy for discreetly delivering love notes to off-limits beauties.
Permission of the *Washington Post*, spring 2007.

Colorful map of the provinces of Georgia showing traditional costumes of the regions. The name "Georgia" for the country is strictly British and not recognized by Georgians, who call their country "Kartli." The author's favorite Georgian red wines, made from the Saperavi grape, similar to a Syrah, are from the Kakheti and Imereti regions. Whites, like Pheasant's Tears, are used for toasting, and are from the amber-colored Rkatsiteli grape. The camels in the lower right corner show how Georgia was the last stop on the famous "Silk Road" from China to Europe.

The author's handsome grandson Lele, Leland Alexander King, examining a miniature replica of an upside down Georgian *kwevri*, or clay wine barrel. With the pointed end down, huge *kwevris* are buried in cool ground so the wine inside will ferment and age slowly.

wine-tastings, and he would try somehow to make it up with a date-tasting. In his large kitchen he produced seventeen bags of different dates of all sizes, colors, and varieties, each from a separate oasis he owned. I have never experienced anything like it. Some little tart ones made good appetizers. The biggest, fattest, darkest ones were perfect for dessert. It was a day I'll never forget. As mentioned elsewhere, I've spent much of my adult life as a wine columnist and judge at international wine contests, but that date-tasting was unique. Col. Ali and I corresponded by old-fashioned, handwritten letters for several years. He even sent me Christmas cards.

New Insights from a Legal Mission in Oman

We met with newly appointed US ambassador John Craig and his staff. Our team included US district judge Edward Rafeedie of Los Angeles (born an Arab in Palestine); Michael Hager, director of an NGO in Rome; and Tarek Riad, a Cairo attorney educated at Harvard who practices in New York and all over the Middle East.

Ambassador Craig stated that we were his very first meeting as ambassador and that our mission was important, being set up personally by Sultan Qaboos and former US ambassador Frances Cook. Ambassador Craig said he was very familiar with the goals of our mission and its potential, noting there was reason not to be optimistic about any immediate achievements because other countries had tried the same approach in Oman without success.

The ambassador is an experienced Arabist who has served as our ambassador to both Syria and Saudi Arabia and was head of the Gulf Region Desk at the State Department just prior to coming to Muscat. He stated Oman was unique in the Gulf region by being independent, peaceful, forward-thinking, and open to the outside, all while remaining religious and socially conservative but not radical. He noted our image in Oman was fairly positive and we were not perceived as trying to control their country as the British were. The Omanis' main resentment against us was that we tended to deal with them too much through the Saudis and to treat them as secondary, except in regard to their critical strategic position at the mouth of the Straits of Hormuz, which control access to the Persian Gulf.

The ambassador told us that our mission was basically open ended, i.e., to ask the Omanis in an inoffensive way what assistance they believed they needed based on how their system of justice functioned, both in theory and in practice. Despite his experience and book knowledge of the region, Ambassador Craig stressed that we really knew very little about how their legal system functioned in practice, and nearly anything we could learn would be a plus. Because he was not yet officially accredited, he could not make official contacts for us and thought that in any event it might be better if we were informal and private rather than an official embassy delegation, since that approach tended to invoke all sorts of time-consuming formalities.

DCM Gary Grappo, who was acting as chargé d'affaires, concurred that people-to-people contacts tended to open more doors than official visits. He also stated, as an example of our remarkable lack of knowledge of the legal situation in Oman, that our embassy wanted to know whether Oman even had a bar association. It also wanted to know what the Omanis, both ordinary and elite, really think about their own legal system. The sultan's new program of Omanization relies heavily on creating public trust in the legal system, which in most Muslim countries is not traditional. He suggested we go slowly and steadily work our way up the official ladders of the various ministries. Our highest aspiration should probably be to speak with one or two ministers, or wazirs, although even that might be too optimistic.

The ambassador felt our most important contact at the outset would be Sheikh [shake] Zahir [zah-HEAR], deputy minister of justice and a serious Islamic scholar. Sheikh Zahir visited the United States last year via USIA as a "religious visitor" and was apparently well impressed. Sheikh Zahir was leaving his vacation home on the Indian Ocean coast for sultry Muscat solely to meet with us, a very good sign. The ambassador stressed that Oman is unique among Gulf States in being neither strictly Sunni nor Shi'ite, but Ibadi [ee-BAH-dee], a small and moderate sect of Islam that is conservative but stable and nonfanatical. Their religion is apparently one of the most critical factors in the Omanis' open and relaxed lifestyle as compared to the militant Saudis.

The initial meeting concluded with Omani coffee, which is flavored with cardamom and rose water, surprisingly thin, and served in tiny cups without handles. You wiggle the cup slightly if you want a refill. It was served by Batool [bah-TOOL], an embassy secretary and a rare Shi'ite in Oman who had her hands completely painted with dark-red henna in elaborate designs for the Islamic festival of Aïd. The ambassador promised to host a social function toward the end of our visit, inviting all of our interlocutors as a sort of "harvest" of contacts, and to judge how well we did from who attended.

We met first with Ahmed al-Mukhaini [moo-KAY-nee] of the embassy, who briefed us on Omani culture and its legal system. I had read six books on the country before arriving, but one is never sure what to believe or whether it is up to date. Ahmed was a native of Sur on the coast, but had lived half his life in Kuwait and was educated in the UK. His English was excellent, and he enjoyed explaining Omani history and analyzing the national character. He felt that Americans would be readily accepted in Oman, which needed help building modern institutions, including its new college (Sultan Qaboos University). He felt Omanis might even accept the concept of juries but that it would take time. He suggested three ways to approach Omani officials about assistance. First, provide courses suggested by them rather than us; second, offer plenty of US visits, particularly to follow cases through US courts from beginning to end; and third, maintain direct US-Omani personal contacts, the only way they would have faith in foreign assistance, because that is how their culture works, person-to-person.

Oman was having difficulty adjusting to its decreased revenue from petroleum. Not only were oil prices down, but Oman was quickly depleting its modest remaining oil reserves. Oil was slowly being replaced by natural gas wells but not fast enough, and natural gas was much more difficult to liquefy and export. He felt that Omanis would only be agreeable to cost-effective trips, such as long-term apprenticeships in the United States combined with study at US professional institutes under government grants. He felt that the lavish new Law College and the Ministry of Education would fund Omani students on a long-term basis if the US government would get the program started.

Under new statutes, most Omani courts would be placed under the Ministry of Justice, which while influenced and even staffed by Muslim clerics, are generally well educated, most having law degrees, although some hold only degrees in religious law. The Sharia courts' jurisdiction had been much curtailed, limiting them primarily to family law matters, called "laws of personal status." They were thus actually somewhat like our chancery or equity courts.

The criminal justice system was a strange hybrid. In the coastal cities, criminal cases were handled through the magistrate court. Many cases in rural areas, however, were handled the traditional Muslim way, i.e., via family negotiation. The traditional chancellors, or qadis [KAH-deez], no longer hear criminal matters. Most Omani law is based on the Napoleonic system taken to Egypt in the early nineteenth century and spread from there throughout the Middle East. Onto that "civil law" system in Oman there is also engrafted part of the old British model. The police conduct an investigation, make an arrest, collect all evidence, and submit it to the prosecutor. The head of the system is not the prosecutor but the inspector general of the police. Until fairly recently there were no prosecutors. The police themselves, without law degrees, fulfilled that function as in the old British colonial system of constables.

By American standards, Oman had a truly low crime rate. The previous year, in this nation of over two million, there were only seven murders, which would be just a drop in the bucket, so to speak, in the city of Los Angeles alone. According to Ahmed, the death penalty applied to most of the same offenses as in America, particularly murder, but is actually used, unlike in the US. A three-person panel must approve all death penalties: the minister of justice, the chief judge of the magistrate court, and the grand mufti, an interesting religious officer unique to Islamic countries. His position on what might be called the "death sentence review commission" was apparently to guarantee nondiscrimination among the three Islamic sects in Oman, i.e., Ibadi, Shi'ite, and Sunni. The grand mufti was appointed by the sultan and must be an Ibadi.

The prison system was relatively humane. Located not far from Muscat in the Batinah region, the main prison had separate facilities for juveniles and for women. Persons not yet convicted were not housed with convicted criminals. Various Omani officials later offered to let me visit the prison, but time constraints prevented it.

According to Ahmed, Omanis in general felt that the criminal justice system was fair unless a powerful person were involved either as defendant or victim, in which case it was assumed influence would be used, as in the rest of the world's countries frankly. Traditionally an accused first attempted to exonerate himself by having the most influential males in his family speak with police officials. Sometimes, especially in the interior, imams were enlisted to lobby on behalf of the accused. Once the case reached the prosecutor, the view was that there was little chance of escaping. Interestingly, Ahmed said that false accusations were few because of the continuing danger of tribal revenge and retribution. Tribal ties, even in the cities, remained extremely strong. The final name of each Omani was the name of his tribe.

The assessment team asked about the sensitive question of corruption in Oman. The staff noted that in the early days of development under the current sultan, the pool of qualified Omanis was so small that cabinet ministers often had conflicting outside interests in government projects and enterprises. This led to a public perception of unnecessary conflicts of interest. After the Basic Law was enacted, however, most ministers resigned their positions. Unfortunately, many simply put their children in their former positions.

With respect to whether the government itself may be sued, Ahmed noted that this was not much of an issue in Oman since government liability insurance generally compensated injured parties informally and citizens voice few complaints.

Michael Hager asked about NGOs. Ahmed noted that the term was not used much in Oman, in part because there remained very tight restrictions on any type of organization which might have led to instability in the country, particularly labor unions and any sort of militant advocacy group. Oman did not allow branch offices of any organization headquartered outside Oman. There was, for that reason, no bar association. At that time a draft code was being circulated that would relax the situation regarding "social, cultural, and charitable organizations," but Ahmed suspected it would be one of the last to be adopted.

Most lawyers practicing in Oman were trained in Egypt, Jordan, or Morocco, although a few studied in the UK and US. The only Middle Eastern country with a "common law" legal tradition was Sudan, which was long ruled by the British. Because of continued violence during the dictatorial rule there of Hassan al-Turabi (ironically a former law school dean), many Sudanese judges and attorneys fled the country and became expatriates practicing in Oman; several were judges and legal consultants to various ministries, bringing at least some Anglo-Saxon legal traditions to Oman.

As for Islamic fundamentalism, Ahmed noted, as had the ambassador, that Omanis were highly conservative and traditional on religion. On the other hand, there was almost no tendency toward fanaticism, due largely to the nature of Ibadi Islam, which although in theory is closer to Shi'ism, is in reality the most moderate of Islamic sects. Some tribal leaders in the interior had even asked their imams to excommunicate militants. I heard some loosely compare Ibadism to Quakerism in the US. I listened every morning just before sunrise to a muezzin in a minaret less than a block from my hotel. In contrast to the tormented sounds of much Islamic prayer, usually in a minor key, Ibadi prayers are melodic and rather cheerful and peaceful-sounding. Nearly every one of our interlocutors prayed regularly five times a day, but it seemed low-key, discreet, and natural, and they made no big point about it as too many other sects often do.

Ahmed characterized Omanis generally as "highly commercial and outward looking." They had a long tradition of trade by sea with both the Indian subcontinent and the entire coast of East Africa. They looked abroad far more than the Saudis. Omanis liked commerce but feared foreign influence. Ahmed characterized their internal conflicts as wanting to compete globally, but without being swallowed up by immoral foreign influences. Oman had always had lots of trade, but little production. A secondary problem was, thanks to the Ottomans, a strongly entrenched bureaucracy and bureaucratic habits of inefficiency that were hard to break.

We next met with His Excellency Sheikh Zahir, undersecretary of the Ministry of Justice, at his office. The sheikh began by saying that our mission came at a "most important time" for Oman, because it was reorganizing its entire judicial system. He stated that they needed expert professional training for all sectors, especially for the prosecutors and police in the directorate now referred to as the Royal Oman Police, which was headed by the inspector general of police, who was *over* the prosecutor general. Sheikh Zahir asked that we meet personally with all of those officials.

Sheikh Abdullah of Sudan, a colorful black man who spoke fluent English and wore a white turban with an all-white, floor-length dish-dash, spoke quite candidly of the problems of Oman. He said that at that time there was essentially no organized judicial system in Oman, but that the new laws circulating in draft form among the ministries proposed to set up a sound judicial system if the conflicts about how it should operate could be resolved. Most of the draft legislation was written by Egyptians with a strong civil law base, but the sultan and others wanted to inject more common law elements, especially as to trial procedures.

Sheikh Abdullah asked if we had Arab speakers in our group, because most staff members of the ministries involved did not speak English. Unfortunately, none of the draft laws were available in English, which made it especially difficult for them to explain to us the issues on which they needed help and difficult for us to offer them the kind of detailed assistance they really needed. I proposed that as to all legal translations, a two-person team of bilingual translators was needed, one a native Arab speaker and one a native English speaker, working closely together, so that final versions in each language would be in perfect form. All three sheikhs agreed with that approach.

In a symbolic gesture which we came to realize was a sign of trust and goodwill, Sheikh Zahir removed his sandals and told a few topical stories, one of which involved the idea that Monica Lewinsky and O. J. Simpson might make a perfect couple. The sheikh himself bore a surprising but very noticeable resemblance to the late comedian John Belushi, suggesting origins in Baluchistan. Staff brought us a large dish of halwa [HAHL-wah], the classic Arab snack and dessert, which is thick and intensely sweet, like fudge with fat added. Its history indicated that Bedouins used it for quick energy after long treks across the desert. My wife compares it to what we call in the Mississippi Delta "go-home pudding," i.e., after they serve it, you are supposed to leave.

While we were having our halwa and coffee, I asked Sheikh Mohamed about his excellent English and his American rather than British accent. He said that he had a BA degree from the University of Arkansas in business and an MBA from the University of New Hampshire. He amazed me when he said he had visited Elvis's home in Memphis.

The next day, Sunday, January 24, the team met at the new law school with the acting dean Nasser al-Fazari [fah-ZAH-ree] and the director of the library Ahmed Bilal [bee-LAHL]. Other professors joined us during the informal meeting. The tenor of this meeting was utterly different from that with Sheikh Zahir. We were told that the former dean had just been removed from his post with the implication that he did something politically incorrect. The officials who met with us seemed nervous and the whole program was disorganized but very cordial.

The acting dean explained that the new law school accepted students straight from high school, as in the civil law system, law being an undergraduate degree. Their law school was in a totally separate facility from the large and well-established Sultan Qaboos University, which was several miles away. The new law school had 120 first-year students, 120 second-year students, and 17 faculty. At that time it taught both civil law, including procedures and commercial law, as well as Sharia law. The professors were primarily Egyptian and Jordanian, with only two or three Omanis. All courses were taught in Arabic except part of commercial law, which was taught in English. Most students had studied English and understood it well enough to derive some benefit from lectures in English, but did not have a "mastery" of it, according to the dean.

The dean and professors stated that the program would be a four-year one leading to an LLB degree, with the first class graduating in 2001. The last three years were to be divided between Islamic law and secular law. The second-year class had seventy students in secular and fifty in Sharia. All tuition and room and board were paid by the government. There were sixty women law students. We noted an extra door at the back of each classroom, which they explained to us was a separate entrance for the women, whose conservative parents sometimes insist that they not mix with the men in class. The women customarily sat in back for that reason. We suspected, on the contrary, clerical pressure.

Classes lasted from 8:00 a.m. to 3:00 p.m. five days a week. Not all classes were in law alone; there were "supporting" courses in politics, computer science and "general" English as well as several lectures on sports, an interesting point. US students would love it. We visited the computer lab, which was impressive. The computer professor got us on the Arabic internet, did a little research on Yahoo, converted the results to English, and printed them out. It made us wonder how that resource might be used to facilitate translations. All students were required to be computer literate. The lab had fifty modern computers for the 240 students.

Unfortunately, most students had gone home for the three-week Eîd holiday, but I got to speak with a few of them privately, as well as one Sharia professor from Iraq, who was wearing most impressive conical headgear with stars and quarter moons that made him look like one of the three Biblical wise men from the East. I was more impressed with the openness and enthusiasm of the students than the administrators assigned to meet with us, who seemed somewhat intimidated and nervous.

The faculty was unanimous that what they needed most was teacher training. They specifically asked if we could send them visiting professors from the US to teach practical courses like moot court and mock trials. We visited a beautiful and well-appointed moot courtroom, constructed almost identically to an American courtroom. The professors recognized that they had excellent facilities and motivated students, and they indicated that professors were well paid but simply needed more experience and guidance in setting up a sound curriculum. They stated they would like to be a "partner" with the US and with US universities in workshops and other training. They proposed sending their professors to the US in a sort of "training the trainers" plan. They would also have liked to start their own law review along American lines both to train their students in legal research and writing and to do useful analysis of Omani legal problems to circulate among practitioners. They seemed remarkably open to new ideas and techniques.

A big deficit was that in order to be admitted to the bar, Omani students had to spend as much as two years abroad, usually in Egypt, Jordan, or Morocco, to be qualified to take the exam. That problem would be eliminated under the new system and replaced with two years' apprenticeship in Omani law firms. The faculty expressed serious concerns, however, about whether that goal could be accomplished because there were so few lawyers in Oman and most of them were foreign. Ironically, many foreign lawyers feared they would no longer be able even to practice once the new "Omanization" decrees were fully implemented to discourage practice by foreign attorneys.

The team next met with my new friend and host Col. Ali Nasser al-Bualy, director of public prosecutions, Royal Oman Police. Ed Guard, the regional security officer, attended in the capacity of law enforcement liaison. Col. Ali was very enthusiastic about his recent visit to the US, sponsored by the USIA. He had two items of ours he wanted to adopt quickly: (1) a speedy trial rule for "minor cases" (the idea of a misdemeanor was hard to interpret here, because under Omani law anything under a three-year sentence was a misdemeanor); and (2) our version of the exclusionary rule, which he said his boss, the inspector general of the Royal Oman Police, had not yet accepted. Only much later in the visit did I learn that what he was talking about was actually the "good faith" exception to the exclusionary rule recognized in all federal courts in the US under a Supreme Court ruling.

Col. Ali explained that he was the supervisor of the eleven lead prosecutors for the eleven waliyas, or regions, of Oman. Five magistrate courts of one judge each heard misdemeanors. All felonies were heard by a three-judge court located in a single courtroom in Muscat. That court also heard appeals from misdemeanor convictions. There are no appeals from felony convictions, the theory being that since three judges had already heard the case, it had already been reviewed. Col. Ali personally disagreed with that system, but was again in a minority position.

The criminal law environment in Oman sounded ideal for prosecutors. They received higher salaries than judges and in most cases were better trained, being required to study in Cairo plus serving an apprenticeship. The law on bail had been recently changed. Previously judges set bail, but since July 1998 the prosecutor sets the bail. Col. Ali said that criminals were for the most part "humble," and that in one recent year, for a population of over two million, there were only about four thousand criminal cases, including all misdemeanors and only twelve murders. The murders were punishable by death unless the victim's family asked for leniency, which was considered by a three-person panel.

Col. Ali Nasser was very open to additional training for his prosecutors, either in Oman or the US. He requested help in making suggestions for changes to the draft criminal law and procedure codes which were being circulated through the ministries. We suggested DOJ seminars, especially for anticorruption prosecutions, as well as sending Omani prosecutors with sufficient English skills to the Justice Department Advocacy Institute in Columbia, South Carolina. He stated that would be highly desirable, but few spoke enough English.

Col. Ali explained that Oman had its police and prosecutors together because of British influence, especially since Sultan Qaboos, who graduated from Sandhurst in England, took the throne in 1970. Under the new codes, one proposal was that all prosecutors be put under the minister of justice, an idea he strongly opposed because that ministry was perceived as being too much controlled by Islamic clerics. Interestingly, he preferred either a freestanding prosecution service as in England or remaining under the police. Col. Ali said that conflicts between prosecutors and police were growing, and he wanted our help in resolving them. I explained to him our law enforcement coordinating committees and how federal agents were permitted by rule to sit by the prosecutor's side during trial. He remarked that we seemed to have much practical experience that could be useful to the Omanis. When he explained the curriculum for training prosecutors in Egypt, Tarek Riad said that they received much better training than the judges since they attended the University of Cairo Law School, where Tarek's father-in-law was the dean. He said they only accepted 120 applicants per year out of 1,500.

Col. Ali explained that at present thirty men and ten women police officers from Oman were attending law school in Cairo. They would later be used primarily as investigators with legal backgrounds. Their prescribed course was two years. He discussed his own education, saying his father was the first Omani ambassador to England, serving from 1972 to 1980. He had private English teachers and studied geology as a major, planning to be in the oil business, but liked police work so much that, over his father's objection, he became the first chief prosecutor in the country. His father was also for many years the head of the sultan's diwan, or cabinet, and one of his closest advisors.

On the following Monday our team met with J. Alistair Jeffrey, solicitor with Fox and Gibbons, Legal Consultants, to obtain a foreign practitioner's impressions of the Omani judicial system as it operated in practice and what changes the new codes were likely to bring. Mr. Jeffrey had practiced in Muscat for ten years. His office consisted of eight lawyers, four Arabic practitioners and four Westerners. Jeffrey seemed most worried about the toughening registration requirements for foreign lawyers. The advocacy law enacted in November 1997 required Omani partners in all firms by December 31, 1999, and that they be associated with a registered civil law company, essentially strengthening Omani control. Foreign lawyers would now be required to have ten years' experience.

On Tuesday I met alone again with Col. Ali to plan my seminar, while the other members of the team met with Ms. Suad al-Lamki, legal advisor, Ministry of Legal Affairs (MLA) to learn about the functions of the ministry and to discuss possible training. Ms. al-Lamki was born in Zanzibar, educated in Cairo, and holds a law degree from Trinity College, Dublin. After serving as a judge in Dar es Salaam, she emigrated back to Oman in 1975 and worked for Petroleum Development Oman and the legal department of the Abu Dhabi National Oil Company before joining MLA. Ms. al-Lamki said that her department had drafted an initial bill which was submitted to the Ministry of Justice. Under it all courts in Oman except the Sharia would be combined in a single court system under the supervision of the Ministry of Justice.

Our team met again with Sheikh Abdullah al-Jazuli, legal advisor to the Ministry of Justice, whom we first met with Sheikh Zaher. He was fairly cynical. Our far-ranging discussion lasted more than three hours and was remarkably candid. Broadly perceived, the current laws were typically Egyptian while the aim of the minister of justice was to include elements of the British/American system. Sheikh Abdullah highlighted the shortage of qualified Omani lawyers in the system. At that time in the commercial court there were sixteen Egyptians and one Sudanese. Only the vice president was Omani. However, in the Sharia court all judges were Omanis. The same was true in the criminal court. Nevertheless, judgments were generally written by foreign advisors. When we asked about the law faculty, Sheikh Abdullah responded sarcastically, "What law faculty?"

Sheikh Abdullah believed that the Ministry of Legal Affairs would eventually be abolished. He also was confident that there would be, under the new law, a judicial training institute, probably by the year 2000. He remarked again that the existing system was, in fact, "no system at all." A committee of lawyers in the Ministry of Justice was responsible for admissions to practice. He recommended that we see the legal advisor in the State Council but not the legal committee of the Majlis al-Shura, whom he said "no one listens to." Sheikh Abdullah was amazingly frank, speaking as a Sudanese who had been in the country observing it for seven years. He stunned us as we were leaving by admitting that he simply "took" the title of sheikh to enhance his standing in Oman and that he was not really a sheikh at all.

On Wednesday the team met with Said al-Shahry, senior partner, and Mahdi Ageed of the Said, al-Shahry Law Office, in association with the British firm Richards Butler. The al-Shahry law office had both local and foreign clients. It handled most of the privatizations in the country, beginning with the 1993 power project. The firm was about to open an office in Salalah on the southern coast of the country on the Indian Ocean where an important new deep-water port had been built. It has close relations with such international firms as Sullivan and Cromwell and White and Case in New York. Salalah, a huge, modern port was where the famous Somali piracy case, portrayed in the movie with Tom Hanks, began. It was also, according to some, the home port of Sinbad the Sailor, the hero of one of *The Arabian Nights* legends.

At the end of the week, the team met with His Excellency Sayyid Said al-Busaidi, president of the magistrate court, who holds a law degree from Cairo University, but began his career as a diplomat. He was a member of the royal family and was a leading sponsor of the new law college and a proponent of the judicial training center. The president also spoke quite good English from his years in Cairo.

On Sunday, January 31, the team met with His Excellency Mohamed al-Hinai, minister of justice. Also present were his nephew, director of the ministry diwan, and Sheikh Abdullah, the Sudanese legal advisor. His Excellency came to his ministry with a mostly tribal and religious law background. His father once led a rebel coup against the father of the current sultan. He was a stern, rugged man with the demeanor of a soldier; he also had a keen mind, was a good listener, and asked good questions. As evidence of his interest, he held us in lively discussion for almost three and a half hours.

Later on Sunday, our team met with Ali Haider al-Balushi, legal researcher for the Oman Chamber of Commerce. His name vividly reminded me again of the little-discussed Middle East origins of our famous late comedian John Belushi. The chamber mediated some seventy disputes each year, of which about 50 percent were resolved through the help of the legal advisors. Omani businesses were not anxious to take their cases to the Omani Commercial Court, mainly because of their interest in avoiding damaging publicity. But they also felt that the cases took too long to adjudicate and were difficult to enforce. Companies would usually rather go to foreign arbitration than to their own commercial court. Al-Balushi frankly opined that the court did not have capable judges.

We met on Monday, February 1, with Nicholas Edmondes, resident partner, Trowers and Hamlins, after I saw one of Mr. Edmondes's impressive articles in English in a local business law publication. Mr. Edmondes described the Trowers and Hammonds network, whose headquarters were in London with some 350 lawyers, the fiftieth largest law firm in London, which had a longstanding relationship with the Gulf States. With respect to the College of Law and Sharia, Edmondes believed that it was a big mistake to try to combine the two systems, and he regretted that the school did not accept his invitation to provide lectures. On the other hand, Edmondes was upbeat about the accomplishments to date in the legal field. He said the rule of law in Oman was "reasonably well followed."

On Tuesday, February 2, the team met with His Excellency Sheikh Hamoud al-Harthy, president of the majlis. His Excellency served for six years as minister of justice and had been associated with legal and judicial reform from the beginning. He referred to the College of Law and Sharia as "his baby." Although competent in English, His Excellency conversed mainly in Arabic through Tarik Riad in order for his assistants to follow and record the discussions. Sheikh al-Harthy was the uncle of Said al-Harthy, my personal aide, interpreter, and kindred spirit throughout all our meetings and during my lengthy private travels across Oman. The al-Harthys were a rich, powerful tribe with much clout throughout Oman going back generations.

His Excellency said that our visit came at the right time since both the Majlis al-Dawla and Majlis al-Shura needed legal training, given their enlarged legislative roles. He emphasized that Omani officials needed to be aware of new ideas, especially practical ones. With respect to the judicial reform then under review, he expected the system to be totally in place within the year 2000. He wanted to take personal responsibility for the training workshop to be conducted at the law school.

On Wednesday, February 3, we met again with Sheikh Zahir al-Hinai to brief him on the outcome of our meetings with all the various Omani officials that we'd met and to discuss overall impressions and share ideas for future training both in Oman and in the US. Applauding the Basic Law, I assured Sheikh Zahir that he should not be discouraged if the implementing legislation in the area of criminal law took more than the two years they had planned, emphasizing that they were essentially creating a complete modern legal system from scratch. I again strongly advocated having official bilingual translations of all relevant laws and codes, explaining that this could be done effectively only by having a team of two bilingual translators: one with mother tongue Arabic, the other with mother tongue English. Sheikh Zahir indicated that the new Judicial Training Institute would be located in Nizwa, the old capital of the interior region, rather than in Muscat on the coast. He confirmed plans to have the Institute in operation by June 2001 in time for the first graduating class of the Law College. Finally, he thanked the mission for its visit and graciously presented beautiful, intricately worked silver kanjar daggers and big pots of halwa to each team member. The dagger now has a special place of honor in my library alongside Caucasian daggers from the Republic of Georgia and Java, Indonesia. I ate too much of the halwa, which is as addictive as it is fattening.

There was one other aspect of my Omani time I have to mention. Ed Rafeedie, the US district judge from Los Angeles, was my partner on our "teaching team." Ed was, by his own description, America's most unusual federal judge. Born in the US of Arab parents from Palestine, he grew up working full time in his father's carnival, serving as everything from general roustabout fixing mechanical rides to a barker, or pitchman, luring "marks." Ed's father died when Ed was still a teenager, and he had to take over the carnival business. He had no time to consider going to college till the business survived when he was in his mid-thirties. Finally getting a chance for education, Ed thrived. "John," he told me, "it was like I was born again. I devoured every book on every subject. As soon as I finished college, I headed straight for law school. When I graduated, I ran for a state judgeship, never having practiced law for a day." Having gotten quite a little fame for handling the sensational, highly publicized lawsuit over the contested will of Groucho Marx (children vs. young wife), before he knew it, California's highly independent Senator Hayakawa had appointed Ed a federal district judge, our country's first Palestinian to be so honored. "You are now dining with the only *carnie* ever to become a US federal judge."

Ed also knew his stuff in many other ways. His house in Los Angeles had recently been featured in *Architectural Digest*, and he was under orders from his wife to bring back some interesting items for their home. At the Kashmir shop at the Hyatt Regency, I showed Ed some incomparable silk carpets, which I went by to admire nearly every day. The shop owners could tell I could never afford one and were delighted when I brought them Ed Rafeedie. He bought several. Needless to say, I could not get enough of Ed Rafeedie and his stories of life running a carnival. He had insights into human nature and gullibility you could never obtain in any other forum. We dined together many times, including at the Al Bustan Palace. He was truly an unforgettable character, a real, old-time American original, and greatly enriched my time in Oman, on top of all its other wonders.

On Wednesday, February 3, our team had a closing meeting with Ambassador Craig to brief him and his staff on our mission outcomes. We described our many positive meetings of the past week, emphasizing our enthusiastic receptions and how the entire fellowship program under the USAID grant seemed to be fully subscribed and that there was very positive acceptance of all our workshop offers. The ambassador expressed great satisfaction with the mission's accomplishments, noting that similar missions in the future would be an important way to reach key Omani officials. We promised to send to the embassy, within thirty days, a completed mission assessment report, which was coordinated by Mike Hager with contributions by all members. I personally wrote the criminal law sections and reports proposing future programs for return visits.

SEEKING JUSTICE IN THE ANCIENT
KINGDOM OF MOROCCO (2000)

I met first with Regional Security Officer Nanette Krieger, a veteran of over twenty years with the State Department, who had previously served in intelligence with the US Army and had been *everywhere*. She had a very realistic and hardnosed view of the possibilities of US nationals attempting to teach our system to a culture as different as that of Morocco. She had many insights into the Moroccan situation which could only be gained by experience. Then I met with Richard Johnson, the economic counselor, an intense, fast-talking officer who also had a strong interest in accomplishing *something* for the US in Morocco. He peppered me with questions about my experience in prosecuting US corruption cases and my prior experience with other Muslim and francophone countries and judicial systems. At first skeptical, once he began to see that there were possibilities for the mission, Johnson remained cautious but a little more enthusiastic. About twenty minutes into our discussion he turned positive. By the end of our discussion, he was giving me lists of items he wanted to learn from Moroccan prosecutors and investigating magistrates. His questions were well focused and covered a broad range of possible corruption. He volunteered to attend my seminars, even though he was already attending a concurrent seminar taught by two Americans to other Moroccan officials in the area of commercial law. It seemed at the outset that the post was more interested in commercial goals than in encouraging the combat against corruption because of the belief that corruption was too much a part of the Moroccan way of life to hope to alter. During our discussions, however, the view emerged that the Moroccan commercial system itself could not be made viable for foreign investment without serious anticorruption reforms.

Ms. Krieger next introduced me to Robert Holley, the political counselor. A longhaired, former helicopter pilot in Vietnam, Holley spoke fluent French and was married to a French wife from Bordeaux, where he had been US consul. At first he was even more negative than Johnson, but we hit it off well on a personal level from our interests in wine, food, and other things French, and he began bombarding me in a friendly way with unfriendly questions about why I thought there was any hope to reform corruption in a society like that of Morocco. He too seemed at first to think that corruption in Morocco was hopelessly endemic and that raising false hopes did more harm than good. Later in the conversation he indicated he thought it was nevertheless worth at least a try and agreed to support the mission. He expressed special interest in financial institution fraud in Morocco as the place to start and in the profound problem of election fraud. Little did I suspect then how much experience the world would be having with the American Bush-Gore presidential election contests the following month. What a seminar for them. At least we showed our national habits of patience and faith in our institutions.

Sunday: At the Ministry of Justice

We next met with M'hamed Drissi, the elderly director of administration for the Moroccan Ministry of Justice. Mr. Drissi was lively, positive, and surprisingly optimistic about the practical potential of the seminars. His French was excellent. Although not himself a lawyer, he seemed to be one of the core people close to the minister who held a position of considerable trust in the administration. He suggested that we needed written materials for the Moroccans because it had been decided for reasons of cost to invite only prosecutors and judges serving in Rabat and to distribute transcripts of the seminar to all other prosecutors and examining magistrates across the country.

Monday: Meeting with the Chief Prosecutor

We met with Ms. Krieger and Mr. Ghazali at his handsome office in the Justice Ministry. He introduced us to Mr. Mohamed Mosleh [MOSE-lay], inspector general, as well as Mr. Abdellah Hammoud, chief prosecutor of the Moroccan Supreme Court, who was currently serving as prosecutor general of the Special Court of Justice (more about that interesting court later). It was a very formal meeting, with Mr. Ghazali first giving a highly organized, Sorbonne-style lecture in elegant French from carefully written notes. All three gentlemen were dressed in expensive, double-breasted Parisian suits. I was turned out in an old summer poplin number with shiny elbows. Maybe it made them more comfortable. Mr. Ghazali stressed that these men were his most trusted advisors and that he wanted me to be candid with them. He stressed that he wanted only what I thought was useful and practical.

Mr. Mosleh then spoke in a much more conversational way. It was apparent that he was someone of real authority and trusted by both the minister and even the young King Mohamed himself. He handed me a list of all the persons nominated to attend the seminar with detailed resumés. It was apparent these were all senior officials. I wondered at first if they were too much part of the old regime. Subsequent experience showed me the contrary. All were mature but by no means set in ways which tolerated corruption. All had been handpicked for their experience and good reputations. Mr. Mosleh and I had several pleasant interchanges during which it became apparent that we could work comfortably together. He asked for my views on whom we should meet with preliminarily for informal exchanges of views about what topics should be covered at the formal seminar on September 29–30. I began to be more optimistic about the prospects. The chief prosecutor, Mr. Hammoud, then spoke. He was very impressive. He expressed enthusiastic support for the mission and asked in particular for "bad experiences" I had had, and asked that they not be "seminarized" too formally, but that we speak frankly together as "brother prosecutors."

At the conclusion of the meeting, Mr. Ghazali indicated that the reason more prosecutors from other regions of the country had not been invited was a mixture of cost and convenience. He felt that the group would be too large to interact effectively if we had more than thirty or so. He indicated the Ministry of Justice planned to use transcripts of the seminars and my written materials (not yet in existence) as a sort of train-the-trainers operation, a practice I have never personally favored. I did agree with him about the size of the group, however. All stressed that they wanted a more American-style informal seminar with plenty of give-and-take.

In the afternoon we met with the owner of the translation/interpretation company, a colorful character named Abdelmajid Tamer. He had the schmoozy demeanor of a born entrepreneur. Mr. Tamer insisted I present him immediately with plenty of written materials to translate and proposed to bill us accordingly. Mr. Drissi persuaded us that written materials really were customary and expected for this type of seminar. It was at that point that I frantically called DOJ for copies of such papers, including my own from the DOJ corruption manual. Mr. Tamer and I later adjourned to the bar for some adult beverages and settled our differences over money.

Tuesday: The Inspector General

Nanette and I met for over three and a half hours with Inspector General Mosleh and six members of his staff who were to attend the seminar. While the meeting was in progress, an investigating magistrate with the Special Court of Justice joined us. Three of the inspectors were articulate in French and asked dozens of thoughtful questions. I suggested investigative and prosecutorial techniques that were used in the United States and that I had personally used and found to be effective in corruption cases. They gave me considerable feedback on which topics they thought would be good to discuss before the entire group.

After traditional cups of mint tea, we adjourned to meet with another group the following morning. Ms. Krieger and I realized from this meeting that a major reason the number of participants had been limited was that only a small minority of the magistrates speak French well enough to discuss legal topics. Most of them understand everyday French, but because all court proceedings are conducted in Arabic, most of them are uncomfortable asking legal questions or offering suggestions in anything but Arabic. On occasion they would start a question, then turn to one of the more fluent French speakers to phrase it for them. It worked well in a small group sitting around a table, but with fifty or sixty participants, it would not have worked well at all.

Wednesday: The DCM

Met again with Mr. Mosleh in his office with a second group of six or seven prosecutors and judges. After the meeting, while going over my notes at the embassy, the ambassador came in to ask Nanette Krieger a question. I introduced myself and we chatted in the outer office about my job and my background. When I told the ambassador why I was there, it was clear he was totally unaware that such a seminar was being conducted. For the first time in my many experiences with the State Department, there was neither a meeting nor a briefing with the ambassador either upon my entry or my exit. My meeting with the DCM, however, was more than a good substitute. It was a classic example of a purely political ambassadorial appointment.

Thursday: The Special Court of Justice

Per my specific request of Mr. Mosleh, we were taken to the Special Court of Justice to watch a trial. Since the court had no prior notice of our coming, it was clear that the trial we watched had not been preselected or arranged, which was very fortunate for us. The Moroccan Penal Code had specific, clear and transparent laws outlining corruption. Taking Section 248 as an example, it states, "Whoever, being a public official, solicits or accepts or agrees to accept offers or promises of gifts, presents, or other advantages to perform or abstain from performing an official act shall be guilty of corruption and shall be punished by imprisonment for not less than two nor more than five years and a fine from 250 to 5,000 dirhams [10 dirhams = $1]. Those convicted are automatically removed from office and barred from office for a period of years."

By special decree of the king dated October 6, 1972, the Special Court of Justice was created to hear all crimes of "fraud, corruption, influence peddling, and embezzlement by public officials." Pursuant to the decree, the Special Court of Justice consisted of five judges instead of the usual three. All of the judges, as well as the prosecutors, were personally selected by the minister of justice from among the most experienced and best qualified of the senior magistrates. Most came from the Supreme Court itself. There was no appeal from the Special Court of Justice.

The most controversial provision of the Special Court is the power of the presiding judge to order trials to be *in camera*, i.e, private and closed (*huis clos*). When I interviewed various magistrates who have served on the court, some told me that the courtroom was in fact never really closed; others told me it was closed in only about half the cases. One prominent news editor was quoted as urging the abolition of the court because its "closed court" provision made it too much like a military court and also because it had proved too slow.

The trial we were to observe began promptly at 10:00 a.m. The courtroom, laid out in the traditional French style, had the five judges seated at a beautiful carved and curved oak bench. To the right was a *greffier*, or clerk, who wrote out a summary of the proceedings, as in a French trial. There was no verbatim word-for-word transcript as in the US. This case was unusual in that the primary witnesses, the victims, spoke only French, whereas the judges and clerk spoke mainly Arabic with a little French. The judges wore black robes with green sashes while the attorneys had white sashes. There were palm trees outside the open windows, reminding me again we were not in Kansas. The prosecutor, Mr. Jamel Sarhane of Casablanca, had participated in our preliminary meetings. He occupied a separate desk above us on our left, on the same level as the judges. Moroccans, like the French, call prosecutors "standing judges." Mr. Sarhane was vigorous and outspoken.

The case, a complicated one dating back to 1971, was an excellent illustration of the problems with the system. It was first tried in a regular court, then transferred a decade later to the Special Court. It concerned the theft of two valuable villas in Casablanca. They had belonged to French citizens before Morocco obtained its freedom from the French protectorate. In the ensuing disorder a Moroccan had apparently forged false deeds at the courthouse claiming to transfer ownership of the properties from the French owners to the Moroccan defendant. At some point in the earlier proceedings, it was realized that the deal could not have happened without the assistance of corrupt public officials and only then was it transferred to the Special Court, causing the case to start all over. In two earlier trials the officials were convicted of corruption and sentenced to two years in prison. One was serving his time and the other was still a fugitive. Neither was to be called as a witness.

As in every system inherited from the French, a multitude of small, detailed rules caused things to proceed with painful slowness. Court was to be conducted solely in Arabic, but since the victim and his key witness spoke no Arabic, and there was no interpreting service available, a Moroccan prosecutor with good French skills was drafted to try to interpret. After thirty minutes of attempts to interpret every question and answer as we would do, the presiding judge, who obviously understood French very well, finally just started using only French. The other four judges joined in. This was troublesome for the clerk, who knew no French, and people seemed to keep forgetting all about him in the heat of the questioning

Without further detailing the trial, suffice it to say that the French rules of procedure, with constant overlays of Arabic traditions, caused things to go really slowly. Since there was no marshal attached to the court, several witnesses did not appear. According to the prosecutor, who was excellent, it was the duty of the police to have the witnesses present. Since the questioning was to be conducted entirely by the presiding judge, and there are no adversary duties on the prosecutor and defense counsel to produce witnesses, trials tend frequently to be continued due to missing witnesses.

The accused, dressed in an expensive dark blue suit, had formerly been in prison awaiting trial, but had been released when he claimed he was sick from being in prison. Then for *four* years he could not be located. He was an exceedingly ugly little man with a remarkable resemblance to the former General Noriega of Panama. He was arrogant and aggressive and by no means intimidated by the proceedings. He tried to produce "new" and questionable copies of the deeds to the properties, which the prosecutor persuaded the presiding judge to exclude on the ground that the file was "closed." The third witness for the prosecution did not appear. It was represented that he had been in hiding for the past two years. A lengthy argument ensued with the court asking, of all people, both the victim and the accused, not the lawyers, which law *they* thought should apply to transfers of property of French persons who had juvenile children with possible rights to the property under French law. That legal issue had not been foreseen or briefed. This court session concluded when it was announced that they would have to wait for translations of the French documents to be prepared and for the other witnesses to be found. For the victim, it was obviously not encouraging, since he had paid his own way once again from France to attend yet another legal proceeding. Trial was to continue on November 21, 2000.

The positive side of the trial was that it seemed to be open, the prosecutor and judges were working seriously toward a just result, and fair play seemed *intended,* although not achieved. The accused was certainly not intimidated or abused. On the other hand, a ponderous procedural apparatus frustrated all real progress in the case, aggravated especially by the language problems. On balance, I was encouraged only by the desire for justice exhibited by the participants despite the chaotic methods of proceeding. Although this case was not one in which politics were in any way involved, it seemed clear that Morocco had the personnel and means to support an effective system of criminal justice to combat corruption if only its ways of trying cases could be made much more practical and efficient.

In the lobby of the Hotel Latour Hassan I ran into American Sandra Shuster, who was organizing another embassy-sponsored seminar on business law. It had been scheduled on the same days as mine, causing conflicts for the only available competent interpreters. It appeared to me that we Americans were as disorganized as the Moroccans.

Friday: Dinner with a Famous Andalou

This day was spent preparing my lectures for the next two days of seminars, which were moved back to September 30 and October 1 to avoid conflicts with the American commercial seminars. There was a rumor earlier in the week that we would be invited to dinner in the home of the Deputy Attorney General Ghazali, but I had heard no more about it. As I prepared to walk out for dinner on my own, I got a call from Nanette Krieger saying we *were* invited to dinner with Mr. Ghazali that very evening. Fortunately, I was already dressed. When we arrived at Mr. Ghazali's house, we all learned to our great surprise that there was yet a *third* program being presented simultaneously by a retired judge of the US Ninth Circuit Court of Appeals, with no knowledge there were two other US seminars going on at the same time.

Before dinner I sat with Mrs. Ghazali, who was one of the famous Andalous from Fez. Popular lore in the books I read on Morocco had it that the most influential group in Moroccan society were the descendants of the Moors who fled the Arab empire in southern Spain when the Christians retook the country. Mrs. Ghazali is an outspoken member of that group. Her father was a judge famous for politically unpopular decisions he made. She was one of the founding members of Transparency Morocco, an organization spearheading the fight against corruption in modern Morocco. She served us, perhaps for emphasis, a *kosher* red wine from Marrakech.

As dinner was being served buffet style, Mr. Ghazali asked me to join him and Richard Johnson on the terrace, where we ate apart from the others. Mr. Ghazali used the familiar "tu" form in addressing Mr. Johnson, indicating familiarity and trust. After ten minutes or so, he began using it with me. Mr. Ghazali convinced me by his remarks that he was sincere about reform. I asked him about the position and influence of Berbers in modern Moroccan society. He could tell my question was sincere, because it was so unsubtle. He chuckled and said that if I had known *he* was Berber he suspected I would have asked it differently. He went on to explain that he had succeeded his father as an important Berber chief in southern Morocco in the Sahara, where his family is influential. He said that credential gave him credibility among urban Arab Moroccans because they must have the loyalty of the rural Berbers, of whom he was one of the premier leaders, however urbane his manner. Mr. Ghazali was clearly a key to our dealings with the Moroccans on corruption.

Saturday: Seminars in French and Arabic

First Seminar

Both seminars were held in the large, ballroom-like conference room of the Ministry of Justice. I was seated between the inspector general and the prosecutor general. We all had microphones and simultaneous translations were conducted from French to Arabic and vice versa. The interpreters were outstanding. When, on occasion, I tried to explain an English legal term in French they were able to translate that as well.

Based upon our earlier informal discussions, we had a good mutual understanding of what topics would be fruitful and which we should avoid. We began with brief opening statements, assuring each other that we were all brother jurists in search of mutual education and improvement. The Moroccans were interested in establishing a system of written financial disclosures and in using administrative discipline before criminal sanctions. We moved quickly to tracing money. Morocco had provisions for audits, but nothing as effective as our FDIC and bank examiners. When I explained to them how we subpoenaed bank records, they seemed surprised at our power and at the organization of our financial institutions. They liked the idea of Currency Transaction Reports, apparently having nothing of the kind. When I explained to them about FINCEN (our centralized national Financial Information Center) and how we could obtain elaborate financial background reports on suspects, they were definitely interested in how to establish such a service, although they also expressed reservations over how such an institution might be abused in their country by one political faction against another. A seminar on investigating and prosecuting bank fraud by officers would be much welcomed by the Moroccans. Election fraud is still too controversial and sensitive to be approached by foreigners. And frankly, we don't seem to be very good at that ourselves.

These discussions led to questions about how anticorruption campaigns in Morocco tended to be mainly used to embarrass political opponents. Although we did not discuss it at length in the open sessions, I was amazed at how Morocco's relatively free press abused its freedom by printing false and scandalous attacks against political opponents. One of the judges said, "Freedom of the press is freedom to lie." When I asked them how this situation came about, they explained that there are truly no "independent" papers in Morocco in our sense. Each paper represents some party or interest group, whose object is not to print objective truth but to obtain political and economic advantage for its allies. This situation is very reminiscent of America in its earliest days, as reflected in Ben Franklin's description of journalists in his day as "infamous scribblers." Morocco clearly has more press freedom than Tunisia, but the results were disappointing to me.

As always in dealing with lawyers in other countries, they could not resist contrasting some of our institutions, which they were familiar with from CNN, with their own. They were especially intrigued with plea bargaining, witness protection, wiretaps, and undercover agents, all of which were mostly forbidden in their system as in most continental systems. When I described to them how plea bargains were in writing and could be rejected by the court, they were a little more receptive. When they realized that we had to present a sworn factual summary of our evidence at the time of the plea, they seemed even more receptive. The Moroccans did not seem to like the idea of witness immunity; it was always a hard sell to someone from a system with no Fifth Amendment where all witnesses could be forced to testify, even defendants.

When I told them about state and local Crime Stoppers programs, they seemed puzzled and did not think it was needed. They confirmed the rumor I had heard to the effect that most everybody informed about most everything in Morocco, and they volunteered that they wouldn't be surprised if a full one-third of Moroccans had at one time or another acted as informants for the police. They said it was simply part of the culture and no payment was expected. They also told me frankly that this program made them uneasy and caused the police to be mistrusted. They felt they already had "crime stoppers" enough for now, and if money was offered, informants would probably *invent* their tips.

Sunday: An Attack of Laryngitis

Second Seminar

After totally losing my voice to laryngitis at the end of the first day, the inspector general introduced me on the second morning by saying he hoped "no one would say that the speaker was afraid of *speaking out* against corruption." The questions moved to the *causes* of corruption as a way of identifying and uncovering corruption. While not technically the focus of the seminar, these questions showed sincerity in fighting the problems by identifying them. The judges deplored a tendency of Moroccans, especially in cities, to small-time extortion of a kind I had personally witnessed, i.e., when you park your car on the street, men ask you for money to "guard" it. If you refuse to pay, it is obvious they will harm your vehicle. I told them of the "broken window" theory enforced successfully in New York City which stressed attacking low-level criminality as a basis for reforming corruption. The participants agreed, some having heard of this practice on the news.

I had planned to spend at least a third of the second day's seminar on using the press to expose corruption and gain the support of the population, which had been critical to us in the United States. The Moroccans, almost unanimously, felt the press could not be counted on to help them. Although there was considerable press freedom, there appeared to be great sensationalism and little responsibility. From what they said and what I saw, the press tended to be so biased and inflammatory that the Moroccans had little to no faith in it. At the conclusion of the second seminar, the inspector general immediately appointed a three-person committee to report to Mr. Mosleh on what type of follow-up the group wanted in future seminars. They agreed unanimously that they wanted future seminars.

Monday: Dinner at Dinjarat Restaurant to Discuss the New King

That evening, by appointment from the previous day, Mr. Mosleh picked me up at my hotel. He apologized for not inviting me to his home in Sale [SAH-lay], across the colorfully named Bou Regreg River, but it was late and his wife was ill. By Arab standards of hospitality, this was a friendly invitation indicating trust beyond mere professional courtesy. Mr. Mosleh drove me to the home of Mohamed Moatassime, an old and close friend of his and a member of the constitutional court. He is also of Berber origin, like Mr. Mosleh. We drove to the beautiful and intimate Dinarjat Restaurant, a local favorite. After a couple of hours of interesting discussions and lots of Moroccan wine, Mr. Mosleh drove me back to the hotel.

During the drive home, Mr. Mosleh began to volunteer quite a bit of in-depth insight into the current corruption situation in the country. He talked of his close personal relationship with the new king. It was apparent that he wanted me to know these things, a sign of trust and that he thought we needed to know these facts in order to work with the Moroccans. Mr. Mosleh described how the old king was very selfish in his old age and cared little for the people. He made it clear that the existing corruption had grown because the old king was perceived not to care about it. Clearest evidence of this attitude is the enormous Versailles-like mosque that King Hassan had built to honor himself in Casablanca, as well as his celebrated appearance on national television to dedicate it dressed all in white like the Mahdi.

Mr. Mosleh stressed how different the young King Mohammed is from his father. He also volunteered several things I had not heard. The first was that the old king favored his younger son, and had not spoken for a long time to his older son, the new king. He stressed how the new king received his legal education in Nice, France, and how he had a much more modern and activist view of corruption than his father. He continued in a personal vein about how the king and the minister had insisted that he stay on past his retirement date. He seemed to be, like Mr. Ghazali, exactly the sort of person we could work with in being of assistance to his country in this area. Apparently the king and the current ambassador get along well together.

Tuesday: Departure

After a hearty lunch, for once alone, I departed for Paris and home.

EXPLORING THE EXOTIC REPUBLIC OF INDONESIA: FROM JAVA TO THE ISLAND PARADISE OF BALI (2002)

The purpose of my mission to Indonesia was set forth in a memo from OPDAT director Carl Alexandre, a native of Haiti, who requested that upon our return we would report in depth on our experiences and impressions and offer insights for developing further programs. The team consisted of US District Judge Helen Gillmer of Hawaii, Adolfo Trevino of the clerk's office in Miami and myself.

The team met in Washington with Michele Crawford and other OPDAT officials for briefings, including (1) the confusing Indonesian legal systems; (2) summaries of ancient and modern Indonesian history; (3) a 2002 Human Rights Watch report on Islamic militants in Banda Aceh [AH-chay], the northwest corner of the westernmost island of Sumatra, near Malaysia, where separatist violence was occurring; and (4) the violent attempted secession of Catholic East Timor from the rest of Islamic Indonesia. In an unusual historic event, Aceh would soon bear the brunt of an enormous tsunami tidal wave in 2004, which would wipe out both the entire town of Banda and much of the province of Aceh as well. It was said by some to be, in that sense at least, a real *political* storm.

Our team met at the State Department with the Indonesia desk officer, who gave one of the most cogent briefings in my long experience of these missions. He noted how each of the last three Indonesian presidents: Soeharto, Habibie, and Wahid, was removed from office and replaced by his vice president. The current president, Mrs. Megawati Sukarnoputri, daughter of the first Indonesian president, was popular with Indonesians generally, but was married to a businessman regarded as utterly corrupt. Having only a high school education, she was perceived as incapable of running a large, diverse, and fractious country with a long tradition of political corruption. Her vice president, Hamza Haz, had been politicking to obtain the support of Islamist militants; some feared he would defeat her in the next election, a potential disaster for the United States. Typical of Hamza's statements was his comment that the

September 11 bombing of the World Trade Center might "cleanse America of its sins."

The desk officer gave us a good picture of the complexities of the current situation. After nearly four hundred years of Dutch Colonial rule, Indonesia only obtained its independence in 1947. Until 1998, it was a relatively stable society considering its diversity and huge population, fourth largest in the world. In that fifty-year period, it had only two "leaders": its first president, Sukarno, and its second, General Soeharto, who replaced Sukarno following the bloody suppression of a Communist coup attempt in 1965.

On the positive side, Indonesia had made great progress in modernizing, remaining intact, and developing a common language, called Bahasa, a sort of lingua franca spoken throughout the country. Bahasa has no past or future tenses and makes liberal use of foreign words, e.g., commission in Bahasa is "comisi," corruption is "corupsi," and to express agreement with someone, you simply say "sama-sama" or "same-same," meaning "it's all the same to me." They gave me a two-week crash course in it at the Schultz Foreign Service Training Center in Virginia. It is one of the few easy languages I can ever recall encountering.

Indonesia was basically a rich country full of poor people. Its resources were enormous, being blessed with ample oil, rich farm land, multiple minerals, and a climate suitable for all types of agriculture. Its problems were equal to its riches: a tradition of passivity in the face of aggression, rampant endemic corruption, and a sort of passive-aggressive mentality where people would endure all manner of abuse, then suddenly rise up and violently overthrow their abusers. The situation at the time of our visit seemed particularly muddled. Since independence in 1947, the country had basically been ruled through the army by two strongmen, Sukarno and Soeharto, both in the tradition of feudal Javanese princes. The recent yearly turnover of leadership was new and troubling. There were also pockets of radical Islam being fueled by *pensantren*, Islamist seminary schools similar to the *madrasahs* that had wrought havoc elsewhere in the Islamic world from North Africa to Pakistan.

Our mission, to assist in discouraging corruption by introducing standards of professional conduct, budgetary accountability, and professionalism in the civil service, was thus a considerable one. Given the fact that Indonesians generally believed their government to be totally *founded* on corruption, it was hard to convince them (and even ourselves) that the police and judiciary could do it. The real disaster came with Soeharto, who permitted his children, siblings, cousins, and in-laws to take over nearly every major government agency and private organization in the country. As a result, there was almost no institution in Indonesia which had enough honest public servants to act as a base for an effective campaign against corruption. Nevertheless, Indonesians said they were looking for an "island of incorruptibility" as a base to attack the corruption, nepotism, and cronyism that were the legacy of Soeharto.

An example of the problems was the unique budgetary process of Indonesia. Tax collection was spotty at best and came nowhere near financing the operations of government, particularly the salaries of public employees. Every agency from the Ministry of Justice to the army was financed mainly by "private donations" from individuals, companies, and interest groups. It was as if the US government were financed entirely by lobbyists. Without gratuities, public employees could not possibly live on their salaries. An audit by the *Straits Times* newspaper of Singapore estimated that 60 percent of the budget of the Indonesian Attorney General's Office came from private "donations" from businessmen. Under such circumstances, it was hard to conceive of fair and independent prosecutions of corruption by such an office.

On the positive side, Indonesia has a very free press, which articulately criticized corruption problems and called loudly for reform. The biggest problem appeared to be deciding where to start. As Archimedes said, you cannot move the earth unless you have a place to stand and put your lever. I told them this anecdote, which they thought accurately described their plight. The failed presidencies of Habibie and Wahid both promised reform, and many young law graduates joined prosecutors' offices hoping to clean up the mess. From 1998 to 2002, however, little seemed to have been accomplished and the anecdotal evidence was that most honest prosecutors and judges had given up and were seeking other careers.

Before this background, we began our series of meetings with embassy personnel, nongovernmental organizations (NGOs), and the Indonesian Commission to Audit the Wealth of Public Servants, popularly known by its Bahasa acronym KPKPN [KAH-pay KAH-pay ENN-nay]. Since most Bahasa verbs and nouns come from lengthy Malay words, nearly every institution and company in the country was referred to by its initials in the form of easily pronounced acronyms like KPKPN.

2:00 p.m. to 4:30 p.m.

In what was described as an "orientation to the KPKPN" at its headquarters near the American Embassy, the team found ourselves on the dais with the chairman and a Mr. Chairul Imam facing a large hall that included every member of the KPKPN save one who was ill. We were asked to make brief opening statements as to our backgrounds and experience, and each commission member did likewise. They were a fascinating group, representing all major islands and ethnic groups of Indonesia. In addition to the chairman, who was Sundanese from West Java, I spoke personally with former prosecutor Imam from the island of Madura; a prosecutor from Jakarta; an attorney from Sumatra, who was also a two-star police general; the chief corruption prosecutor, who is from Bali, and his best friend, a fluent English speaker who was head of enforcement for the Indonesian IRS; the vice president of the National Buddhist Organization, another fluent English speaker who was chairman of the Council of Christian Intellectuals; a Polynesian attorney from Ambon in the Moluccas (formerly the Spice Islands); a lady bank examiner in full Islamic garb minus the veil; a former UN peacekeeper in Cambodia who spent two years at the University of San Francisco; and the head of the Indonesian Planning Bureau, whatever that was. I could go on, but you get the idea of the quality and diversity of the group.

The discussions were lively, enthusiastic, and almost entirely in English. It was evident that the people in Indonesia most interested in reform and most capable of taking effective action to achieve it were those who had visited the West, particularly the United States. It was not just a matter of language but of exposure to a different culture, where corruption was not the norm. During breaks and at the conclusion of our scheduled meetings, many informal side conversations were taking place, with both the Indonesians and our team reluctant for the interchanges to end.

Thursday, June 13, 2002, 9:30 a.m. to 12:15 p.m.

I spoke on how we uncovered and investigated public corruption in the US and how our investigators and prosecutors have learned to work together. Trying to help the participants adapt our procedures to Indonesian culture, I gave them a Top Ten list of points to consider:

First, choose carefully your defendants, selecting people already thoroughly disliked who did something that everyone agreed was totally corrupt and wrong. They should be defendants who have little chance of claiming they are being prosecuted for political reasons.

Second, choose assistant prosecutors who are young enough to be uncorrupted but experienced enough to handle such challenging cases. KPKPN representatives should meet with prosecutors privately, away from their offices, and keep the matter secret as long as possible. The members who make the presentations to the prosecutors should be those with enough experience in their own backgrounds to gain the confidence of the prosecutors.

Third, the same method should be used by choosing police officers to work with the prosecutors who have already worked with those prosecutors, and at the very least should be energetic, courageous, and experienced enough to handle the case, but not old enough to be part of the corrupt old regime.

Fourth, the KPKNP should begin immediately developing positive social relations with key supervisors and decision makers in the Attorney General's Office.

Not wanting to be too lengthy, I nevertheless gave them five more key ideas:

Fifth, pick a handful of only the best cases first. Do not try to convict everyone at once.

Sixth, members of KPKPN with appropriate experience should be assigned to develop close ties with key members of the press, both written and radio and T.V., and get to know them well enough to form relationships of mutual trust and confidence because the press is an essential tool and a source of true information as well as a powerful ally in fighting corruption by exposing it and demanding action from public officials.

Seventh, informal investigation can often be more effective than formal. Don't try to overstretch your powers; always use a friendly approach first. Enemies, while not reliable, often are excellent sources for *leads* to evidence, and ex-girlfriends and ex-wives know more than anyone about an opponent's weaknesses.

Eighth, always see a corruption case from many perspectives at once: What will the man on the street think? How will parliament feel? Will this make the president or others look like honest reformers, in which case you will get their support, or will it make them look like the prosecutions are a political vendetta, which could cost the prosecutors their jobs? Putting it in Mississippi terms, as the Choctaws say, always try to "walk in the moccasins of your prey."

Ninth, coming from a state that is 38 percent African American, I explained to them how critical it is to recognize ethnic feelings and that I assumed that the same applied in Indonesia, considering some of the comments I had already heard made by Javanese and Sumatrans about each other. The audience howled at this comment, obviously being familiar with the same problems we both face.

Tenth, and last, I suggested that the approach should always be *positive* and appeal to Indonesian pride in their long and noble history rather than looking at things negatively as if rooting out corruption were an embarrassment. I told them how Mississippi officers would sometimes tell us that we were embarrassing the police and making them all look bad when we prosecuted one for corruption, and how I explained we were just removing a few "bad apples" from an otherwise good barrel. They liked the comparison. I had to explain constantly to the press that corrupt officers were hopefully the exception and that the officers working to fight corruption in their ranks should be commended, not criticized.

In response to questions suggesting that corruption in the US was easier to fight than in Indonesia because it almost never existed in our *federal* judiciary or *federal* government, I outlined the successful prosecution of former Federal Judge Walter Nixon of Mississippi for corruption and the impeachment of Federal Judge Alcee Hastings of Florida for taking bribes from drug dealers (and, sadly, of how he was then elected to Congress from Miami, where he still served). I mentioned the recent investigations of Presidents Clinton and Reagan and their associates and of how, prior to the resignation of President Nixon for obstructing justice, his vice president, Spiro Agnew, had been convicted of bribery for receiving cigar boxes stuffed with cash from businessmen while in the White House. Our mutual difficulties seemed to reassure them.

I told them of sheriffs and chiefs of police in Mississippi I sent to prison for taking bribes and who then returned from prison and were reelected to offices by the voters. I also explained the ABSCAM investigation, resulting in several US congressmen being sent to prison for receiving bribes in an undercover FBI sting operation. I outlined for them how much more violent was the corruption I had witnessed in Russia than in Indonesia, stressing that Indonesians were not alone in their fight and that human greed and the instinct to steal were universal and would never be abolished, but must be kept under control, which could only be done by leaders like the KPKPN, since the general public in all nations and at all times mostly complained but did little to help.

I took the liberty of using humor and told them a couple of stories about the politician in Boston who said, "People here don't tolerate corruption, they *demand* it," and the two public officials from Mississippi who were caught discussing on an undercover tape what each had done with his half of the hundred thousand dollars they embezzled. One said, "I spent most of it on whiskey and women and just *wasted* the rest."

Without going on too long, I discussed how we had obtained records from such places as Switzerland, despite bank secrecy laws, how we infiltrated and destroyed powerful criminal gangs like the Black Stone Rangers in Chicago, and how we foiled a plot by a state judge in our district to blow up the office of a lawyer he didn't like, and how we try always to protect our witnesses, both formally and informally. I gave them my father's old cautionary quotes from his hero, Confucius, who stressed realism in life, saying, "Eggs should never fight with stones," and "Before you kick a dog, learn his master's name." They seemed to relate to this Eastern view of caution in the pursuit of idealism.

My three presentations on Thursday, each of which took one and one-half hours, were divided into an hour of lecture followed by thirty minutes of questions, which were quite lively, although tiring. The three "rest" breaks were all taken up with crowds of Indonesians asking follow-ups and expressing optimism about their possibilities of making progress.

Mr. Y Made Yasa [EE-MAH-day-YAH-suh], the assistant attorney general from Bali supervising all corruption prosecutors, asked several good questions through his interpreter, making important points to KPKPN members via his questions: (1) his office had recently charged fifty-three public officials with corruption; (2) he needed help because unlike us, he could not subpoena *any* bank records because the president of the National Bank of Indonesia had the legal right to quash all his subpoenas, which he had repeatedly done; (3) Mr. Yasa would personally support efforts by KPKPN to get more authority to gather evidence; (4) he was thwarted from investigating cases by vagueness and contradictions in existing law which must be removed; and (5) he and KPKPN needed enforcement powers to compel public officials to answer questions. Many public officials claimed KPKPN had no effective powers because theirs were all conferred not by statute but by mere regulations. As shown in the illustrations, Mr. Yasa was a photogenic man and would make a good poster boy and role model for corruption prosecutions.

3:15 p.m. to 4:30 p.m.

The chairman opened the floor to questions from all participants to all members of our team. Our main difficulty was in trying to transpose certain legal concepts from the continental system, which the Indonesians inherited from the Dutch, to our Anglo-Saxon system. We had to change one incompetent interpreter, and on occasion it took two or three tries to obtain the correct explanation of a legal term such as the "predication" needed to open an investigation of an American public official versus the power to issue a grand jury subpoena, the quantity of probable cause needed to obtain a search warrant, or the slippery concept of "reasonable doubt" to be applied by juries. These difficulties were overcome, however, and the workshop ended on a high note with the chairman presenting each of us with a blue velvet box containing our own personalized brass KPKPN membership plaque commemorating our roles in the seminar, which now holds a place of special pride in my study at home.

That evening we dined together at the Hilton with great enjoyment. I sat between Mr. Hartoyo of Sumatra and Mr. Hehámahúa of Molucca. We were highly entertained by Mr. Chairul Imam of Madura, an island noted for its storytellers and sense of humor. Chairman Syakir invited us to his office the following morning to say goodbye.

Impressions

My first impression of Indonesia, upon driving in from the Jakarta airport, was of a crowded country that was physically modern. Jakarta could in fact be mistaken at first glance for Houston, Texas. The people looked more Westernized than in most of Islam. At least in Jakarta, I seldom saw women wearing the scarf, or *hijab*. Our meetings were never interrupted by the usual lengthy breaks for prayer and there were few loudspeakers to awaken one for annoying early morning prayers before sunrise. In essence, at least in Jakarta, I observed a fairly secular society.

Nevertheless, the biggest danger I perceived to American interests in Indonesia came from militant Islam. A primary impression one received in Indonesia was of confusion and instability. No one knew who would hold what office tomorrow. There seemed to be much more certainty that, whatever change happened, the corruption and the traditional underlying feudal system would survive. That conclusion included the military, which was likely to take power and control the country if the Islamists did not. Indonesia did not seem to me to be fertile ground for democracy, although a certain kind of rule of law would be acceptable, just not necessarily our Anglo-American one.

A handful of incidents might better explain my conclusions. Early in my stay I saw a young Indonesian woman on the street wearing a long gown with a head scarf. On top of the scarf was a New York Yankees baseball cap. I asked my interpreter from the embassy to ask her about the cap. He returned and said that her mother had recently "gone religious" and forced the daughter to wear the scarf, but "she never told me I could not wear an American cap on top of it."

In a second incident, I thought a couple of young Indonesians were giving me dirty looks across the sidewalk. I asked my interpreter if he would mind asking them, politely, if there was a problem, urging him not to initiate one. He spoke with them for an instant. They immediately began smiling and waving to me, saying "USA" with a "V" sign. The interpreter said they had been giving me dirty looks because they thought I was Australian, and that the Australians had tried to "break up" Indonesia by helping East Timor secede. When they heard I was American, they began expressing support for our soccer team in the World Cup. When I asked my interpreter about that issue, he said, "Oh yes, Indonesians appreciate the respect the Americans are showing the rest of the world by finally fielding a good international soccer team." For some reason I would have supposed the opposite, that they would resent us trying to dominate yet another part of their lives, but throughout my stay in Indonesia, both in Jakarta and in Bali, the Indonesians rooted openly for the American team.

Recommendations for Action

My overall impression was that America and Americans had a generally positive image in Indonesia. Every Indonesian I spoke with either wanted to visit America or to revisit it. Our government, however, was viewed with more of a jaundiced eye and was suspected of meddling for its own interest whenever it felt like it. Having been in the country such a short time, I hesitated to make any confident recommendations, but I did offer these ideas:

(1) We need to send a long-term resident legal advisor to Indonesia. Their culture does not adapt well to superficial visits. Recognizing our budgetary limitations, however, if we send an intermittent legal advisor (ILA) for ninety days as proposed, he/she needs to spend far less time discussing the intricacies of US laws and customs and more time studying Indonesian history, modern and ancient, in order to understand what he/she is dealing with. Several useful books on those subjects are included in the Further Readings section.

In that regard, Nobel-Prize winner V.S. Naipaul's books give the best insight into current Indonesian mindsets. Dutch writers have the best descriptions of the multitude of personalities one will encounter in Indonesian officialdom. Their extreme pessimism about the future is typical of the Dutch, however, who seem to think Indonesia will never survive without them. The famed British administrator Sir Samford Raffles makes valuable comparisons with India and is helpful in seeing Indonesia as the unique place it is, and not just another ex-colony. Professor Schwarz is the easiest to understand regarding the thoroughness of corruption and cronyism in present Indonesian society, as well as the importance the Chinese of Indonesia play in crony capitalism. The importance of traditional hostilities between ethnic Chinese and ethnic Indonesians is best explained by Sukma. Without some background in the local culture and history, an ILA speaking to Indonesians as if to an American audience might as well be speaking to an empty room. The ILA needs to be realistic and flexible.

(2) Indonesians will listen to the voice of experience, but resent proselytizing and readily suspect foreigners are meddling in their affairs. The ILA will always need to work closely with our knowledgeable embassy personnel and its talented interpreters, because if you do not speak the language, they are your only way of becoming acquainted with Indonesians, especially those who count.

(3) It is especially unwise to treat any existing institution in Indonesia as an automatic adversary. Lines of communication and engagement need to be kept open. If nothing else, we can dispel some of the mistaken impressions some Indonesians have of America. This suggestion particularly applies to our negative attitudes to the military and the police. We need Indonesia as an ally for strategic reasons, both during the current terrorist phase and when it has ended and the possible "clash of civilizations" continues.

(4) One of the most important things we could do to improve the judicial system, ethics and accountability in Indonesia would be to sponsor frequent and lengthy international visitor programs to America for carefully selected Indonesians. Nearly every enthusiastic reformer I met had visited or studied in the US.

While our visit to Jakarta was brief and somewhat unsettling as to just how profound the problems are in Indonesia's basic institutions, it was encouraging to see that Indonesians are open to knowing Americans better and adopting into their culture those aspects of ours which they admire and which they feel would make their country better. DOJ should be commended for what it has done so far, and encouraged to do everything possible to cultivate and assist this interesting and vital nation.

On a More Personal Note

I developed in Jakarta, at the Hilton especially, a great love for Indonesian food, notably the complex soups like *buburayan* chicken porridge and *sarapan pagi* noodles, my new favorites for breakfast. Indonesian food was, to me, considerably less spicy than either Thai or Indian. I had tried it in San Francisco with my daughter Lydia at the elegant ethnic Borobodur Restaurant before leaving and knew I'd like it, but had no idea how much. For a good, short introduction to Indonesian cuisine, I recommend "Tableful of Spice," by James Oseland, in the Fall 2002 edition of *Saveur*, founded and edited by my old Paris friend Dorothy Kalins, whose writings on food are always worth seeking out. She now produces books under the name Dorothy Kalins Ink, including three beautiful books about my favorite New Orleans chef, John Besh.

In meetings with Mr. Yasa and his English friend and translator, I learned several new, practical Indonesian proverbs, such as "Wisdom is knowing what to do next." They gave us quite a bit of trouble trying to explain our ideas of what constitutes "proof" let alone truth. Their way of thinking reminded me a lot of the way former President Barack Obama described his own lengthy education in Indonesian ways from his respected Indonesian stepfather during his youth there.

Mr. Yasa explained the five basic Principles of Pancasila [pahn-kah-SEE-lah], a sort of Ten Commandments or mini-constitution of beliefs which all citizens must swear to obey. Primary in the principles: There is only one God. Several religions are accepted, however, including Islam, Catholicism, Dutch Protestantism (basically Lutheran), and, remarkably, Hinduism, despite its hundreds of gods, the Pancasila reasoning that Hindus' only *true* God is

Vishnu. Most notable omission from the five accepted monotheistic religions is Judaism, which they claim, based on the Torah and Old Testament, mentions many gods, thus disqualifying Judaism. This omission is apparently a product of Islamic prejudice as Islam is overwhelmingly the country's main religion.

Before my visit to Bali I'd read two key books on that fascinating, mysterious island. *A House in Bali* by Colin McPhee (2000) is a beautifully written, accessible study I found invaluable. *Island of Bali* by Miguel Covarrubias (1946) is a dense, in-depth study of the intricacies of Balinese culture and history. I was first warned by the cover of the book where his paintings of the women of Bali all looked distinctly African, nothing like Balinese women. An interesting book for serious scholars, but not for the faint-hearted. Upon my return from Bali I discovered the wonderful little volume from Lonely Planet, *The World Food Guide to Indonesia* (2002), which is invaluable in re-creating at home all those Balinese dishes I loved. As for my own house in Bali, each of the twelve bungalows in our compound was named for a different flower, mine for the Camboja. My assigned guide and translator was Pande [PAHN-day], a member of a unique clan of ancient sword-makers for Balinese kings, who hold a special status outside all Hindu castes and thus can go into any village or home. This special flexibility makes them the perfect guides to the island. His name means "Three," as in the Third Son of His Father's third wife, sort of like the old "Number One Son" in old Charlie Chan movies.

At first Pande was always cheerful, guiding me barefoot along raised berms between deep-green rice fields bordered by the balsawood trees, which grow with such speed and to such great heights that they can be harvested every other year. Being nearly as light as paper, logging them is extremely easy. In fact at first, everything about Bali seemed easy. The climate is so mild and moist year round that they basically live out of doors. My own little house was more western, with concrete walls, but my "private" shower was totally outdoors, kept private only by being surrounded by thick walls of bamboo. Most Balinese houses have walls only of palm fronds with roofs of tightly wound palm leaves tied together with strong native vines. Basically the only cost for building a house in Bali is labor, which is usually familial and communal. The materials all being natural and free, in theory housing in Bali should be carefree. The catch, however, is with the land. By tradition it is held by families and almost never sold. That has for years kept out most tacky resorts while welcoming foreign tourists, but it also makes it difficult for young Balinese to obtain land on which to build houses for their families.

After several blissful days in my little bungalow, one morning Pande showed up looking sad. When I asked if he had troubles, he said, "Yes. Money troubles." He then proceeded to explain his situation. To my surprise, he told me he has a degree in civil engineering from Jakarta University but could not get a job in Indonesia because you had to pay a huge bribe there for any job. On Bali he lived well within his little income as a guide, but on Bali they had no need for his kind of engineer. Another problem on Bali was the constant round of festivals, some 210 days out of 365 in a year. For each festival you had to make cash and other donations for the local gods and for festival expenses. Pande now lacked the funds. When I offered him a small sum, he politely refused saying that would be begging. Without paying much attention, I had noticed that the woman who cared for my bungalow left an offering every morning, before I got up, to my house deity, as shown in the illustrations. The woman was a gem who gave me a long hour and a half full-body massage every morning for just five dollars. In the afternoons she scattered aromatic Camboja flower petals (a Balinese kind of orchid) over my bed before I came back. The offerings she left to the deities on a large palm leaf were always pieces of local fruit, nuts, flowers, and an occasional piece of chicken. One day I asked Pande what she did with the offerings when she took them away in the evenings. Were they thrown away? "Oh no, they are given to the poor. The gods eat only the *spirits* of the food, not the substance." Of course. A brilliant spiritual system, I thought.

The Alam Sari Keliki resort, where I stayed throughout my visit, belonged to a New Zealand couple, both school teachers, who commuted by plane to their island paradise with their three children. It seemed to me an ideal existence, despite the commute. They agreed entirely, except for the ten-year wait they had endured to buy the land, needing unanimous approval of all the elders of the local village. It was especially hard because the land was so valuable, being so close to Ubud [OO-BOOD], the unspoiled cultural and artistic capital of Bali. The couple eventually prevailed, largely because, as poor school teachers, they persuaded the local village council that they were not greedy and would protect, and even enhance, the property like a sacred trust. Probably a proper price for paradise.

Everywhere on Bali there are temples to the many gods worshipped there, most of them taken from India with a few changes. My favorite was, and is, Dewi Sriwa [DAY-WEE SREE-wah], goddess of rice and wisdom. I brought home two statues of her, one of teak and the other of "whitewood." I feel they bring me luck. I also brought back a rainstick, a three-foot long hollow piece of bamboo intricately carved and stained. Inside there are dozens of seeds, so that when you shake the stick it makes a soft rattling sound, very similar to a soft Balinese rain falling on a palm-stalk roof. On the top of the rainstick is a smart little turtle, which symbolizes to the Balinese the earth itself. The ancient Balinese pre-Hindu creation myth posited that the earth itself is a giant turtle, as evidenced by its occasional movements and the fact that it obviously has a curved surface. The Indonesians warned me, mostly in jest, not to shake the rainstick too hard or too often or I would bring floods to America. I've been careful about that.

Balinese temples all have beautiful little ponds filled with a variety of colorful pet fish. To enter the temple you should wear a full gown, but Christians like me were allowed to get by with a simple sash around the waist. The walls of the temples are made of beautiful, brownish-orange soft clay bricks dug out of the beds of local rivers. I brought home with me one of those bricks along with a traditional black-and-white-checked prayer cloth, which is placed under Dewi Sriwa and other gods and goddesses to guarantee that the forces of good and evil, black and white, are balanced and thus in harmony during prayers. I still follow that tradition, keeping Dewi and her cloth in front of my big-screen-television table.

Probably the most trying, and ironic, event in the mostly peaceful history of Bali happened on October 12, 2002, just over three months after my visit, when Islamic terrorists bombed a seaside resort on the south side of the island, killing 202 people. I had just been telling everyone in my office, where I was the antiterrorism coordinator, how peaceful Bali was. We've had more terrorists in Mississippi than you would think, as I recounted in my two previous *Guntown* books, not to mention the Ku Klux Klan. But there had been warnings. I already had a file of clippings from the *New York Times* and *Washington Post*, but especially online reports from the BBC, about terrorists trying to infiltrate Indonesia, but almost no one anticipated such acts on peaceful Bali. The terrorists, who laughed and mocked the judges at the Balinese murder trial when prosecutors, led by my friend Y Made Yasa, mentioned at length earlier, asked that they be given the death penalty. I felt pride when the five-judge panel imposed the ultimate penalty. I will not elaborate on them here, but there are excellent accounts of the investigation and trial. One of my favorites, "Back to Bali," was published in the Condé Nast *Traveler* of May 2003, which stressed how foreign travel to Bali, after a brief fall-off, had if anything increased, as Australians (the main victims of the attack) were returning to Bali to show support for the Balinese, who depend so heavily on tourism. The attack certainly did not deter me from wanting to return either.

The most profoundly cynical comment on the bombing, expressed by the unrepentant militant leader and so-called "martyr" Amrozi, was his boast that he was following the teachings of the Holy Koran never to kill innocent Muslims while exterminating *kafirs* [kah-FEERS), or "infidels," because he knew there were virtually no Muslims on the Hindu island. Only local Hindus worked at the beach resort, which was mainly frequented by vacationing Christian Australians, devotees of Bali's famous "high surf" seacoast. The peaceful Balinese do know how to defend themselves, however. Their legal system worked. There have been *no* repeat acts of terror on Bali.

The symbol at the heart of Balinese religious beliefs, which are truly ancient, lies in the sacred mountains, especially the triad of central peaks and, most of all, the "Mother" mountain, the Gunung Agung. The nearby Gunung Batur erupted with great violence in 1963, thus perhaps proving the Balinese belief in its power. It is a firmly established Balinese custom to sleep with your head toward Gunung Batur. My bed was placed that way, and I certainly did not change it. As we were flying away from Bali, our pilot for Indonesia's state airline, Garuda, kindly circled the sacred mountains, and I got some unusually good pictures of their majestic, cloud-capped sides.

The Balinese literally worship their sacred mountains, despite the occasional volcanic eruptions. Mountains to them signify heavenly life and peace. Ironically, although on an island, Balinese fear the ocean and try to avoid it, believing it to be the "realm of death." Perhaps there is some basis for their fear. To the east of Bali is tiny Lombok, where beautiful porcelains are made. All of my bathroom furnishings come from Lombok. Despite this proximity, Bali and Lombok have among the most radically different climates and topographies on earth. Bali is mild, moist, and incredibly green, resembling southern India, for which Indonesia was named by the British. "Nesia" [NEE-zee-yuh] is a modern corruption of the Greek word for "island," thus indicating how all its islands were once settled by Indians. The Muslim takeover of Indonesia was slow and peaceful, entirely by traders from the Middle East rather than by the sword, largely explaining Indonesia's (so-far) peaceful, more moderate version of Islam.

Lombok, on the contrary, is an extremely hot, dry, arid island featuring cactus and plant life more like Australia. Scientists say the reason for this bizarre contrast is an enormous fissure in the earth's crust under the ocean between the two islands, one of the deepest in the world. The Lombok islanders resemble the Balinese in one respect: their tremendous respect for sacred volcanic mountains. One of my favorite treasures from Bali is a beautifully hand-carved teak chest, wide at the bottom and tapering to a point at the top, like the sacred mountains. The islands also share traditions of beautiful, intricate *ikat* weaving, of which I also include here an example.

Two older parts of Balinese culture known worldwide are its famed dances and its unique and mysterious shadow plays. When I was a student at the Sorbonne in Paris, my brilliant theater professor, M. Simon, was a true French chauvinist, in love with French plays and players from the Renaissance to the mid-twentieth century. He also loved the lively physicality of the eighteenth-century Commedia dell'Arte of Italy. But above even France and Italy were the plays he saw performed on a long-ago visit to Bali as a young actor-in-training.

He hardly ever taught one of our weekly classes that whole year without reenacting a little of what he saw on Bali. He praised the brilliant colors of their famed legong dances, generally done by groups of young girls in brightly colored silk costumes and so intricate in their hand movements that young girls older than fifteen no longer have fingers and wrists flexible enough to perform them. He reveled in telling us of the Balinese comedy dances, early LGBTQ pioneers, where big male dancers with lots of lipstick perform pretty daring homosexual courtship rituals. Really.

His highest praise, however, was always saved for the shadow plays, in which puppets reenact the most famous Indian epics like the Ramayana. I was skeptical of his descriptions until I saw those remarkable plays in action myself. So much did I enjoy them that I went back night after night to watch several different ones. I also agreed with M. Simon on the remarkable large-scale, multi-actor dance that acts out a violent war between a group of endangered humans being attacked by a band of big, black monkeys. Just as the humans looked about to be killed, a group of white monkeys (actors painted white with powder) appeared from the shadows to rescue them. The contrasting shouts from the booming, roaring voices of the contending warriors, backed by deep drumming, moved in unison in lively, coordinated waves across the stage, giving me the very chills M. Simon said they would.

No visit to Bali would be complete without witnessing a wonderfully unique insight into the sophisticated Balinese psyche and their strange primitive idea of their ancient and unique history and culture. To a naïve, modern American, it seemed at first decidedly politically incorrect, but I probably lacked proper context. The Balinese did however mention that their large colonies of native orangutans have red hair and pink skin, while their native mountain gorillas have black skin. I just left it there.

Throughout my *Guntown* career as a federal prosecutor, I repeatedly applied to be the RLA (resident US legal advisor) to the US ambassador in Paris. Each time I won the competition and received an offer, but I had to turn the job down because DOJ insisted that after a three-year stint in Paris I would be under contract to work for five full years only in Washington on the French Relations desk. From the department's standpoint, it was perfectly reasonable. For me, however, it was totally impractical. I could not take my children out of their excellent public schools and away from their lifelong friendships. Nor could I ask my wife to give up her hard-won job as a French professor. Also, the cost of living in crowded Jakarta and a long, painful urban commute for me were not exactly selling points for that job either.

Then, in 2004, the Paris job came open one more time. My girls were in college and my wife nearly ready to retire, so I decided to try again. The same live-in-Washington rule was retained, however, and I eventually had to pass once more. Then Michele Crawford, head of the RLA program called: "John, would you do us one small favor? In part due to your suggestion, we are choosing an RLA for Jakarta, but only have four applications and the regulations require five. Would you, with both of us knowing you would not actually *take* the job since the only job you really want is Paris, be the fifth interview, just for purposes of the regulations?" I of course agreed, but that evening when I discussed it with Regan, she reminded me of how much I had loved Indonesia, especially Bali, despite the bombing. I called Michele back and asked if time in Bali would be part of the job. "Of course," she said, "lots of weekend time in Bali; it's a key to Indonesia."

To my amazement, I was offered the job, I accepted, and I went to a scary three-week State Department Academy training school on how to avoid kidnappings, detect car bombs, and practice defensive driving. As mentioned earlier, I even felt pretty good about learning to speak Bahasa after just three weeks. I received my diplomatic passport (with full immunity) and two round-trip tickets for Regan and me to Jakarta.

Then I had long talks with some other AUSAs and DOJ employees who'd taken similar jobs abroad. They explained how the pay somehow came under the State Department, not DOJ, and I'd basically lose three years of my retirement. Others reminded me I'd have to commute by bus an hour and a half each way to the embassy each day in wild Jakarta traffic and would certainly not live in the Hyatt Regency. Nor were trips to Bali so frequent, only three or four times a year and mostly just for weekends. Regan and I reconsidered and decided that Indonesia and Bali would have to come from cookbooks and films like the wonderful *The Year of Living Dangerously* from 1982 with Mel Gibson and Sigourney Weaver, which I still highly recommend as a very accurate depiction of the *feel* of living in Indonesia. For me, for now, Bali is unfortunately just another dream. But life is long, so who knows?

SPECTACULAR GEORGIA, THE MOUNTAIN REPUBLIC IN THE CAUCASUS: LAST STOP ON THE ANCIENT SILK ROAD FROM CHINA

EXCERPTS FROM *THE LORD OF THE PANTHER SKIN*
The National Epic Poem of the Republic of Georgia, by Shota Rustaveli,
Translated by R. H. Stevenson

Gifts remain yours; all else is lost.

Evil is but a shadow that passes; good is enduring.

How sweet it is to look upon beauty; the eye longs to behold what is fair.

She was beautiful as a carpet of Cathay.

She was a friend truer than a sister.

Her words, though few, were each of the worth of ten.

As carefree as boys, like very goats we used to wanton together.

She would tremble like an aspen in the wind.

Then she deserted me for her husband.

My heart was pierced by lances of jealousy and melancholy.

Grief took me over like wine.

I feared to die a stranger in a strange land.

I wished that the shoes of his horse would serve her for earrings.

But the mad must be left to their madness.

And wrath is but a net for sorrows.

One can pour from a pitcher only that which it holds.

Mistaken is the man who does not prepare for troubles at every turn.

Because the sun shines alike on roses and dunghills.

And yet, even in Hell, a little financial consideration can settle most things.

First Mission to the Republic of Georgia, February 2003

February 21, 2003 (Friday)

I arrived in Tblisi on time from Istanbul at 3:05 a.m. in almost total darkness, with lots of helicopters and military aircraft all over the large airfield. It was snowing hard and there were incomprehensible words in the ancient and unique Georgian alphabet written on everything. The airport staff consisted entirely of soldiers, most short and stocky with heavy new fatigue uniforms, caps, and boots. All spoke English. The atmosphere was Russian macho, but more efficient and less menacing. Several of the slimmer soldiers in uniform were attractive Georgian women with almond-shaped eyes. The camo uniforms looked American. Compared to Moscow and Chişinău, the airport was clean, smelled good, and was not at all scary, missing the thugs of Moscow and the Soviet decrepitude of Chişinău. The overall impression was modern, well kept, and Western.

Although I had read several background books about the Caucasus, I had few preformed ideas of what Georgia itself would look like. The airport to the city was lined with snow-covered evergreens reminiscent to me of Flagstaff, Arizona. There were rows of sycamores and hedges, very neat. The road was blacktop, multilane, and smooth. I was accompanied in the hired van by a Thai couple who were in Tblisi to teach computerized banking to the Georgians. My greeter explained in good English that he did not use his real name, Irakli, because it sounded too much like a Turk or an Arab. This was my first exposure to a Georgian. He was twenty-three, planned to go to law school, and volunteered that he intended to be a "private" lawyer because most government employees were corrupt, and one had to be corrupt to work there. This statement surprised me because, in other former Soviet countries I had visited, people never mentioned corruption so candidly. It would not be the last time I heard such comments. We arrived at the hotel at 5:00 a.m.

My schedule provided for a meeting at 10:00 a.m. with Deputy Prosecutor General Giorgi Tvalavadze [tuh-VAH-lah-VAHD-zee] and an afternoon meeting with the prosecutor general's drafting team for the new Law on Prosecutors, written to comply with the standards of the UN and the Council of Europe. As I kept discovering, Georgian names are a little easier to pronounce than they look. Tvalavadze, for example, if taken slowly is simply "tuh-VAH-lah-VAHD-zee." The emphasis is always on the next-to-last syllable, like English. But I also learned that some Americans here gave up and just referred to Georgians by the first letter of their last name as in "Mr. T.," claiming, wrongly I thought, Georgian was too hard to pronounce.

I kept wondering how the utterly different US and European legal systems could be successfully meshed by the Georgians, who were being told what to do in great detail by opinionated parties from Western Europe, Russia, and the US with wildly different views about procedures. I was about to learn: not so well.

Awakened at 8:00 a.m., I was told that a severe form of the flu called "Finnish" flu was spreading across the area. My original assigned driver was sick with it, all schools were closed for two weeks, and many areas were quarantined. All my interviews were canceled, so I called about my Monday meeting with US IRS agent Doug Scott, an old friend who was in Tblisi for a year with the US Department of Tax Revenue to write a new Inspector General Law. He moved my Monday meeting back to Friday, being already over the flu himself. My loyal replacement driver, Temo [TEH-moh] Migreshvili [mee-gresh-VEE-lee], and my interpreter, Mrs. Nino [NEE-noh] Karashvili [kah-rahsh-VEE-lee], drove me to Doug's office. The streets of Tblisi were Soviet: potholed everywhere. Fortunately, Temo owned his own rugged silver Mercedes.

We talked with Doug for two hours. My driver and interpreter seemed amazed to be invited to join us. Georgians often feel excluded when Americans talk with other Americans. Doug spoke candidly in front of them. He was discouraged about making progress against corruption in Georgia. His favorite adjective was "Georgianized," which generally meant stalled. After six months in Tblisi, with six more to go, he described every transaction as "beginning with great idealistic good humor and flattery and plenty of Georgian wine and ending in no progress whatever." He was disappointed in how his plans were not going forward. I had read his draft Inspector General Law before my trip and thought it was excellent and could work well, but only if adopted largely unchanged.

Doug said the law itself was more or less agreed upon; the big dispute was about who would appoint and control the inspector generals. His preference was that they *not* be under the control of their own ministers but should answer strictly to the president because there was so much corruption within the ministries. Most ministers of course disagreed. The minister of defense wrote him that they had "too many investigations already." He would support the law only if he controlled the hiring, firing, and supervision of "his" inspector general.

Another problem was with the head of the Law Enforcement Reform Committee, a well-known politician. He had asked to be allowed to review the proposed law, which Doug had sent him with a request for a response months earlier, but he had never received any response and was told privately he would never get one. President Shevardnadze [sheh-vahrd-NAHD-zay] had stated he agreed with Doug's entire IG package, but word was again sent to Doug informally by a "back channel" that the whole bill was a "dead duck" and would never be adopted by parliament.

Doug asked the Ministry of Finance sponsor to present, or "front," the bill for him, but no one would even meet with him to discuss it. There was already a plethora of internal audits embedded in all ministries, but they followed the Soviet system by investigating and reinvestigating until everyone was tired, the case was old and they then simply closed it out. Doug was recommending that all other internal inquiry and investigation bureaus and laws be abolished in favor of one inspector general for each ministry. But he was not optimistic. He said that many people had been caught in corruption, but because of informal networks and alliances, no one was ever fired, let alone prosecuted. Corruption, he said, was not only in the system, it WAS the system.

Doug said that what Georgia needed was a government-wide code of ethics, but that whenever he mentioned it, he got only negative responses. He stressed that former Soviet states did not have to be like this. He had already visited Bulgaria at length, and it seemed to be progressing much faster. The Georgians, having been oppressed so long, were now especially sensitive about anyone telling them what to do. They preferred receiving equipment such as computers, faxes, telephones, and copying machines, almost any modern office equipment. Doug did not feel this was so they could steal them, as in some countries, but because they favored efficiency and economy. During my visits to Georgian offices, I noticed all officials had numerous antique telephones that never rang. Several volunteered that they had to have several before they could get one that worked. Everyone relied entirely on cell phones, personal rather than official. How did they afford those on their salaries?

Just to show that not all the problems were on the Georgian side, Doug noted that American bureaucracy and statutory schemes often prevented us from giving the Georgians our available excess equipment that we would otherwise readily give them. He cited how customs had to search for a loophole under the Border Freedoms Act even to provide hardware to Georgian law enforcement. This problem needed either legislative attention or, more likely, some clever public servants in Washington to find ways to send the Georgians what they needed by getting around our existing statutes.

When I asked if there was anything positive to report, Doug mentioned SAIC, which stands for Science Applications International Corporation, the private outfit Mike Nicholson ran under contract with the embassy. Doug said they had successfully funded the Anti-Corruption Council, law libraries, the crime lab, and training programs in cooperation with DOJ resident legal advisor Peter Strasser of New Orleans. Other positives were the foods and wines. Doug had even developed a liking for Stalin's favorite wine, the red-labeled semidry Kvanchkara [kuh-vahnch-KAH-ruh].

Doug's office was a fourth-floor walk-up. The hallways were unheated and his office was comfortable only right beside an American-imported oil heater. Bulbs were bare, and the unfinished parquet floors were not glued to the subfloor, so it was like walking across a field of loose dominoes. Most Georgian elevators worked well when the electricity was on, which was not often.

I decided to spend some time getting useful background from some young Georgian friends of Temo and Nino. We went to an inexpensive local cafeteria. Expecting a grim, dirty Soviet-style place, I was pleasantly surprised to find a clean, well-lit restaurant where I tried a half-dozen Georgian specialties for less than six dollars with a three-dollar bottle of good red wine. I bought and brought home a neat little paperback in English called *Georgian Dishes*, which listed no publisher or date. The group seemed well informed on politics and social and economic conditions in Georgia and were outspoken in their opinions on the widespread corruption in Georgia. Some favored a return to an ironfisted leader like Stalin or Putin. Others preferred Western-style reforms and democracy.

One young woman was from the famed city of Sukhumi, the Black Sea resort in Abkhazia favored for generations by Russian leaders for their holidays. She described Abkhazia, recently taken over by Russian troops and now inaccessible to Georgians, as the best part of Georgia and that Georgians badly want it back. They compared it to the US losing California. The Russians, on the contrary, were constantly pressuring Georgia to become part of Russia again. The whole situation reminded me of Moldova, where the Russians took by force the eastern region of Transnistria, next to Ukraine, and still occupied it and where the southern wine region, Gagauzia, populated mainly by Christianized Turks, had tried to secede while I was there in 1995. Georgia, like Moldova, is multiethnic, multilingual, coveted by the Russians, and subject to being Balkanized unless the US assists the Georgians.

Perhaps this is as good a place as any to describe what I perceived as the role of women in Georgian society. The young Georgians I met with did not know each other well. The young men were polite and even courtly toward the women, who were outspoken while very feminine. Despite hearing stories that Georgia and the Caucasus were the original home of medieval chivalry, I had not quite expected Georgian women to be so Western. They are vastly more liberated than Moldovan women, who are generally subdued and subservient. Throughout my stay Georgian women were treated with great respect and much more equality than either Moldovan or Russian women. Several senior prosecutors were women.

One young man from the region of Kakheti agreed strongly with the young women that this was a sad, confusing period for Georgians. They feared for the future. They loved Georgian independence and looked entirely to America for help. They did not believe any European nation could or would defend them against the Russian army, which would quickly overwhelm them, as it did after their only other spell of freedom just after the Russian Revolution. With that exception, ending in 1921, they had been ruled by the Russians since 1801. (This was proved true in 2008 when the Russians suddenly invaded, destroyed most of the Georgians' US-supplied military equipment, and then quickly withdrew. The message was clear: "We still control you whenever we want.")

The Georgians told me that there was extortion and bribery throughout the government. Salaries were so pitifully low and taxes so unrealistically high that almost no one paid them. Everyone simply paid off whatever government official was involved, and the money went on up the line. When I asked about "mafias," they said there was really only one: the government. There was street crime, but nowhere did I see tattooed gangsters with retinues of prostitutes like I saw in Moscow and Chişinău.

The Georgians were confused about where to begin fighting corruption. The economy was in such bad shape that people hung onto old Soviet ways just to survive, although most would rather have been straight. It did not seem that corruption was cultural and expected, as in Indonesia, but the product of economic conditions. The Georgians' great fear was that the Russians would continue to use ethnic tensions with the Abkhaz in the west, the Ossetes in the north, and the Chechen menace in the northeast to pressure Georgia and eventually invade it again to "protect" minorities and finally take over Georgia wholesale. (Again prophetically. Putin's Russia did it in Crimea and eastern Ukraine in 2015.) No one felt they stood a chance against the Russian army militarily like the Finns once did.

The Georgians were temporarily encouraged by the presence of five hundred US Marines in the Pankisi Gorge on their border with Chechnya to "train" Georgian troops, and they believed the Marines were really there to, in effect, protect them against a Russian invasion, at least temporarily. I later visited the Marines there briefly, in secret, and agreed with the Georgians' assessment. But we Americans were having trouble deciding what to do next. We did not want armed conflict with Russia.

After a long lunch, the Georgians proposed to show me Mtskheta, the original capital of Georgia a few miles north of Tblisi on the strategic hills across and above the river. This visit gave me a chance to see the countryside and how people lived. Tblisi was, even in the dead of winter, a beautiful city. To me it resembled Luxemburg, with its steep hills, winding river, and dramatic vistas. The typical Soviet suburban apartment towers were better maintained than those in Moldova, but the number of unfinished, windowless buildings and rusting factories across the landscape was stunning. Incredibly, Georgia's biggest export was *scrap metal* from junked factories and vehicles.

Poorly dressed people walked the roads in small groups, most going to warm themselves a little in the numerous ancient churches, only recently reopened. The roads were decent in places, but sometimes almost impassable. Flocks of sheep wandered across the roads near the capital, and big white pigs and numerous well-fed cows wandered loose in the countryside. The biggest consolation seemed to be eating well. I saw no signs of hunger.

On the streets of Tblisi, gypsy children begged aggressively. Interestingly, whenever an adult Georgian tried to beg, the Georgians shouted at them and drove them away, saying, "Get a job, you lazy bum." At the churches, however, they always gave coins to the old women begging, saying "with freedom they lost their Soviet pensions and need the money badly and are too old to work."

My first night I rested with a delicious room-service dinner of kharcho (spicy tomato soup with walnuts), chakhokbili (roasted chicken with herbs and polenta), and a bottle of excellent dry red Prince of Imereti Saperavi, which was somewhat like a Syrah.

Saturday

At 10:00 a.m. my interpreters Irakli and Nino picked me up at the Marriott. We went straight to the Procuracy Office to meet Mr. Tvalavadze. As in Soviet times, we waited in an unheated blockhouse by the gate while the guard took my passport and gave us a dirty scrap of torn paper as a receipt. The old guard had a large, battered desk covered with papers on which he was working feverishly. The temperature inside could not have been over forty-five degrees Fahrenheit. He explained he was grateful for his government job, which paid little but gave him lots of time to work for his church. He worked directly for the patriarch, the Georgian equivalent of the pope, who was reconverting all the old Georgian churches from Soviet museums and warehouses back to working churches. He gave me several postcard-sized copies of traditional Georgian murals which the patriarch personally painted on the walls of the main Sioni Cathedral in Tblisi.

Mr. Tvalavadze, a very busy man, kept us waiting one and a half hours in his heated anteroom. During that time I questioned Irakli, a bright twenty-three-year-old whose mother is a lawyer, about the system. He said both he and Mr. Tvalavadze had once worked in the city administration. In theory it oversaw its government department but in reality was a useless remnant of the Soviet system where no one really did anything except enjoy full pay. This issue launched Irakli into a general discussion of the justice system, which he described as almost purely Soviet with little thinking, lots of pseudoscience, no pragmatic sense of getting anything accomplished, and which thrived on rigidity and petty performance of technicalities regardless of results. This mentality was obviously hard to break, as I witnessed in Russia and Moldova. It was all form and no substance.

Mr. Tvalavadze welcomed us cordially, apologizing sincerely for the delay. Throughout our two-hour meeting with him, his cell phones rang incessantly about a wide variety of official issues. He was in his late twenties and said that he had worked for government, beginning as an intern, since he was sixteen years old. He said, as people in my office do, "I love my work and would do it for free if I didn't need the salary." He described his personal history as follows: He majored in international law at Tblisi State, began as an investigator, became a prosecutor in corruption cases, joined the mayor as head of law enforcement and human rights, and ended as inspector general. He reminded me of an up-and-coming, young US congressman.

Mr. Tvalavadze had been with the National Procuracy only since December 2001. He was at the time of our meeting the deputy procurator over international relations, the press center, investigations of police misconduct, and what he referred to as the equivalent of our Secret Service. He said there was a special staff for human rights cases with five prosecutors who report only to the prosecutor general. They were trying to improve communication with their main supporters, the human rights NGOs and the public defenders. He claimed success in training prosecutors to take the new qualification exam, saying he had himself scored 99 out of 100. He believed the prosecutors were sufficiently talented and could be trained to the point that they could have a good system. He was grateful for what our RLA Peter Strasser has done in this area. I knew Peter from his days as an AUSA in New Orleans, where he successfully prosecuted corrupt former Louisiana governor Edwin Edwards, sending him to federal prison.

The biggest current problem was an almost total lack of equipment in prosecutors' offices. Only two of his ten telephones were operative and he relied entirely on private cell phones. The procuracy had only *one* computer per region, or thirty total computers for a nation of six million people. All were old and slow. I suggested trying to give them some of the many computers recently "excessed" by US Justice, such as the forty-five sitting in storage in our office in Oxford alone. My US contacts said it was hard to deal with US regulations on this matter and that the electric converters they had been using for US computers cost three hundred dollars each. Others thought conversion from 110 to 220 was not that expensive, but computers were special because of frequent power outages and surges. They also needed fax machines, copiers, and telephones, given the poor roads and lack of other communication equipment. Salaries were due to rise for prosecutors by 400 percent in April to 90 percent of judges' salaries. This would mean salaries of $200 to $300 per month where the minimum cost of living is approximately $50.

Regarding human rights, I asked what concrete steps had been taken toward improvement. Mr. Tvalavadze said the problem had two parts. First, abuse of persons arrested was widespread, mostly to obtain confessions, and partly just out of old bad habits. He had recently ordered that each prosecutor personally visit each defendant in custody for signs of beatings immediately after arrest. Special medical officers were to check those in custody for abuse and to treat them and report it to the Human Rights Unit. At the end of each day, his staff collected all news articles about abuse and gave the information to the Human Rights Unit for investigation the next day. He believed that complaints were going down.

The most surprising problem was physical violence arising from religious intolerance. This unusual problem was led largely by one man, a defrocked Georgian Orthodox priest named Father Basili Mkalavishnili [kah-lah-veesh-NEE-lee]. Even after being officially kicked out of the church by the patriarch, Basili continued to lead in Tblisi a sect of over a hundred followers who consistently beat up and even killed Jehovah's Witnesses. They used, most strikingly, large steel crosses in the beatings. Father Basili had been convicted three times but judges were afraid to punish him because he had too much popular support. On two occasions he had actually beaten Jehovah's Witnesses *in court*, and on another occasion his followers even kidnapped two policemen who were trying to protect the victims. Mr. Tvalavadze set me up meetings with the lead prosecutors of those cases.

Upon receiving a call to accompany the prosecutor general to the parliament, he had to leave but wanted me to help him with one thing especially: setting up an inspector general system to fight corruption within the departments. He wanted an inspector general appointed only by the president. He was aware of the legislation drafted by Doug Scott and was strongly in favor of it, but felt it was hopelessly stalled. I failed to ask what he thought would happen in 2004 when President Shevardnadze was scheduled to leave office due to term limits. The obvious danger from putting everything in the hands of the president, rather than relying on a messy separation of powers like we have, is the possibility of getting a corrupt president. Sadly, we Americans are now getting vivid experience with what an ignorant and unethical president can do, and how difficult it is to combat, most people seeming to react with fear or indifference, or both.

Mr. Tvalavadze said he wanted to take me to visit a prosecutor's office at Telavi in the Kakheti region (said to produce the best wines). We talked of our mutual interest in wines, as well as the fact that we both played basketball, me in high school and college and he for the National Academy of Sports. He promised to call me at 4:00 p.m. to organize a trip for Sunday. Like nearly every prosecutor I interviewed, he worked at least six days a week, and often seven. Some said he was too involved in PR and image-making, but it was hard to argue with someone who worked as hard as he obviously did.

Mike Nicholson of ICITAP police training was waiting for us at his office in the colorful Betsy's American Hotel, where he also resided. Betsy's was unusual, having some rather good nude paintings of women on the walls. Mike was full of energy and the most positive person I met. He tried phrases in Georgian on his lively young staff, was interested in recording Georgian polyphonic music, and seemed to be accomplishing a lot. His program needed to be extended and expanded. He had the sort of can-do attitude that was needed under the discouraging circumstances of a post-Soviet state, as well as the strong military background needed for what was partly a hardship post.

From 3:00 p.m. to 5:00 p.m. I met with the drafting team of the prosecutor general: Venedi Benidze [buh-NEED-zay], who presided; Khatuna Kalandadze [kah-lahn-DAHD-zay], head of investigations; and Vazha Jankarashvili [john-kah-rahsh-VEE-lee], head of prosecutions for the Inspector General Office. Mrs. Kalandadze complained about all the disruptions the changes were causing. She was right about one thing, however: we compared the English with the Georgian texts directly and found stunning multiple mistranslations, omissions, and important words added in English that did not exist in the Georgian version, and vice versa. A concrete example will illustrate. Article 20, Chapter 4, titled "Acts Issued by a Prosecutor," read as follows in the English version: "A prosecutor is authorized to issue the following acts: the request, the submission, the protest, the resolution, the agreement, the complaint, the order, the instruction and the information."

Upon comparing the Georgian text, we learned what those terms really mean: "Request" meant to request the appointment of an expert; "submission" meant to demand corrections; "protest" meant to ask that acts be overturned; "resolution" meant a plea bargain using prosecutorial discretion; "agreement" meant approving investigative techniques; "complaint" meant an appeal of court decisions; "order" was a word that did not even appear in the Georgian text, and no one knew what it meant; "instruction" meant to order investigators to do certain investigative acts; "information" meant to make written reports to parliament. In effect the English translations put us in the position of having no idea whatever what the new laws actually meant or how they worked. This needed urgent action.

A glance at the chart of the Procuracy Office showed its divisions titled in English as "Unités." While it may be true that it takes a paragraph of English to explain one word of legal French and a paragraph of French to explain one word of legal English, the above "definitions" do neither, and the entire procuracy statute as translated was full of gibberish. One of my primary recommendations, if not *the* primary one, would be that the embassy establish, by agreement with the president and parliament, *two-person* translating teams, with one native bilingual English speaker and one native bilingual Georgian, both with some knowledge of legal vocabulary and procedures, to make OFFICIAL, CERTIFIED copies of all legislation. With the drafts that were being presented, it was a certainty that confusion and serious legal problems would result from passage of laws no one could possibly understand.

Mr. Jankarashvili was a bright and serious person who seemed sincerely interested in legal reform. He invited me to meet with his entire staff later in the week, which was done. I learned from him that prior US seminars and information were well remembered. As we were speaking about speedy trial requirements, one team member asked me about our Speedy Trial Act. I told them that defendants had to be brought to trial no sooner than one month and no later than two months after first being publicly charged, rounding off the exact days. Mr. Jankarashvili immediately said that he had been told we had seventy days rather than sixty, and I had to admit he was correct. They noted that they have ninety days instead of seventy. We had a good chuckle over his catching me being imprecise.

Another interesting point was the more than six hundred amendments that had been made to the previous reform codes. The drafters were adamant that those amendments were not regressive as charged in the press, but were made simply to remove useless layers of bureaucracy added by other drafters who had no actual experience of investigations and trials in the real world. They stressed that the earlier new laws were drafted by Russians, not Westerners, and were making their jobs impossible.

At 5:00 p.m. I met with the very impressive Dr. Shota Papiashvili [pah-pee-ahsh-VEE-lee], head of the new Prosecutor Training Center. Although he had white hair and appeared to be older than the others, Mr. Papiashvili gave an enthusiastic one-on-one presentation about his training practices, including his use of simulated cases, real cases, and what we would call mock trials. He held a special chair on the law faculty at Tblisi State, which permitted him to publish legal research and allowed him to recruit trainers from the best law faculty there. He had access to twenty professors, forensic scientists, researchers, and scholars. He apologized for having been trained in Moscow and for not speaking English, but stated he would love to visit the US to learn our system and to be trained further as a trainer in our US facility at Budapest, where he had already attended an FBI seminar, taught by my old friend and Mississippi FBI agent Kevin Rust. Kevin had recently retired and relocated to Oxford and from there now travels the world investigating money laundering for private companies, a prize job.

Mr. Papiashvili said the main goal of his center was to retain the best young attorneys and specialists like criminalists. He said his center had been promised its own building, but that he had no money for it and did not foresee any. It had been suggested to him by the Europeans that he train his prosecutors at the facility for judges. He said that he knew that was the French model, but he favored American-style separation of powers and would not train his prosecutors to be interchangeable with judges. Perhaps he was saying what he thought we wanted to hear, but he said he was familiar with the French model and did not wish to follow it.

Mr. Papiashvili held a doctorate and had always taught criminal law and procedure in addition to his governmental duties. For six years he was a member of the Court of Attorney Discipline. He stressed the importance of keeping judges independent by not mixing them in investigative and prosecutive roles. But he did hold European views against undercover operations, plea bargains, and polygraphs, which he said were "a substitute for work." I didn't argue with him—yet.

I asked him for examples of problems with the new statutes and what had caused the amendments. He said that mixing continental and Anglo-Saxon systems had caused anomalies, such as once a "suspect" is named, investigators are limited to only two "investigative acts" without prosecutor and court approval, totally stymying vigorous investigation. He asked if I would be willing to speak to the criminalists from his department during my visit, and I said of course I would.

Saturday evening Giorgi and Irakli took me to the Dzveli Sakhli (Old House) restaurant and introduced me to dedas puri (momma's bread), khachapuri (a sort of quiche), aromatic Abkhazian sausage, tsikani (goat shish-ka-bobs), eggplant with pureed walnuts and pomegranates, and other exotic but delicious Georgian specialties. My greatest discovery was tkemali, a wild plum sauce used with meats and which comes in both red and green varieties. It made catsup and Worcestershire sauce taste pretty dull. I even bootlegged a big plastic bottle of each back to the US, where it tasted as good as it did in Georgia and made even dried out chicken breasts palatable. Irakli and Giorgi and I talked for hours about conditions in Georgia.

Sunday

Temo, Irakli and I toured Tblisi, visiting synagogues and an Armenian church and attending a two-hour service at Sioni Cathedral. As in Russian Orthodox churches, parishioners tended to wander in and out during the service. They were not as effusive in their devotions as recently religious Orthodox modern Russians, who fervently kissed old icons on the walls, but they did burn regular forest fires of votive candles. Unlike Moldova, where men stand on one side and women kneel on little prayer rugs on the other, in Tblisi no one knelt, and men and women mingled freely. The cathedral was packed the whole time. Built in the form of a cross, four small choirs sang beautiful, complex, polyphonic hymns in turn from the four corners. Their ancient-sounding music clearly deserves greater fame. I brought home several CDs of them, which the people in my office really loved.

The Georgian nuns' clothing was very interesting. Instead of the puritanical wimples of Roman Catholics (*ora pro me*), Georgian nuns wear handsome black headdresses that look like something medieval queen Eleanor of Aquitaine might have worn. They all spoke both French and German. They gave me a small framed picture of St. Nino of Cappadocia, a female slave who began the Georgian church in the third century AD, bringing Jesus's Aramaic alphabet with her.

After church, we tried to drive to the ethnographic museum above Tblisi, but the roads were too icy. The museum consists of reconstructed houses typical of each region of Georgia. Failing that, we discovered the only remaining wine bar in Tblisi, which has just reopened next door to the opera. It had a great variety of wines for sale and color brochures in English and would soon open for light meals and tasting of wines to be purchased. The proprietor told us that at one time, before the Soviet occupation, Tblisi had over a hundred such wine bars and they were a thriving business which he and others hoped to reestablish.

The beautiful, restored opera house was showing a matinee of *Absalom and Etere*, an opera written by Georgian composer Paliashvili. The audience was filled with children who got in for the equivalent of a nickel. The 150-year-old house held a thousand. It was cream colored with gold trim and a blue ceiling, and it had lots of carved wood, resembling a Venetian palace with a Persian stage. President Shevardnadze had a bulletproof glass box at the base of the balcony. The opera house looked like the one in the famous French-Georgian film *A Chef in Love*, although it was filmed farther west in Kutaisi (the former Colchis where Jason got Medea and the Golden Fleece). *Absalom* was filled with beautiful choral numbers, lots of dance, spectacular costumes, and a classic Caucasian ending when the queen stabs herself to death with a dagger she had given the king as a wedding present. He had just died of a broken heart. With bodies all over the stage, Shakespeare came to mind.

That evening we had dinner at a popular regional Mingrelian restaurant in the countryside. Beside a roaring fire and a man playing a pandoori, a sort of lute, we ate heartily of cheese grits (*ghomi*), skewered pork shaslik, homemade catsup, and the best tomatoes I have eaten in years, dressed only in parsley and lemon juice. While discussing the beautiful woods on the hillsides behind the restaurant, Irakli noted that unfortunately, to raise hard currency, the Georgians were now cutting down most of their ancient forests and selling the wood for hard currency to the Turks. They say Georgia is an acquired taste, and that evening I knew I was acquiring it.

Monday

At 9:00 a.m. we met with Greg Olmstead, regional security officer, at the US Embassy. Greg was impressive, a straight talker who had been in Georgia for four and a half years and knew it thoroughly. When he arrived he was RSO for the entire Caucasus region. Now he had only Georgia and two assistant RSOs, which showed the importance now being accorded to Georgia and perhaps also indicated that it was more unsettled than it looked from Tblisi. The embassy was one of the most beautiful I have seen inside and out, but it was tightly guarded. When I pulled out my camera to take a picture of the pastel blue front, a guard grabbed me before I could even focus it.

Greg made me an appointment with the ambassador for 3:30 p.m. on Wednesday for a preliminary report on my mission. He liked the idea of a visit to Kutaisi or Gori, birthplace of Stalin, and was very helpful. He told me not to expect a joint meeting with the press officers of the Interior and Security Ministries, saying they were as competitive as the FBI and IRS and would probably much rather talk to me than to each other. Sure enough, it was the only scheduled meeting that was canceled at the last minute by the Georgians, who said they would meet me privately and separately and would even meet me with reporters off-the-record, but not with each other together. Time was unfortunately too short for all that.

At 10:00 a.m. I met with Inspector General Prosecutor Vazha Jankarashvili alone for about an hour. He explained that his office began in April 2000 with the primary goal of *preventing* corruption. He explained, "We are poor in operations," meaning the office had little discretion and few tools. The law prohibited it from gathering intelligence and from keeping anything secret. He believed inspectors general in other ministries had more latitude. Before he could take any investigative action, he had to notify the suspect, which totally dried up the evidence and any potential cooperation. He said that he had just gotten information that a prosecutor in a leading Georgian city was in league with certain Russian gangsters called "thieves-in-law," but feared he would have trouble proving even enough to remove him from office.

I asked if he had achieved any results. He said that the previous year his office had successfully fired ten employees for bad behavior, including an assistant prosecutor for falsifying documents. It also brought several successful complaints based on reports from citizens and the press. This year it had fired two prosecutors already. The office could give administrative punishment and had specialized prosecutors who could in theory prosecute other prosecutors. He just fired two weeks earlier the "high" prosecutor who supervised all investigations in western Georgia for being improperly close to known gangsters.

Mr. Jankarashvili said that he knew there was misconduct, but felt that 90 percent of it would stop if salaries were higher. Most prosecutors were honest but found it hard to live on their salaries. They also needed improvement to their system of financial disclosure declarations. Although prosecutors were required to file them, failure to comply was not substantially punishable, the maximum fine being a hundred dollars, which was usually less than the bribe offered. The prosecutor general did not have the right to propose new laws to parliament. He was responsible for drafting them, but a member of parliament must personally present the law (much as in the US) and there were tons of lobbyists ready to influence parliamentarians with cash.

Mr. Jankarashvili brought up one problem I had thought about but that no one else had mentioned: the inspector generals themselves could easily become centers for corruption. With exclusive powers, they could easily extort employees with threats of investigations as under the Soviets. He mentioned that in April prosecutor salaries would triple. It took a real fight with parliament to get the increase and that they used "all legal means," including the backing of the first deputy prosecutor, whose husband was the chairman of parliament.

"Mr. Vazha," as I began to call him, began calling me "Mr. John," southern-style, and we discussed Georgian wines and my experiences as a wine judge and columnist over the past thirty years. He was interested in that industry and its underdevelopment. He even found me a book in English on Georgian wines. He also swapped me a Georgian Security Service (read "KGB") cloth patch for an Oxford Police Department shoulder patch.

Monday evening I was invited to a supra dinner ("feast") at a beautiful restaurant in the country outside Tblisi with Mr. Papiashvili and his friend Dr. Kozmanashvili. Mr. Papiashvili acted as támada, or toastmaster, offering in excess of twenty-five toasts, all praising America, our families, Georgian and American women, and hopes for future cooperation. Fortunately the glasses only held about two swallows each. It was a long, slow, splendid evening of the kind where positive relationships are cemented in wine. We talked a lot about our countries and our personal experiences. Unlike Russians, whom I still enjoy, Georgians do not often drink to excess. Being drunk is frowned upon, and I saw little drunkenness during my stay.

Dr. Kozmanashvili spent considerable time in the US, especially California, and was a member of the US Academy of Forensic Science. Irakli was extremely helpful as an interpreter. From my own experience interpreting in similar circumstances, I know it is very tiring, and the poor interpreter has no time to eat and cannot afford to drink, so his services were much appreciated and contributed a great deal to the big success of the evening.

Tuesday

At 10:00 a.m. we met Mr. Vazha and Mr. Papiashvili and traveled for an hour in two cars to Gori, home of Stalin, where we met the prosecutors and police. The road to Gori gave quite a vivid view of life in the Georgian countryside. It began with six lanes, soon narrowed to two, and became a lot bouncier. Most cars were large because the roads were too rough for smaller ones. We encountered frequent roadblocks but no hassles because of the high positions held by our companions, but there was no obvious reason for the roadblocks other than to shake down drivers. One image of travel in Georgia was of the small barns made entirely of stacks of hay and grim bus shelters made of the shells of burned-out buses. All along the road were plastic gas cans with hand-painted signs advertising gas for sale—clearly stolen and of dubious quality. Temo said the two biggest businesses in Georgia were junked cars and "informal" gas stations, which "spring up like mushrooms after a rain."

The Georgians have a fetish for dark-tinted windows of the kind theoretically illegal in the US, but common. Although covered in snow, there were vineyards and fruit trees all along the valleys and hills and freshly dressed chickens hung up in rows for sale beside baskets of good-looking apples. Villages were at the base of the mountains or halfway up. Georgian life had contrasts like the car radio: You could listen to either raucous, annoying techno-pop or, as Temo did, switch to a Vivaldi CD.

In the country there was far more Russian writing on signs, and many houses were left unfinished with no windows. The farmland looked rich with plowed fields, but the people looked as poor as the most rural Mexicans. At a checkpoint we met our hosts, a carload of Gori prosecutors in a black ZiL. Vazha and Shota were in a black Volga. Public officials did not appear to lord it over other citizens with their cars as I saw in other Soviet countries. Having a car, driver and cell phone did, however, make life infinitely easier. The suburbs of Gori were like the worst housing projects of northeast Washington, DC, but several parts of downtown Gori were beautifully restored.

At the time, the writ of Georgian law did not run beyond twenty kilometers north of Gori where South Ossetia begins. Formerly (and still officially) part of Kartli province, South Ossetia had effectively seceded from Georgia. The Ossetes were only recently moved to the area from Russia by the Communists. Previously the area was 100 percent Georgian. Although orthodox Christians, the Ossetes spoke a different language, akin to Persian. The Roman writer Livy once said that to trade in Caucasia the Romans had to carry 120 different interpreters with them. Some say Stalin had an Ossete father. Until the collapse of the Soviet Union, there was little ethnic conflict in South Ossetia, but since then the Russians have repeatedly incited it to encourage secession. They have even built a large tunnel through the Caucasus to encourage settlement in Georgia of more Ossetians loyal to Moscow.

In 1992 after liberation, when Zviad Gamsakhurdia [gahm-sah-KOOR-dee-yah] was president, over 450 Georgians were murdered in this region. The prosecutors referred to it as a "zone of non-law." Ossetes carried Russian passports rather than Georgian. Criminals, the only ones who profit, cooperate across the border in banditism. President Putin had recently cracked down in South Ossetia, driving many of the worst criminals back into Georgia. In February of 2002 unlawful elections were held, and an Ossetian named Eduard Kokoid was elected president of the "Republic of South Ossetia," promising criminals informally, "If you don't commit crimes here, but only elsewhere, we will give you asylum."

The road we passed just before Gori led to Tskinvali [ts-keen-VAH-lee], the regional headquarters for Georgian prosecutors in South Ossetia. Since they could not actually enforce the law there, for all practical purposes the Georgians had no role there. The only law and order was provided by Georgian and Ossetian soldiers who worked together informally to keep down ethnic conflict. The Ossetes refused to "extradite" prisoners to "Georgia." The prosecutors stressed that the situation was far worse than reported in the international press.

The military road to Russia was the biggest haven for smugglers in all of Georgia. It was said to be some of the most beautiful country in Georgia but "law enforcement there is just a theory." Since both sides needed the road open, there was little violence but no law. The factories there were ruined and farms deserted. Crime was the only industry. The locals called it the "Republic of Contraband." No taxes or customs duties were collected by the governments, and transporters of wine were regularly extorted. Local residents of this region were utterly disheartened; the prosecutors called it "criminogenic." Like Abkhazia, this region reflected the Russian desire to reconquer all of Georgia.

Before this depressing background, the prosecutors expressed great gratitude to former US legal advisor Jack Gleason, whom they called a "valued colleague" who got them xerox machines, fax machines, computers, and even a law library to "ease our work." The new prosecutor for the city of Gori, there just two months, was former military. He said having separate courts for "military" cases was critical, because in disputed parts of Georgia the situation was too unstable for civilian courts. Two additional prosecutors served as inspector generals over human rights and police abuse. Another was the criminalist, who handled all crime scenes. He said, "I don't have a gun, just a camera."

For the last hour or so of our meeting the electricity was off, underlining their statements that they had no funds for investigations, the Ministry of Finance having just cut them to zero. They said their biggest problem was gangs and banditism with twenty-four robberies and two murders on the roads in the previous few months. They stated they were ashamed of the poor state of their country and were terribly grateful to America for helping them. They asked me how we caught corrupt prosecutors and judges, and when I told them about undercover operations, body wires, plea agreements, and the like, they just shook their heads and said, "We are not really allowed to do those things."

Despite their circumstances, the prosecutors and police seemed to have decent morale and a strong sense of camaraderie. After our meeting, they took me for a visit to the beautiful and surprisingly un-Stalinist museum honoring Stalin. It was twenty-five degrees outside and snowing, but the museum was totally unheated and unlighted. The guide turned the lights on for a few seconds so I could photograph the beautiful stained-glass windows and chandelier. The guide, who said she was fifty, had been a guide for over twenty years, mainly for Russians, but that no one came any more except Americans. In the past few years she had learned on her own to speak quite good English with a rich vocabulary, an interesting commentary on Georgian adaptability and survival skills. She said she really enjoyed guiding Americans. "They are so open and candid."

After the museum, we were invited to another big supra dinner. The local prosecutors deferred to Mr. Vazha to be támada since he was "much more eloquent." A recital of a few of the toasts was enlightening. They drank first to the victims of September 11; to the United States as a world leader; to Georgia as a member of the anti-terror coalition; to all the prosecutors of the world because "we understand each other at the highest level;" to the rule of law; to love and beauty, although "beware of beauty, it is a dangerous thing"; to our family names; to the everyday life of our families; to the virtue of faithful wives; to *pictures* of our mothers-in-law; to John Ashcroft ("be sure to tell him he was the subject of a toast"). Mr. Vazha noted at this point that he knew 937 toasts, but mercifully chose not to use them all. He toasted Temo and Giorgi, our drivers, reminding us they were designated drivers and had not touched a drop of wine.

Mr. Vazha closed with a toast to the memory of Stalin and asked me to respond to his toast. I said that in America we follow the Latin rule of never speaking ill of the dead, so I would just say that despite his misdeeds Stalin was a great military leader who was our valued partner in defeating the Nazis, and we happily honored him as such. Mr. Vazha then drank to "advanced codes of law," which he hoped would help Georgia, which was "living in a cruel hour" and "sorry to be seen in this piteous situation." He claimed that Czar Peter the Great was actually a son of Georgia because his Russian mother allegedly had a Georgian prince as her lover. He concluded that with our help Georgia would return to its former glory. On that note we rode triumphantly back to Tblisi.

The next evening I shopped for souvenirs at the open-air "Dry Bridge" flea market, located under an old bridge over a dry creek, which protected it from rain and sleet. It had everything an open Russian *tolchuk* market has except the dancing bears and chimpanzees. I bought several fine Circassian daggers, drinking horns, Cossack boots, and some beautiful old Cossack prints.

I left my hotel the next morning at 4:00 a.m. to catch the 6:00 a.m. flight to Istanbul and Amsterdam, arriving in Memphis at 7:30 p.m. central time. I was back in the US Attorney's Office in Oxford, Mississippi, for an 8:30 a.m. criminal staff meeting the next morning. I never did catch the Finnish flu.

Second Mission to the Republic of Georgia, July 2003

In March 2003 the Georgians we'd worked with asked RLA Peter Strasser to invite me back for a second series of seminars, this time focusing on prosecutor-press relations. The Georgians apparently were amazed at how well our office was supported by local media, both television and newspapers. Their experiences had been far less positive, in fact, downright hostile. I agreed to the trip immediately, but my US attorney was reluctant to let me be away for very long so soon after my February trip. However, I managed to persuade him, a staunch Navy man, that I had to be away for a few days anyway to attend the graduation of my older daughter Allison from Naval OCS at Newport, Rhode Island, when she would become a military doctor, having already been assigned to be chief US naval medical officer at the famous base in Sasebo, Japan, from which our former enemies launched the fatal attack on Pearl Harbor. After lengthy negotiations I finally got permission to travel on to Georgia after Newport in July 2003. The trip was much more challenging—and exciting—than I had dreamed in my wildest fantasies.

Our loyal government unbelted for a $7,900 round-trip ticket for me (if you are in the air over fourteen hours you get to fly business class) plus $9,900 in expenses. A once-in-a-lifetime trip. My wife Regan could of course not miss Allison's graduation, but being of thrifty Scottish Highland stock (Clan McGregor), she insisted on going by Greyhound Bus and did so. Airline tickets cost a fortune, and there was no flight to Newport at all. The bus ride was not all roses. To soften her arrival, I booked us a fancy room at the Four Seasons Hotel in Newport and rented a Mercedes to pick her up in at the bus station. She arrived tired and nauseated from the road food. Unfortunately, Allison's

OCS experience had not gone as planned. Navy friends had promised her that OCS for new Navy doctors at Newport was a lazy two weeks, lying in the sun all day, eating endless lobsters on the Navy tab at night. Her friends did not know the base had a new commander who had decided doctors needed a full OCS experience, complete with underwater survival training, pistol range, hand-to-hand combat drills, and the like. Allison was too busy even to meet Regan and me at the ceremony itself, which took place on a soccer field. We were astonished at her appearance: deeply suntanned, her lovely, curly blonde hair cut boot-camp short. She later explained she had to use a razor blade to police the edges. She looked great and we were so proud of her.

Regan and Allison visited several Newport mansions while I took a shuttle one-way to Logan airport in Boston. En route my fellow passenger for the two-hour drive was, by a huge coincidence, a fellow Ole Miss graduate. My trip had been very happy so far. DOJ had agreed to let me take four or five days of extra leave while there, and I planned to see everything I could, despite a few warning signs. Peter Strasser sent me several news clippings about problems foreign visitors in Georgia were having. On June 5 three United Nations observers in Georgia for local elections near the Kodori Gorge had been taken hostage by local "bandits," who were demanding a one-million-dollar ransom—for each. Georgia, following US and UN policy, was refusing to pay.

I was scheduled to arrive in Tblisi on July 3 and go on to Mt. Kazbegi and the Gudauri ski resort (much better in summer) for July 4. Peter tried to reassure me that no hostages had been harmed in Georgia to date. Kidnappings of foreign visitors in June and December 2000 and October 1999 had all resulted in the release of the hostages with, of all things, an apology from the kidnappers, who said it was "only about money."

Then on June 17 the BBC reported that Georgian police had found, in a taxi at the Tblisi airport, a suitcase bomb filled with nuclear "dirty bomb" materials. Al Qaeda was claiming responsibility. Papers in the suitcase indicated the bomb was destined for the volatile Pankisi Gorge area, where I was scheduled to meet with local prosecutors. Nevertheless, I had been so charmed by Georgia that I followed my usual course of excessive self-confidence and on July 2 flew out of Boston to Detroit and on to Amsterdam, where I caught an AirZena flight with Georgian airlines.

The Georgian passengers followed the same traditions as many Middle Eastern passengers: When a plane lands successfully, they greet the event with wild applause. On that flight my only real problem was about the seats. They were simple metal folding chairs, bolted to the plane's floor, but "flexible." It was fortunate that there were only a few empty seats, because whenever the plane hit an air pocket or raised or lowered its flight path, all the empty collapsible metal folding seats would fold up and crash loudly to the floor. The

Georgians paid them no mind beyond an occasional chuckle, and the flight attendants just let them lie there; probably wise since that way they no longer made those metal crashing sounds when they were already lying on the floor. We landed uneventfully.

Peter Strasser had made me great reservations at a classic old Tblisi hotel called the Kopala on Chekhov Street. Its walls and stair rails were of exquisitely hand-carved, well-aged wood, reminiscent of the classic old buildings constructed by WPA workers during the Great Depression of the 1920s in the US. The hotel in fact reminded me eerily of the old Hotel Timberline on Mount Hood in Oregon, where I had once participated in a magnificent judging of Oregon Pinot Noirs. Late that night, the other judges and I left the comfort of a roaring wood fire in the hotel's great fireplace and tried to climb the gentle but icy slope of Mt. Hood in tennis shoes. After a few hundred yards, I slipped on some ice and fell hard, dislocating my right shoulder. A college football player working at the hotel for the summer put his foot on it and yanked it back in place. It hurt so bad that first night that my only relief was lying in bed singing loudly to myself song after old song to take my mind off the pain. It suddenly occurred to me that if I could get into that kind of trouble in the peaceful USA, I'd better be more careful in Georgia. But the shoulder is fine now, so . . .

After a night of wonderful Georgian food and wine, we headed out the next morning via the famous Georgian Military Highway, the only route all the way through to southern Russia via Vladikavkas (Caucasus City). When we reached the base of Mt. Kazbegi, I could see at its top the famous twelfth-century Trinity Church, an elegant stone structure outlined against a bright blue sky. It being July, the valleys were deep-green velvet, like the finest Alpine valleys of Switzerland but larger. You could easily see, with the naked eye, white mountain goats climbing and leaping across the lower peaks as wild horses roamed the valleys.

When the paved roads gave out, we switched to a beat-up old Russian military jeep which seemed to have neither springs nor shock absorbers. The seats were not padded, just a thin strip of foam rubber over metal. We constantly hit bottom with our bottoms and the metal, unpadded top of the jeep with our heads. With my history of back problems, I wondered how much success we'd have getting me to a hospital (by helicopter, I hoped) for a back operation. Fortunately, every time my head slammed into the metal ceiling, it took my mind off my back. Peter Strasser's son had brought along a small bicycle helmet, which, at some cost to my ears, I pulled over my head, cushioning the blows somewhat.

We arrived at the famed Lake Annanuri, perhaps the most beautiful mountain lake I've ever seen. Its beauty removed all my pain, and I shot several successful rolls of film of it. It has been a fetish of mine through all my travels, which I now regret, that I rarely take pictures of myself, foolishly not wanting to look like a tourist. For that reason, there are few pictures of me among my magnificent gallery of photos from my missions, but Peter's son insisted on taking several of me at Annanuri and on Mt. Kazbegi for which I am eternally grateful.

When we got to the Trinity Church, our driver produced a big, dented fuel can full of a cloudy liquid. Utterly thirsty, I cautiously drank a glass. It tasted OK. "Good apple cider," I said. He was offended. "This is good Georgian wine, made by my family." To assuage him, I drank three or four more glasses, which I later regretted before we could reach a bathroom. We spent a few days wandering the Caucasian villages. It often occurred to me that after thinking of myself as a Caucasian—just a synonym for "white" after all—I was now among real Caucasians.

We checked into the lovely, modern Gudauri Hotel, a ski resort built by an Austrian consortium, but which apparently had met with greater success with summer visitors than winter skiers. There were lots of ski resorts in Europe, but in my experience nothing as spectacular as the alpine meadows of Mt. Kazbegi.

After several days and nights of partying, I was to give a lecture on press/ prosecutor relations at 9:30 a.m. on July 10. The previous day, after another major stomach incident, I decided it was perhaps the pure-looking, delicious mountain water that had some insidiously hidden, anti-American microbes that were causing my distress, so I drank for lunch a couple of murky but delicious Georgian beers, which I'd never tasted before. When John Cooper, one of the American presenters saw me with the beer, he said, "Oh, John, no, no. That stuff is full of strange bacteria. Not even the Georgians can drink it."

It was not long before his words proved true. I vomited for hours like never before in my life. Finally, after a nap, I woke up, looked at my watch and saw that it was nearly 9:30. "I've got to give my talk; where are the videos of me with Mike Wallace on *60 Minutes*? Where is that film of me with the Blackstone Rangers in Chicago? I can't fly all the way here and then let these people down by not even making my presentation!" I was nearly hysterical. Everyone looked at me funny, but no one helped me. I felt desperate, hopeless. Finally, one of the Georgian reporters took pity on me. "My friend. Cease your worrying. There is plenty of time for you. It is now 9 o'clock at *night*, not 9 o'clock in the morning. Your talk is tomorrow." I went straight to sleep, got up early feeling great in the bright, clear Caucasian morning, and my presentation went fine. Well, mostly fine except for one vigorous fistfight, as explained later.

During that visit, I had arranged to rent a helicopter to take me to Svaneti, the most ancient and remote part of Georgia, on the Russian border. We could only go in by helicopter because there were no paved roads. I had watched the great French-Georgian film *A Chef in Love*, with yellow English subtitles, which features great shots of Svaneti with background music from its polyphonic Renaissance-style male choirs. The landscape there is dotted with tall stone watch towers dating to the Middle Ages, still in use when clan wars break out. I just had to visit Svaneti. Sadly, just before we were to leave, the Georgian police told me that a wiretap had revealed a plot to kidnap me and hold me until the police released one of their clan leaders then held in jail. They did not want money. "Don't worry. They will treat you very well, with respect and plenty of good food and wine, even women if you want." For better or worse, that new adventure was canceled. No trip to Svaneti. I still regret it.

In the morning, after my lecture, I met with Mrs. Rusudan Kazumashvili [kah-zoo-mahsh-VEE-lee] deputy director of the Press Center for the Procuracy. She made a smooth, prepared presentation for about fifteen minutes about what her office did, basically "coordinating news dissemination to the public and information services," including print journalists and television. It offered to Georgian society both an "objective contact" and "rational information" from the procuracy. Over sixty journalists were accredited to attend procuracy press briefings and were authorized to ask free-wheeling questions, both orally and in writing.

Mrs. Kazumashvili said that the main "negative aspects" of her job were that most journalists had no knowledge of law and most were not well informed on current events. They always asked for the most scandalous information first (sounded familiar). Her main conflict was trying to protect the integrity of investigations while keeping the public informed (not an unfamiliar dilemma to DOJ press officers like me). "We try to be accurate," but journalists consistently used "bad methods to trip us up. We have to re-explain legal vocabulary to them every time we meet. We want to give two- or three-day seminars for journalists, but so far this is mostly an ideal. We have no money and need sponsors," she said. I offered to write to my old friend and editor, Charles Overby, CEO of the Freedom Forum in Washington, which had done much with several Eastern European countries in this area. At that time the electricity went off totally for a few minutes. Luckily I had two small but powerful flashlights from the US which I always carried in my pocket, having been forewarned. We were thus able to see our notebooks, and her briefing continued.

Mrs. K. made a summary of what the press wrote each day about the procuracy to read its "tendencies" and furnished it to the prosecutor general. She asked me, "What do you do when the press writes false, insulting, or libelous articles?" I waffled. She volunteered that the center tried to prevent them or answer them, but avoided "authoritarian measures." Mrs. Kazumashvili had university degrees in law, economics, and philology and volunteered, "I love my job." She said that she and her boss had both attended US-sponsored seminars the previous September on "law, media, and the military" at the parliament building. She said the seminar was outstanding, featuring simulations of press conferences and other tricky situations. She said it showed that the principles and problems of a prosecutor's press office in the US and one in Georgia were very much the same: we tried to tell the truth and protect investigations while journalists always wanted more colorful facts and more scandal.

Mrs. Kazumashvili said that the Georgians had sponsored a seminar in November featuring a contest for the best head of a press center among all ministries. Her boss Dali [dolly] won a free trip to Washington, where she was staying at the time of our interview. At the conclusion of our interview, she asked if she could be of help in getting us access to other meetings. I asked her if we could meet the Jehovah's Witness prosecutor, whom we had had trouble reaching, and whether I could visit a prison. She immediately arranged both, seeming to have quick access to the prosecutor general's personal staff.

At 12:00 p.m. We met with Ranaz Jgenei [ee-GEN-ay], who had investigated most of the Jehovah's Witness cases. His office had a large bookcase with lots of finely bound leather volumes, the only one I saw in a government office. He said he still had twenty-six open criminal cases on Father Basili Mkalavishvili. He explained the problem. The "Watchtower" Jehovah's Witnesses groups were not registered in Georgia as a religion. Their propaganda was given out door to door, and they used food and money to "brainwash" young Georgian children to leave the orthodox faith, which was just recovering from Communist atheism. Many Georgian parents agreed with Father Basili. Eight of his cases had gone to court; nine were to be combined in a new conspiracy charge, but three of the cases against Father Basili were still being blocked by a city judge.

Mr. Jgenei said that on January 24 followers of Father Basili had attacked some evangelical Baptists, which had never in history happened in Georgia. The country was generally tolerant of all Christians, Jews, and "even Muslims despite all they've done to us," but Father Basili's group hated all Protestants. Mr. Jgenei believed that Basili had finally overplayed his hand and would be jailed this time around. His followers had expanded from one hundred in Tblisi to around nine hundred nationwide, but once they started burning books and nativity scenes and attacking buses, the matter became a national embarrassment; it would probably be impossible for a judge to let them off again. Mr. Jgenei expressed mock nostalgia that they could no longer make Basili simply "disappear" as the Soviets used to do. He asked if the US could help with witness protection because the Jehovah's Witnesses were too fearful to testify. Most of their money came from the US, even though some of their leaders were Georgian. Mr. Jgenei believed that with Basili in prison his movement and its violence would quickly fade away. The Orthodox Church certainly opposed the group.

Mr. Jgenei concluded by saying that he had recently passed the prosecutor's exam and thought that salary increases in April would help decrease corruption. He said that if his office had only one request, it would be for computers. He expressed great respect for the United States, saying his son graduated from the University of Alabama and had worked in the Georgian Embassy in Washington for the previous five years.

At 1:15 p.m. we visited the Juvenile Detention Center, arriving via several miles of ruined buildings and nearly impassible streets at a clean, modern facility where a young, clean-cut warden in a tie met us. He said no one had called him, but he showed us around anyway. He said of the twenty-six inmates, aged fifteen to seventeen, all but one were there for theft. He said none were there for selling drugs and none were in gangs. Prisons were called "colonies" in Georgia. All the inmates worked in the evenings and went to school all day long. He said their main problem was poverty. There had not been much recidivism, but his facility was an experiment. Striking proof of the terrible condition of the roads were the rusted car doors standing up in the biggest potholes to warn drivers against falling into them.

At 3:00 p.m. I met for an hour and a half with US Ambassador Richard Miles, one of the most productive and enjoyable meetings of my long career visiting US embassies. A former Marine, Ambassador Miles was a blunt-spoken, bright, and articulate advocate for the United States. I had seen his picture and read about him in the English language papers nearly every day on a variety of subjects throughout my stay. He was just the same in person, the kind of firm but generous father figure we needed to improve our image abroad. He peppered me with pertinent questions about what I had seen and heard and my recommendations, comparing them to similar missions I had done elsewhere.

In a nutshell, I told the ambassador that I thought progress in Georgia would have to be incremental, with which he agreed. We also agreed that it was easy while on the scene to become discouraged, but the United States had sufficient long-term strategic interests in Georgia that we needed to stay the course, listening to the Georgians on what their needs were and making sure they were doing their best to make progress toward the rule of law and a relatively free and democratic judicial system.

At 4:30 p.m. approximately thirty-five prosecutors and Tblisi State professors were invited by Dr. Shota Papiashvili to attend a seminar on how the press in the US handled corruption. The seminar was to be given by me at the Procuracy Office. It had to be moved from the university, which was under quarantine because of another alleged flu epidemic. Most of the officials I had been unable to meet with individually were present. I wondered how many really had the flu but were there anyway. Mr. Papiashvili was coughing profoundly and obviously had the flu, but he carried on. I told the group I would rather use the time to answer their questions than to make a speech. They asked short and well-phrased questions for a few minutes, then asked that I give at least a short speech. After a few minutes a shouting match erupted near the back. As I was asking them to quiet down, a fistfight broke out, which Mr. Papiashvili finally suppressed. He explained sheepishly that several prosecutors were actually yelling disagreement with me for speaking too positively of "those dog journalists," and the others were defending me. It was unsettling, but at least they were paying close attention.

Mr. Papiashvili then said he hoped to publish, with our help, a brochure on the subject of preventing corruption by using the press, with contributions from prosecutors, investigators, criminalists, the military, and experts on human rights. As far as I could tell, every Georgian prosecutor I had met with except Mr. Tvalavadze was present, as was Ms. Kazumashvili from the Press Center. Most waited around afterward to shake my hand, apologize for the fight, and thank me. They were a very courteous people, however impulsive and easily angered.

At 6:00 p.m. after the seminar, I met in her office nearby with Tamar Iaseshvili [YAH-sesh-VEE-lee], the new chair of the Commission on Human Rights of the Procuracy, an independent division answerable only to the prosecutor general. Until two weeks prior she was chief assistant to the prosecutor general and the only one actually prosecuting human rights violations. Mr. Jgenei apparently just supervised investigations, not prosecutions. She seemed full of enthusiasm and determined to make a difference. She had just established a hotline on her desk for citizens to call. If the case was not near Tblisi, she could order local prosecutors to handle it and review the results. She said the American Bar Association had agreed to assist by translating laws and reviewing her work according to international standards. She used to be a supervisor of police. She knew somewhat how our IG system worked, but said Georgian conditions were much more difficult.

She proposed to work closely with public defenders to "sneak up on police without prior notice" using a team of prosecutors and public defenders. She said it was critical to catch witnesses immediately before they and the evidence could be tampered with. She felt she could enforce a code of behavior on the police because of her long experience as one of them and could persuade them to cooperate before they were influenced not to. Her husband was the powerful chief of police at Mtskheta, across the river from Tblisi. A handsome woman in middle age, Mrs. Iaseshvili had several pictures of her teenage daughter on her desk, which I compared with pictures of my own fifteen-year-old. She also swapped me a metal Security Service (formerly KGB) badge of her husband's for several of my US police cloth patches.

My last night ended at a great family dinner with Peter Strasser, his wife, and their two beautiful children. Ted Greenberg of the Asset Forfeiture and Money Laundering Section of DOJ joined us. It was a good opportunity to see the hardships of living in Georgia. Peter's car was locked inside a big, thick steel case with razor wire because of theft and vandalism. While later the experience will be wonderful for them to look back on, it was apparent that Peter's children missed America and its safety and conveniences. Peter showed me the generator the embassy furnished him for his house because the electricity constantly would go off. His own fifteen-year-old daughter wanted to apply to a high school in England, but as in Soviet times, they could not simply mail off the application because the postal service in Georgia was so unreliable. Peter asked me to carry it with me and mail the application for him when I got to Amsterdam on my way back, just as people used to do in Soviet countries. I was happy to do so.

That incident reminded me of my own most painful postal experience. After looking all over Tblisi for a place to buy stamps to mail the eighteen postcards I had already written to friends in America, thinking how exotic the postmark would be and what beautiful stamps they would have, I spent forty-five minutes standing in line watching true inefficiency at work in a Georgian post office. It being the only place you could buy stamps, the clerks dawdled and denied they had any stamps. When my interpreter Irakli yelled at them and told them he would report them to superiors, a surly clerk finally produced some, but in denominations so small I had to layer them all across the sides and even on parts of the front of the postcards. When we asked when they would arrive, the clerk said smugly it would take "one or two months." Not one of my postcards ever arrived.

On July 13, I flew home by Fokker T-70 jet via Vienna and Amsterdam, well satisfied with my time in Georgia and hoping to return. So far I haven't made it, but my den is crammed with beautiful souvenirs of that unforgettable country.

EPILOGUE: A VISION OF DEATH
AND ONE LAST ADVENTURE

Late in the summer of 2011, my wife Regan and I took an unusual trip into the deep French boondocks. Known officially as Auvergne [oh-VERN-yuh], it is an ancient province in remote central France, little visited even by the French. Created by volcanoes thousands of years ago, its soil is some of the poorest in France, good only for pastureland, but those deep-green pastures produce extremely fine cattle and sheep from which the locals make some of France's finest cheeses, including Roquefort, Cantal, Saint-Nectaire, and bleu d'Auvergne. Visually, Auvergne is spectacular, marked by towering *Puys* [pweez], circular volcanic craters filled with startlingly beautiful, deep-blue mountain lakes.

Remote Auvergne was the place in France where the Gauls made their last stand against Julius Caesar and his Roman legions. After losing, they fled west to Brittany, Wales, Galicia, and Cornwall. It was only after Rome fell a few centuries later that a Germanic tribe, the Franks, conquered France under their famous leader, Charlemagne. The Franks tried unsuccessfully to speak Latin, leading cynical modern linguists to refer to their language, which we call "French," as "Latin spoken badly by Germans."

Regan and I had another reason for wanting to explore remote, historic Auvergne other than just to taste the cheeses. We wanted to visit the little-known castle of the greatest French friend America ever had: the Marquis de Lafayette. Of all the Frenchmen who ever loved America, Lafayette, whom the French called *l'Américain*, was certainly the most important. George Washington is said to have considered Lafayette the son he never had. Ironically, because of the conflicted leadership role Lafayette played in the bloody French revolution in 1789, he is much less known and revered in France than he is in the US.

After a long and sometimes scary ride over narrow, winding mountain roads, Regan and I finally found a modest hotel/restaurant in a tiny mountain village near the castle. The next day we drove all over the area, marveling at the magnificent herds of local sheep and their vast, deep-green pastures, which in winter make some of the best—and least visited—ski slopes of all France.

Because of a knee injury, Regan was unable to visit underground pens where the sheep were kept and milked, but I visited dozens of them, breathing in great volumes of sheep dust.

At the end of our trip, Regan stayed on in France to supervise repairs on our eighteenth-century limestone house in the Cognac region while I flew on home. As soon as I got there, I developed a huge cough, which I foolishly assumed was some sort of early-fall allergy. "Must be some French pollen," I told myself, forgetting all the sheep-poop dust I'd inhaled. The cough soon got worse. A nurse-practitioner at the Oxford hospital tested me, after making me drink two full quarts of a thick liquid that looked like a milkshake but tasted like suntan lotion. The nurse gave me his opinion: "From those books written by that English vet with the popular television show (*All Creatures Great and Small*), what you have looks to me like that old disease farm hands used to get from breathing in dust from cow or sheep poop. They call it 'Anthrax,' but nowadays you hear of it only when terrorists distill it and refine it way down to make that poison powder they send people through the mail."

Within a week I was back in the hospital with a high fever. This time I was sent from Oxford to Tupelo at the North Mississippi Medical Center, the largest "rural" hospital in the United States, which has far more specialists. They soon had a solid diagnosis: bacterial pneumonia. Soon several bags of liquid drips hung everywhere and multiple needles were stuck into me all over, but my temperature continued to rise until it reached 105 degrees. My body was badly swollen and discolored. My skin looked ready to split open in several places. My daughter Allison, a medical doctor in the US Navy then stationed in the seaport of Sasebo, Japan (from where the attack on Pearl Harbor was ordered), persuaded the Red Cross to fly her and her husband and their year-old daughter, Abbey, to the hospital in Tupelo, where Allison had done a three-year residency and had clout.

A Catholic chaplain had offered to administer to me my last rites, the doctors having told him I would probably not make it through the night, my eleventh in that hospital. My wife Regan had flown immediately home from France and had spent all those nights sleeping in a really uncomfortable chair by my side while I ranted crazily in my sleep. At times I could think and speak clearly, but much of the time I was delirious and incomprehensible. While the Catholic chaplain tried to get some sort of deathbed conversion, our beloved Presbyterian pastor from College Hill Church in Oxford, Alan Cochet, entered my room. Having served for many years as a Marine Corps chaplain and visited combat-zone hospitals all over the world, Alan asked if one of those hanging plastic bags contained the Lasix needed to reduce the excess liquid from my system. The answer was no. Alan ordered that Lasix be added immediately.

Within an hour my temperature started dropping. My speech stopped slurring and my head cleared. I began thanking Alan, the doctors, Regan, Allison, and our other daughter Lydia, who had arrived from Nashville, telling them of a "vision" I'd had during my delirium. First there were thousands of flashes, like film clips on an old projector, of events from all my past life: sports, friends, children, every event in my life seemed to be stored somewhere in my head, exactly as in a computer. There was no sound, but it was all in color and starkly clear.

I told them of how at one point it had all slowed down to normal speed. I was sitting in a little rowboat being rowed by a man facing toward me, pulling on the oars. The water was perfectly still and calm. All around us were tall, shiny, white and crystal stalagmites and stalactites, beautiful to look at. Above us was an open blue sky. On my right I could touch a rough limestone wall as we moved forward. As the boatman rowed calmly on, I could see about fifty yards ahead of me "the farther shore," as if a voice had said it, although there was no voice. It was a sort of low, sandy beach. I knew immediately what it meant: I was going to die, but die happy. In my mind I felt calm and happy. I thought what a wonderful, lucky life I'd had and how I was now ready for it to end peacefully. I had never looked forward to the pains and embarrassments of old age anyway. I was ready to go.

Then I thought of Regan and Allison and Lydia. I thought not of how sad I would feel, but of how they would feel. "No. No," I said. "Turn back now," I told the boatman. He began pushing toward me on his oars instead of pulling, moving us away from the farther shore. Slowly I began to think, "What in the world will I do as I get older? I'm healthy now, but maybe not for that much longer. What will I do with all that time?" So far there was only one grandchild, one year old. But there could be others. Happily, there are now three, all healthy and beautiful. My greatest pleasure now is my time with them and Regan and our children. But what to do with the rest of my time? Then I thought of the thirty-five boxes of files of old criminal case files I'd lugged home when I retired and stored behind my wine cellar, thinking I could possibly, but not likely, write a book about my more interesting cases. After several more days they released me from the hospital.

The Mayo Clinic finally reported that my blood tests, which showed a low white-cell count and irregular platelets and red blood cells, were consistent with lupus, the dreaded autoimmune disorder that normally strikes mostly young women, almost never men over sixty like me, but the evidence was fairly clear. Lupus is the Latin word for "wolf." The disorder was so named because many patients' first signs of the disease are scaly red patches on the temples, often triangular-shaped, which some early doctors thought looked like the face of a red wolf. I had a few such scales, small ones, just not wolf-shaped.

Little is known of lupus except that it is often triggered by being given massive doses of antibiotics as I had been. Lupus is very hard to treat, and the news from the team of doctors was not good. The infectious disease specialists finally left my case to George, a brilliant, patient rheumatologist, a Princeton undergraduate and Berkeley MD. George had been teaching medicine at the University of Pennsylvania, an Ivy League school, where he met a beautiful blonde nurse originally from Mississippi who absolutely refused to marry him unless he moved to Tupelo. So he did.

My course of treatment was at first unsuccessful. George recommended for me the standard lupus medication, methotrexate, which is very noxious to other organs, requiring constant lab work with needle punches, and which also requires the patient to stop drinking wine entirely. As a lifelong wine judge and syndicated columnist then writing on my second wine book, a series of essays entitled *The Search for Good Wine*, I flatly refused to take it. He then tried me on hydroxychloroquine (Plavix), also a fairly toxic drug, a standard treatment for malaria. Plavix made me worse and caused cataracts to form on both my eyes, later requiring surgery to remove them. Regan said the treatment turned me into a zombie. After two years of trials, I refused to continue taking it. When I told George I was quitting, he finally gave in to my demand to know what that drug actually did to your body, chemically speaking. "It weakens the walls of your cells, especially your white blood cells, thus discouraging them from attacking your good cells, as in your kidneys, lungs, heart, etc." Oh.

During those two years I had had two heart attacks plus pneumonia four times, requiring home-health breathing treatments. George told me that my fourth pneumonia was my next-to-last one. If I had another, it would be my last. The predicted course of lupus was clear: every two or three months I would probably have what they liked to call a "flareup." Fortunately there was a quick, effective, short-term cure: large doses of prednisone, a corticosteroid taken orally by little pills, in bad cases of up to sixty milligrams a day, more often forty, then "stepping down" gradually five mgs at a time to zero. Prednisone worked, but every doctor I talked to, including my daughter Allison, said steroids were themselves toxic and could eventually be even worse for me than lupus itself, and they could damage my vital organs even faster if I took them for long periods. Like many a stubborn patient, I ignored their doctorly orders, stashing extra pills and self-medicating. Every time I went below ten mgs, I had a big "flare-up." For the next two years, I took two five mg pills every morning, and my big flare-ups subsided.

Several weeks after I left the hospital in Tupelo, I was lying in bed at home trying to recuperate. One day I looked over at the bookshelf facing my bed. Prominent in a bright orange cover, a huge tome titled *Majorca: Culture and*

Life got my attention. I'd bought it and shipped it home years earlier, but had never opened it. I looked in the index for the name of the little fishing village where I'd tended bar over fifty years earlier. I quickly found it: Cala Ratjada. When I turned the pages to find the village, on a big color page facing it was a revelation: In full color was a beautiful grotto like the one in my dream and identical to the one I'd visited by rowboat way back then.

I remembered how Louie Cumberledge had gotten a local villager to show me the wonderful, privately owned grotto. Very few people had ever seen it, although cave specialists said it was one of the world's most beautiful. I later learned that nearby was another, nearly identical grotto, open to tourists, the one shown in this book, with the same kind of opening to the sky, the same kind of crystal stalactites and stalagmites, and an identical sandy "farther shore."

So my hospital experience had not been a mystical vision at all. It was far better. It was the real thing, a real memory. That memory or "vision" had a powerful, lasting impact; it motivated me to embark on one last adventure, writing memoirs of my adventures, of which this volume will be the fifth and last. It is now nearly a decade later and my health, remarkably, remains good, better than ever if anything. To say I am grateful would be quite an understatement. My vision of death was a useful warning and reminded me of the motto of my alma mater, Millsaps College, that we should always be aware of and respect "the transitory quality of life and happiness." What remains of my time will be reserved entirely for my wife, my children, and my beautiful grandchildren, to whom this final volume is dedicated.

ACKNOWLEDGMENTS

In addition to my two fantastic secretaries, Brenda Gill and Linda King, who typed this book beautifully from my rough, handwritten legal pads, the following are an even one hundred people who made a positive impact on my life:

Antoine Adam, Geary Alford, Ghislaine Audebert, Zina Baeshen, Eddie Barton, William H. Baskin, James Bear, Walter Beard, George Beatty, Gisele Berthelon, Neal Biggers, Alice Booth, David Reese Bowen, Nancy Buchanan, Con Buckley, Pamela Cameron, Joan Case, Bernard Chang, Paul Chen, Richard Clayton, Janice Cleveland, Alan Cochet, A. B. Cullen, Luke Dove, Mireille Ducluzel, Lewis Eliot, A. E. Elmore, Doug Evans, Françoise Fersancourt, Roger Filliatreau, Cynthia Foster, Don Galleano, Christian Garrison, Craig Gill, John Grisanti, Gilbert Hahn, Hal Haney, Paul Hardin, Joe Hart, Nellie Hederi, Mitt Hobbs, George Housley, Fred Johnson, John Johnson, Dorothy Kalins, William C. Keady, Leo Kelberg, Mary Kemmer, Gerald Kiger, John Kiger, Orel Kiger, Clint Kimberling, Bill Koch, Henry Lackey, David Lake, Chad Lamar, John Langston, Twinkie Lawhon, Tommy Mayfield, Anita McGehee, Pearl McGrew, Edith Miller, Jim Miller, Alysson Mills, Bill Mooney, Al Moreton, Emerson Mutterspaugh, Joe Nacrelli, Bob Norman, Charles Overby, Rex Paul, Wilma Phillips, H. M. Ray, Claude Ringuet, Paul Roberts, Tom Royals, Jack Ryan, Annie Sarpoulet, Bill Schilling, Peter M. F. Sichel, Henri Simon, Bob Small, Don Stacy, John C. Stennis, Inez Stephenson, Shane Gong Stewart, William E. Strickland, Delphine Suit, Ilene Sutton, Richard Sutton, Margie Tama, Bertie Trulock, Jim Vail, William F. Watkins, Fred Weck, Mary Wells, Parham Williams, William Sledge Woods, Steve Yates, Joe K. Young, Larry Zabriskie.

FURTHER READINGS

Readings on Travel—General

Books

Bedford, Sybille. *The Faces of Justice: A Traveler's Report*. New York: Simon and Schuster, 1961.

Brooks, Geraldine. *Nine Parts of Desire: The Hidden World of Islamic Women*. New York: Anchor, 1995.

Brenner, Michael. *A Short History of the Jews*. Princeton, NJ: Princeton University Press, 2010.

Crossette, Barbara. *The Great Hill Stations of Asia*. Boulder, CO: Westview Press, 1998.

Desai, Boman. *The Memory of Elephants* (a portrait of the Parsis). London: André Deutsch, 1988.

Escalas, Jaime. *Guide of Majorca*. Stanford: Condor, 1963.

Fleming, Peter. *News from Tartary*. New York: Houghton, Mifflin, 1964.

George, Don, ed. *Better than Fiction: True Travel Tales from Great Fiction Writers*. Melbourne: Lonely Planet, 2012.

Glubb, Sir John. *The Life and Times of Muhammad*. Chelsea MI: Scarborough House, 1970.

Goodwin, Jason. *Lords of the Horizon: A History of the Ottoman Empire*. London: Vintage, 1998.

Hailman, John. *From Midnight to Guntown: True Crime Stories from a Federal Prosecutor in Mississippi* [especially the chapter "Faraway Places with Strange-Sounding Names"]. Jackson, MS: University Press of Mississippi, 2013.

Hailman, John. *Return to Guntown: Classic Trials of the Outlaws and Rogues of Faulkner Country* [especially in the chapter "Fancy Frauds," section with international variety]. Jackson, MS: University Press of Mississippi, 2015.

Hailman, John. *The Search for Good Wine: From the Founding Fathers to the Modern Table* ["A Worldwide Joyride," per wine columnist Barbara Ensrud]. Jackson, MS: University Press of Mississippi, 2014.

Hailman, John. *An Illustrated Survey of Law & Literature from Confucius to John Grisham* [unpublished manuscript]. Oxford, MS: University of Mississippi Law Library, 2010.

Hailman, John. *Thomas Jefferson on Wine* [with stories of his travels in France, Italy, Germany]. Jackson, MS: University Press of Mississippi, 2006.

Hammer, Ute Edda, ed. *Majorca: Culture and Life*. Cologne: Konemann, 1999.

Hourani, Albert. *A History of the Arab Peoples*. New York: Warner, 1992.

Huntington, Samuel P. *The Clash of Civilizations and the Remaking of World Order*. New York: Simon and Schuster, 1997.

Further Readings

Kaplan, Robert D. *Eastward to Tartary, Travels in the Balkans, the Middle East, and the Caucasus.* New York: Random House, 2000.

Kapuściński, Ryszard. *Travels with Herodotus.* New York: Vintage, 2008.

Kurlansky, Mark. *The Basque History of the World.* New York: Walker, 1999.

Lawrence, T. E. [T. E. Shaw, pseud.]. *The Odyssey of Homer.* Oxford: Oxford University Press, 1932.

London, Ephraim, ed. *The World of Law.* Vol. 1, *The Law in Literature.* Vol. 2, *The Law as Literature.* New York: Simon and Schuster, 1960.

Luhrmann, T. M. *The Good Parsi: The Fate of a Colonial Elite in a Postcolonial Society.* Cambridge: Harvard University Press, 1996.

Maclean, Fitzroy. *Eastern Approaches.* London: Penguin, 1949, 1991.

Maalouf, Amin. *The Crusades through Arab Eyes.* New York: Schocken Books, 1984.

Marco Polo's Silk Road. Introduction by John Masefield. London: Watkins, 2011.

McGee, Jim, and Brian Duffy. *Main Justice: The Men and Women Who Enforce the Nation's Criminal Laws and Guard Its Liberties.* New York: Simon and Schuster, 1996.

McPhee, John. *La Place de la Concorde Suisse.* New York: Farrar, Strauss, 1984.

Pelton, Robert Young. *The World's Most Dangerous Places.* 5th ed. New York: HarperCollins, 2003.

Rice, Edward. *Captain Sir Richard Francis Burton: The Secret Agent Who Made the Pilgrimage to Mecca, Discovered the Kama Sutra, and Brought the Arabian Nights to the West.* New York: Scribner, 1990.

Sattin, Anthony. *The Young T. E. Lawrence,* New York: Norton, 2014.

Sichel, Peter M. F. *The Secrets of My Life: Vintner, Prisoner, Soldier, Spy.* New York: Archway, 2016.

Snow, C. P. [Charles Percy]. *The Affair.* Strangers and Brothers Series. New York: Scribner, 1960.

Spencer, Robert. *The Politically Incorrect Guide to Islam (and the Crusades).* Washington, DC: Regnery, 2005.

Stavans, Ilan, and Joshua Ellison. *Reclaiming Travel.* Durham: Duke University Press, 2015.

van Gulik, Robert. *The Chinese Gold Murders.* A Judge Dee Mystery. Chicago: University of Chicago Press, 1959, 1977.

van Gulik, Robert. *The Chinese Bell Murders.* A Judge Dee Mystery. Chicago: University of Chicago Press 1958, 1977.

Winokur, Jon. *Encyclopedia Neurotica.* New York: St. Martin's Press, 2005.

Articles

Karkaria, Bachi. "Why Is India's Wealthy Parsi Community Vanishing?" *BBC News,* January 9, 2016. www.bbc.com/news/world-asia-india-35219331.

Readings on France and Paris

Books

Ackers, David. *How to Renovate a House in France.* Worcestershire, UK: Accent Publishing, 2004.

Bakewell, Sarah. *How to Live, or A Life of Montaigne in One Question and Twenty Attempts at an Answer.* London: Other Press, 2011.

Balzac, Honoré de. *Lost Illusions*. The Human Comedy Series. Translated by Kathleen Raine. New York: Modern Library, 2001.

Busson, Yvon, and René Gast. *One Hundred and One Beautiful Towns in France*. New York: Rizzoli, 2008.

Camus, Albert. *Noces suivi de l'Été* [collection of 1937 essays]. Paris: Collection Soleil/ Gallimard, 1959.

Chauvel, Jean-François. *Algérie, Terre Française*, Paris: Editions Pensée, 1960.

Cole, Robert. *A Traveller's History of Paris*. Brooklyn: Interlink Books, 1999.

Davey, Charles. *The Complete Guide to Buying Property in France*. London: Kogan Page, 2004.

Eliot, Marc. *Steve McQueen: A Biography*. New York: Crown, 2011.

Gopnik, Adam, ed. *Americans in Paris: A Literary Anthology*. New York: Library of America, 2004.

Horne, Alistair. *Seven Ages of Paris*. New York: Vintage, 2004.

Houellebecq, Michel. *Submission*. New York: Farrar, Strauss, 2015.

Lobrano, Alexander. *Hungry for Paris: The Ultimate Guide to the City's 109 Best Restaurants*. 2nd ed. New York: Random House 2014.

Mah, Ann. *Mastering the Art of French Eating: From Paris Bistros to Farmhouse Kitchens, Lessons in Food and Love*. New York: Penguin, 2014.

Mayle, Peter. *My Twenty-Five Years in Provence*. New York: Knopf, 2018.

Morel, François. *The Most Beautiful Wine Villages of France*. New York: Mitchell Beazley, 2002.

Norwich, John Julius. *A History of France*. New York: Atlantic Monthly Press, 2018.

Ogden, Christopher. *Life of the Party: Pamela Digby Churchill Hayward Harriman*. Boston: Little: Brown, 1994.

Raspail, Jean. *The Camp of the Saints*. Petoskey, MI: Social Contract Press, 1973.

Robb, Graham. *The Discovery of France: A Historical Geography*. New York: Norton, 2007.

Robb, Graham. *Parisians: An Adventure History of Paris*. New York: Norton, 2010.

Rowlands, Penelope, ed. *Paris Was Ours: Thirty-two Writers Reflect on the City of Light*. Chapel Hill: Algonquin, 2011.

Steinberger, Michael. *Au Revoir to All That: Food, Wine and the End of France*. New York: Bloomberg, 2009.

Wells, Patricia. *The Food Lover's Guide to Paris: The Best Restaurants, Bistros, Cafés, Markets, Bakeries, and More*. New York: Workman, 2014.

Articles

Allport, Susan. "A French Home, Humble but Sweet in the Charente." *New York Times*, February 23, 1997.

Readings on the Republic of Georgia

Books

Ascherson, Neal. *Black Sea*. New York: Hill and Wang, 1995.

Blanch, Lesley. *The Sabres of Paradise: Conquest and Vengeance in the Caucasus*. New York: Carroll and Graff, 1995.

Khoperia, N., T. Lomadze, and K. Bakradze. *Georgian Dishes* (recipes with photos). Tblisi, Georgia: 1992.

Maclean, Fitzroy. *Eastern Approaches*. London: Penguin, 1949, 1991.

Nasmyth, Peter. *Georgia: In the Mountains of Poetry*. Richmond, Great Britain: Curzon, 2001.

Pasternak, Boris. *Letters to Georgian Friends*. Translated by David Magarshack. New York: Harcourt, Brace, 1967.

Rosen, Roger. *Georgia: A Sovereign Country of the Caucasus*. Hong Kong: Odyssey, 1991.

Rustaveli, Shota. *The Lord of the Panther Skin*. Translated by R. H. Stevenson. Albany, New York. SUNY, 1977.

Said, Kurban. *Ali and Nino*. New York: Vintage, 2000.

Steavenson, Wendell. *Stories I Stole from Georgia*. New York: Grove Press, 2002.

Readings on the Republic of Indonesia

Books

Bastin, John. *Native Policies of Sir Stamford Raffles in Java and Sumatra*. Oxford: Clarendon Press, 1957.

Bayly, C. A, and D. H. A. Kolff, eds. *Two Colonial Empires: Comparative Essays on the History of India and Indonesia in the Nineteenth Century*. Leiden, Netherlands: Martinus Nijhoff, 1986.

Brown, Colin. *A Short History of Indonesia: The Unlikely Nation?* Crows Nest, Australia: Allen and Unwin, 2003.

Clair, Colin. *Sir Stamford Raffles: Founder of Singapore*. Watford: Bruce and Gawthorn, 1963.

Conby, Kenneth, and James Morrison, eds. *Feet to the Fire: CIA Covert Operations in Indonesia, 1957–58*. Annapolis: Naval Institute Press, 1999.

Corn, Charles, *Scents of Eden: A Narrative of the Spice Trade*. New York: Kodansha America.

Covarrubias, Miguel. *Island of Bali*. New York: Knopf, 1946.

Darling, Diana. *Bali and Lombok*. Singapore: Darling Kindersley, 2001.

Draine, Cathie, and Barbara Hall. *Culture Shock! Indonesia: A Guide to Customs and Etiquette*. Portland: Graphic Arts Center, 2000.

Greenway, Paul. *Bali and Lombok*. Melbourne: Lonely Planet, 1984, 1999.

Kingsbury, Damien. *Guns and Ballot Boxes: East Timor's Vote for Independence*. Caulfield East, Victoria, Australia: Monash Asia Institute, 2000.

Heuken, Adolf. *Historical Sights of Jakarta*. Singapore: Times Editions, 1989.

James, Jamie. *The Glamour of Strangeness: Artists and the Last Age of the Exotic*. New York: Farrar, Strauss, 2016.

Jardine, Matthew. *East Timor: Genocide in Paradise*. Chicago: Odonian Press, 1999.

McPhee, Colin. *A House in Bali*. Singapore: Periplus, 1947.

Naipaul, V. S. *Among the Believers: An Islamic Journey*. New York: Vintage, 1981.

Naipaul, V. S. *Beyond Belief: Islamic Excursions among the Converted Peoples*. New York: Vintage, 1998.

O'Brian, Patrick. *The Far Side of the World*. Aubrey / Maturin Novels. New York: Norton, 1984.

O'Brian, Patrick. *The Nutmeg of Consolation*. Aubrey / Maturin Novels. New York: Norton, 1981, 1992.

Further Readings

O'Brian, Patrick. *The Truelove*. Aubrey / Maturin Novels. New York: Norton, 1992.

Ricklefs, M. C. *A History of Modern Indonesia since 1300*. Palo Alto: Stanford University Press, 1994.

Schiller, Jim. *Imagining Indonesia: Cultural Politics and Political Culture*. Athens, OH: Ohio University Press, 1997.

Schwarz, Adam. *A Nation in Waiting: Indonesia in the 1990s*. Boulder, CO: Westview Press, 2000.

Smith, Holly S. *Adventuring in Indonesia: A Travel Guide*. San Francisco: Sierra Club, 1997.

Sukma, Rizal. *Indonesia and China: The Politics of a Troubled Relationship*. Abingdon, UK: Routledge, 1999.

Tanter, Richard, Mark Seldon, and Stephen Rosskamm Shalom, eds. *Bitter Flowers, Sweet Flowers, East Timor, Indonesia & the World Community*. Lanham, MD: Rowman and Littlefield, 2000.

Van Dijk, Kees. *A Country in Despair: Indonesia between 1997 and 2000*. Leiden, Netherlands: KITLV Press, 2002.

Witton, Patrick. *World Food: Indonesia*. Oakland, California: Lonely Planet, 2002.

Articles

Beher, Richard. "The Year of Laying Cable." *Fortune*, July 9, 2001. http://archive.fortune.com/magazines/fortune/fortune_archive/2001/07/23/307376/index.htm [two-time convicted felon and former Arkansas governor Jim Guy Tucker's failed attempt to create a cable television empire in Indonesia].

Gantz, David. "The Foreign Corrupt Practices Act: Professional and Ethical Challenges for Lawyers." *Arizona Journal of International and Comparative Law*, Winter 1997.

"Indonesia: A Cautionary Tale." Cover story of *Business Week*, May 20, 2002.

Renoe, Curtis. "Institutionalized 'Corruption': Implications for Legal Reform in Indonesia and the Need to Make Haste Slowly." *Stanford Journal of East Asian Affairs* 2 (Spring 2002): 102–13. [lawyer/anthropologist who spent fifteen months of field research in Indonesia in 1997–1998].

Rohde, David. "Indonesia Unraveling?" *Foreign Affairs*, July–August 2001. https://www.foreignaffairs.com/articles/asia/2001-07-01/indonesia-unraveling

Movie

The Year of Living Dangerously. Mel Gibson, Sigourney Weaver, Linda Hunt, 1983.

Readings on the Republic of Moldova

Books

King, Charles. *Odessa: Genius and Death in a City of Dreams*. New York: Norton, 2011.

Moldova. Minneapolis: Lerner Publications, 1993.

Van Meurs, Wim P. *The Bessarabian Question in Communist Historiography: Nationalist and Communist Politics and History-Writing*. New York: Columbia University Press, 1994.

Further Readings

Weiner, Eric. *The Geography of Bliss: One Grump's Search for the Happiest Places in the World.* New York: Twelve, an imprint of Hachette Group, 2008.

Articles

Baker, Peter. "Ex-Soviet Republic of Moldova Returns Communists to Power." *Washington Post,* February 27, 2001, p. A17.

"Moldovans Trapped in Deep Freeze; Russian Currency Collapse Key Factor." *Jackson (MS) Clarion-Ledger,* February 7, 2000, p. 9C (AP).

"Stalemate across the Dniester." *The Economist,* June 26, 1999, p 61.

Wines, Michael. "History Ignites a Volatile Tug of War in Moldova." *New York Times International,* February 25, 2002, p. A3.

Readings on the Kingdom of Morocco

Books

Brotton, Jerry. *The Sultan and the Queen: The Untold Story of Elizabeth and Islam.* New York: Viking, 2016.

Lewis, Wyndham. *Journey into Barbary: Travels across Morocco.* 1937. London: Tauris Park, 1987.

McDonald, Lucille. *The Arab Marco Polo: Ibn Battuta.* New York: Thomas Nelson, 1975.

Mernissi, Fatima. *Dreams of Trespass: Tales of a Harem Girlhood.* Reading, MA: Perseus Press, 1994.

Mernissi, Fatima. *Islam and Democracy: Fear of the Modern World.* Cambridge, MA: Perseus Press, 1992.

Kerper, Barrie, ed. *Morocco: The Collected Traveler.* New York: Three Rivers Press, 2001.

Porch, Douglas. *The Conquest of the Sahara.* New York: Knopf, 1984.

Readings on the Sultanate of Oman

Books

Al Taie, Hatim, Joan Pickersgill, and Nassar Al Taie. *Oman: A Comprehensive Guide to the Sultanate of Oman.* 2nd ed. Muscat: Al Roya Publishing, 1999.

Beasant, John. *Oman: The True-Life Drama and Intrigue of an Arab State.* Edinburgh and London: Mainstreet Publishing, 2002.

Fiennes, Ranulph. *Where Soldiers Fear to Tread,* London: Hodder and Stoughton, 1975.

Gardiner, Ian. *In the Service of the Sultan: A First Hand Account of the Dhofar Insurgency.* South Yorkshire, UK: Pen and Sword, 2006.

Glubb, Sr. John. *The Life and Times of Muhammad.* Chelsea, MI: Scarborough House, 1970.

Harris, Sam, and Maajid Nawaz. *Islam and the Future of Tolerance.* Cambridge: Harvard University Press, 2015.

Further Readings

Hawley, Sir Donald. *Oman and Its Renaissance.* London: Stacey, 1995.

Lewis, David Levering. *God's Crucible: Islam and the Making of Europe, 570–1215.* New York: Norton, 2008.

Maalouf, Amin. *The Crusades through Arab Eyes.* New York: Schocken Books, 1984.

Nowell, John. *A Day above Oman.* Dubai: Novitiate Press, 1998.

Rice, Edward. *Captain Sir Richard Francis Burton: The Secret Agent Who Made the Pilgrimage to Mecca, Discovered the Kama Sutra, and Brought the Arabian Nights to the West.* New York: Scribners, 1990.

Sattin, Anthony. *The Young T. E. Lawrence.* New York: Norton, 2014.

Schacht, Joseph. *An Introduction to Islamic Law.* Oxford: Oxford University Press, 1964, 1991.

Spencer, Robert. *The Politically Incorrect Guide to Islam (and the Crusades).* Washington, DC: Regnery, 2005.

Stark, Freya. *The Southern Gates of Arabia: A Journey in the Hadhramaut.* 1936. New York: Modern Library, 2001.

Taylor, Andrew. *God's Fugitive: The Life of C. M. Doughty.* New York: Dorset, 1999.

Thesiger, Wilfred. *Arabian Sands.* 1964. London: Penguin, 1991.

Articles

Fisk, Robert. "Young Britons Hold the Line in Oman." Times (London), April 30, 1981.

Geyer, Georgie Anne. "Opera House in Oman Is a Window to a Wider World." *Uexpress,* October 20, 2016. https://www.uexpress.com/georgie-anne-geyer/2011/10/20/opera-house-in-oman-is-window

Knox, Jack. "The White Sultan." *Times Colonist,* July 14, 2007. https://www.pressreader.com/canada/times-colonist/20070714/281539401550822.

Readings on the Russian Republic

Books

Albats, Yevgenia. *KGB: The State within a State.* New York: Farrar, Strauss, Giroux, 1994.

Blanch, Lesley. *The Sabres of Paradise: Conquest and Vengeance in the Caucasus.* New York: Carroll and Graf, 1995.

Corten, Irina H. *Vocabulary of Soviet Society and Culure: A Selected Guide to Russian Words, Idioms, and Expressions of the Post-Stalin Era, 1953–1991.* Durham: Duke Press, 1992.

Custine, Le Marquis de. *Empire of the Czar: A Journey through External Russia.* 1839. New York: Peabody, 1971.

Dolgun, Alexander, with Patrick Watson. *Alexander Dolgan's Story: An American in the Gulag.* New York: Ballantine, 1975.

Evans, Joseph E. *Through Soviet Windows.* New York: Dow Jones, 1957.

Figes, Orlando. *The Crimean War: A History.* New York: Picador, 2010.

Figes, Orlando. *Natasha's Dance: A Cultural History of Russia.* New York: Metropolitan, 2002.

Handelman, Stephen. *Comrade Criminal: Russia's New Mafiya*. New Haven: Yale University Press, 1995.

Kalb, Marvin. *Imperial Gamble: Putin, Ukraine, and the New Cold War*. Washington, DC: Brookings Institute Press, 2015.

Kapuściński, Ryszard. *Imperium*. New York: Knopf, 1994.

Kashin, Oleg. *Froward [sic], Russia! A Fantastical Tale of Life under Putin*. Translated by Will Evans. Brooklyn, New York: Restless Books, 2010.

King, Charles. *Odessa: Genius and Death in a City of Dreams*. New York: Norton, 2011.

Le Carré, John. *Tinker, Tailor, Soldier, Spy*. New York: Knopf, 1974.

Lermontov, Mikhail. *A Hero of Our Time*. Translated by Paul Foote. New York: Penguin, 1966.

Myers, Steven Lee. *The New Tsar: The Rise and Reign of Vladimir Putin*. New York: Vintage, 2015.

Pasternak, Boris. *Dr. Zhivago*. New York: Pantheon, 1958.

Pelton, Robert Young. *The World's Most Dangerous Places*. 5th ed. New York: HarperCollins, 2003.

Pushkin, Alexander. *The Complete Prose Tales*. Translated by Gillon R. Aitken. New York: Vintage, 1993.

Randolph, Eleanor. *Waking the Tempests: Ordinary Life in the New Russia*. New York: Simon and Schuster, 1996.

Remnick, David. *Lenin's Tomb: The Last Days of the Soviet Empire*. New York: Random House, 1993.

Remnick, David. *Resurrection: The Struggle for a New Russia*. New York: Random House, 1997.

Solzhenitsyn, Aleksandr. *The Russian Question at the End of the Twentieth Century*. New York: Harper Collins, 1995.

Tolstoy, Lev Nikolaevich. *The Cossacks*. 1862. Translated by Peter Constantine. New York: Random House, 2004.

Tolstoy, Leo. *The Death of Ivan Ilyich*. Translated by Lynn Solotaroff. New York: Bantam Classics, 1981.

Ure, John. *The Cossacks: An Illustrated History*. New York: Overlook Press, 2002.

Villiers, Marq de. *Down the Volga: A Journey through Mother Russia in a Time of Troubles*. New York: Viking, 1991.

Articles

Korolkov, Igor. "Secret War against Organized Crime: Why US Federal Prosecutors Came to Moscow." Izvestia, July 22, 1995. [Interviews with US prosecutor re the Ivankov case].

LaFraniere, Sharon. "Russian Courts Give Power to the People: Revival of Jury Trials Marks Shift from Soviet-Style Justice System." *Washington Post*, December 22, 2002, p. A24.

Latynina, Yulia. "Jury Trials Not Reflecting Well on the Nation." *Moscow Times*, May 12, 2004.

Shelley, Louise. "Soviet Undercover Work." In *Undercover: Police Surveillance in Comparative Perspective*, edited by Cyrille Fijnaut and Gary T. Marx, 156–73. The Hague: Kluwer Law Internation, 1995.

"The New Cossacks: A Super-Ethnos in Russia's Ribs." *The Economist*, December 21, 1996.

Readings on Tunisia

Books

Dumas, Alexandre. *Tunis: Impressions de Voyage*. Paris: Editions Ibn Charif, 1848.

Dwyer, Kevin. *Arab Voices: The Human Rights Debate in the Middle East*. Berkeley: University of California Press, 1991.

Kaplan, Robert D. *The Arabists: The Romance of an American Elite*. New York: Free Press, 1993.

Mahfouz, Naguib. *The Palace of Desire*. New York: Doubleday, 1991.

Porch, Douglas. *The Conquest of the Sahara*. New York: Knopf, 1984.

Spellberg, Denise A. *Thomas Jefferson's Qur'an: Islam and the Founders*. New York: Knopf, 2013.

Spencer, Robert. *The Politically Incorrect Guide to Islam (and the Crusades)*. Washington, DC: Regnery Publishing, 2005.

Tomkinson, Michael. *Tunisia*, Oxford: Oxford University Press, 1990.

INDEX

Index

Index

Index

Index

Silverwood, Jim, 86, 91

Simon, Monsieur, 197–98

Sims, Elizabeth, 54

Sioni Cathedral, 206, 211–12

60 Minutes, 221

Slim, Habib, 80, 81

Slovenia, Ljubljana, 49

"Slow Train," 16

Smirnov, General, 141–42

Smith, Orma "Hack," 88–89

Snake River Dam, 12

Snegur, Mircea, 116

Snow, Hank, 16

Snyder, Paul, 9

Soeharto, President, 184–86

Solzhenitsyn, Aleksandr, 129

Sorbonne, 18, 23, 32, 197

South Carolina, Columbia, 167

South Carolina, University of, Law School, 133

Soviet Union, 71, 98, 99, 104, 108, 109, 111, 112, 113, 115–17, 120, 126, 128, 133, 142, 144, 203, 206, 216, 226. *See also individual republics formerly in the Soviet Union*

Spain: Andalusia, 40; Barcelona, 40, 41; Cala Ratjada, 41, 44, 47, 231; Catalonia, 41–43; Granada, 40; Madrid, 26, 40; Málaga, 40–41; Mallorca, 40–47, 231; Múro, 43

Stalin, Joseph, 109, 133, 204, 213, 216, 217

Stefan cel Mare (Stefan the Great), 99

Stennis, John C., 51, 82

Stevenson, R. H., 200

Straits of Hormuz, 159

Straits Times, 186

Strasser, Peter, 203, 207, 218, 219, 220, 226

Strickland, William Emile, 18, 19–20, 21

Sturza, Christina, 100, 114

Sudan, 163, 164, 168–69

Sukarno, President, 185

Sukarnoputri, Megawati, 184

Sukma, Rizal, 192

Sultan Qaboos University, 160, 165

Swan Lake, 141

Sweet Briar College, 18

Switzerland, 19, 62–65, 189; Bern, 64; Geneva, 59–62, 67; justice system in, 60–62, 91; Lausanne, 4; military in, 62–63; Ticino, 64

Syakir, Mr., 190

Symonds, Rhett, 32–34

Syracuse University, 124

Syria, 127, 159

Taillebot, Judge, 95

Taiwan, 4

Tajikistan, 135

Tamer, Abdelmajid, 175

Tanzania: Dar es Salaam, 157, 168; Zanzibar, 157, 168

Tatars, 137

Tatiana (Russian guide), 143–44

Tblisi State University, 207, 210, 224

Tchaikovsky Concert Hall, 12

Tclemcen, University of, 68

Tecumseh, Chief, 10

Tekkari, Bechir, 81–82

Tennessee, Memphis, 13, 14, 51, 149, 164

terrorism, 66, 70, 184–85, 192, 196, 219

Texas, 12

"3:10 to Yuma," 16

Timofti, Miron, 104

Tocqueville, Alexis de, *Democracy in America*, 129

Tolstoy, Leo, 128, 132, 134, 135; *Anna Karenina*, 128; *The Cossacks*, 129; *War and Peace*, 128

train travel, 8–11, 12, 16

Transparency Morocco, 179

Transylvania, 105

Traveler, 196

Tretyakov Museum, 136–37

Trevino, Adolfo, 184

Trinity Church (Mt. Kazbeti), 220, 221

Trinity College, 168

Trojan War, 66

Trulock, Harold, 7

Trulock, Raymond, 7

ABOUT THE AUTHOR

John Hailman is now retired as a federal prosecutor after thirty-three years in the US attorney's office in Oxford, Mississippi. During his time as a prosecutor, journalist Bill Minor described him as "the hardest-hitting federal prosecutor to ever come along in Mississippi," and Judge E. Grady Jolly noted that "his arguments before the United States Court of Appeals for the Fifth Circuit were the best I have ever heard from any of the many United States prosecutors that appear regularly before the court."

Hailman was also an inaugural Overby Fellow in Journalism and for twenty-five years an adjunct professor of law and trial practice at the University of Mississippi. He is the author of four previous books on law and wine: the critically acclaimed biography *Thomas Jefferson on Wine*; the true-crime memoirs *From Midnight to Guntown: True Crime Stories from a Federal Prosecutor in Mississippi* and *Return to Guntown: Classic Trials of the Outlaws and Rogues of Faulkner Country*; and a book of one hundred essays on wine, food, and travel, based on his thirty years of nationally syndicated columns, *The Search for Good Wine: From the Founding Fathers to the Modern Table*, all published by University Press of Mississippi.

Visas

VISIT UP TO THREE MONTHS

IMMIGRATION OFFICER
(186)
18 MAY 1964
LONDON AIRPORT

LONDON AIRPORT

- 4 JUIN 1964
20   FRANCE